The Theory of Value, Capital and Interest

The Theory of Value, Capital and Interest

A New Approach

Branko Horvat

Zagreb Institute of Economics
Croatia

Edward Elgar

Published by
Edward Elgar Publishing Limited
Gower House
Croft Road
Aldershot
Hants GU11 3HR
England

Edward Elgar Publishing Company
Old Post Road
Brookfield
Vermont 05036
USA

British Library Cataloguing in Publication Data

Horvat, Branko
Theory of Value, Capital and Interest:
New Approach
I. Title
330.01

Library of Congress Cataloguing in Publication Data

Horvat, Branko.
The theory of value, capital, and interest / by Branko Horvat.
p. cm.
Includes bibliographical references and indexes.
1. Labor theory of value. 2. Capital. 3. Interest. I. Title.
HB206.H67 1994
335.4'12—dc20 94-16372
CIP

ISBN 1 85898 055 0

Printed and bound in Great Britain by
Hartnolls Limited, Bodmin, Cornwall

Contents

PART V EXTENSIONS

PART VI GENERALIZATIONS

Figures

Preface

The knowledge of the genesis of a book facilitates its understanding. That motivates the following few prefatory remarks.

Rather early in my career, I became a member of the Federal Planning Board. While still studying for my second doctorate in England, I was appointed to a position in the Federal Planning Bureau in Belgrade, where I was soon to become its chief methodologist. At that time I had quite a thorough knowledge of Marxian economics from my studies in Zagreb. In Manchester and London, I acquired a reasonably good command of neoclassical economics. It looked as if the education was satisfactory. But all this scholastic competence proved of little avail.

Marxian economics had no price theory, its value theory was not correct and its analytical techniques were primitive. The potentially extremely useful two-sector reproduction schemata, which were at that time used at most to prove that the Lenin–Rosa Luxemburg 'law' of the faster growth of the first department (output of the means of production) – was just an analytical error.

Neoclassical techniques were more sophisticated, and price theory had something to offer. But there was little useful for my planning business. Margins and welfare theorems were of almost no use. Concepts widely used in model building, like incremental net-capital–income ratio (ICOR) were not only misleading but also meaningless. The use of the production function was definitely misleading. The puzzle of interest rate remained unsolved. In the school I learned that the rate of growth depended on investment and in a poor country the rate of investment could not be increased because that would depress consumption below a tolerable level. This dogma was first refuted in practice (in Yugoslavia high investment rates coexisted with rapidly expanding consumption) before we learned how to refute it in theory (productive investment could not possibly depress consumption). Some social accounting concepts proved misleading and so on.

In our practical work, we mostly used the Harrod–Domar–Mahalanobis model in all possible variants. As the Federal Statistical Office began to supply us with input–output tables, we also used all possible variations of Leontief's input–output analysis. Finally, we made substantial use of theory free econometrics. Having been forced to use partial knowledge in inventing ad hoc solutions, after a number of years I came to the conclusion that what we primarily needed was a good theory. If possible, one that would conceptually integrate micro and macroeconomics.

The core of any economic theory is value theory. Thus, as soon as I was relieved from my official duties in 1970, I began to search for an appropriate value theory. I had a feeling that such a theory, if it is to be useful, must build its concepts and constructs in a similar way as we organized our work in the Planning Bureau. Classical and neoclassical economists studied economizing behaviour of individual agents. Although that remains part of every economic theory, it seems that modern economy cannot be well understood unless the point of departure is somehow reversed: planners would have to study economic rationality of the society. Thus they would have to start considering the system as a whole. In preparing plans in the Planning Bureau, we would be setting up material and value balances for the entire economy. (In this way we were using the *duality principle* without being quite aware of that.) Why not try to work out the value theory in the same way?

By the time I arrived at the above conclusion, a certain amount of preparatory research was already at my disposal. Already as a second-year student, I encountered the phenomenon of replacement (in a growing economy) being substantially lower than depreciation calculated at zero interest rate. My references were Marx and the Soviet economist Notkin. In a paper which won the University prize in 1950, I went slightly beyond Marx but not beyond the knowledge available to Soviet planners as described by Notkin. Without the use of mathematics not much could have been done. Several years later I received a fellowship from Manchester University, where, as a doctoral student, I produced the second paper, which was sent to the *Manchester School* for publication. Harry Johnson, the editor and my teacher, asked to see me. With the earnest expression on his face he showed me Evsey Domar's 1953 article in the *Economic Journal.* To my consternation, Domar's equations were identical with those in my paper. The implication was obvious. How to explain that I have never heard of Evsey Domar and never read *Economic Journal* because it was not available in my Zagreb library? Who could believe that? But Harry was too good a teacher and too intelligent a person to reject offhand even something obviously unbelievable. He stated his condition: if I could prove that my approach was in some way different, he would publish the article. Fortunately (for me) Evsey, who was later to become my dear friend, made a mistake. He wrote that the effect was essentially an accounting one and that with a different accounting procedure it would disappear. I proved that it was a real one which no accounting could eradicate. The paper was published (in 1958).

The problem was fully elaborated in my two further papers in the *European Economic Review* (1973). In these papers I talked of 'depreciation multipliers'. In a more general framework, this concept later evolved into *replacement effect*.

In the 1958 paper, I rediscovered the *principle of synchrony* when I treated replacement of fixed assets as capital cost of current production of a national economy. I use the term rediscovered because whenever we engage in discounting to calculate the present value of an income stream, we use the same principle. It was natural to extend the principle of synchrony to the second factor, labour, and to expect a similar effect. In fact, as a planner I was doing that all the time sharply distinguishing between demographic investment, creating merely jobs for new workers, and investment increasing per capita consumption. In spite of that knowledge, and in spite of what was natural to do, I have not done it. Not until (in 1973) I read the Weizsäcker–Samuelson article of 1971 in which the authors do exactly that and call the result synchronized labour costs. In this way the second, *employment effect* was ascertained as well.

Now I had the necessary conceptual inventory. Next year, while teaching capital theory at the American University in Washington, I produced a mimeographed discussion paper containing the new theory in the nutshell. It was only a matter of time and patience to work out all the consequences. Instead, my work was interrupted for almost a decade.

At that time I realized that trouble was brewing in my native country. Yugoslavia was heading towards a catastrophe. As a socialist, I felt obliged to thoroughly reconsider principles and practices associated with socialism. I wanted to find out where socialism went astray and, perhaps help the country to mitigate the coming crisis. I did the former but was utterly unsuccessful in the latter. The result of the research was *Political Economy of Socialism*, published in New York and Oxford in 1982 and in an enlarged Yugoslav version in 1984 (with an addition in 1989). The two books ought to be considered as an institutional counterpart of the present book.

The interruption of work has had some beneficial consequences too. Some clearing of the ground, which otherwise I could not have escaped doing myself, was done by other economists, in particular by neo-Ricardians following the trail blazed by Piero Sraffa's *Production of Commodities by Means of Commodities*. It is not necessary to be a planner to see that the present paradigm is no longer satisfactory. In this book I endeavour to give credit for all relevant contributions I am aware of, regardless of whether I benefited from them or rediscovered them *ex post* when my own work had already been done. If any one's contribution is to be particularly stressed, I would single out that of Luigi Pasinetti. He saved me a good deal of work.

In 1984/1985 I was teaching at Yale and as a Fulbright fellow was associated with the university's Institution for Social and Policy Studies. The Fellowship provided me with leisure time; good library and the Institution's hospitality did the rest and so I produced a Working Paper with an enlarged version of the theory. Next year a generous research grant of the University of South California, made possible an intensive continuation of work that resulted in another Working Paper. I wish to express my gratitude to all mentioned institutions and to the responsible persons involved. The text was also improved by my doctoral students who were first exposed to the theory contained in the book. That helped me to eliminate certain ambiguities and simple errors. However, as in a game of chess, some oversights and not fully spelled out assumptions are probably still left behind and I shall welcome any professional critique. The study is largely conducted in terms of a two-sector model. Though possible generalizations are straightforward, I have not presented them except in the last chapter because they complicate the argument unnecessarily, open no new vistas and are mostly a play with algebra. Also, the size of the book was limited by the publisher. For the same reason, an entire chapter showing how neoclassical economics can rigorously deal only with the stationary state was left out.

The study was essentially completed in 1989 but the ensuing war in Yugoslavia interrupted the preparation for publication for another four years. As it proved impossible to work as a scholar in Zagreb, where I was kicked out from the University and elected a president of a social-democratic party, I went to the University of California at Berkeley. There I was appointed the Regents' Lecturer. This is a position established for outstanding persons without the academic affiliation. That now applied to me. Ample free time, excellent library and discussions in my class and with colleagues helped to edit the manuscript. Keen interest of the publisher, Mr Edward Elgar – which is quite rare when non-orthodoxy is concerned – did the rest. Thus, my gratitude is also due to a friendly American University and to an openminded English publisher.

The first publishable short version of the theory appeared in Serbo-Croatian in 1987. A number of relevant problems were over time treated in my articles published in various learned journals. The present book is the complete version of the research programme first announced in my 1974 Washington discussion paper. Its methodology is based on two guiding principles: conceptual rigour and expository simplicity. At least that was the plan target. To what extent the target has been reached – that is up to the reader to judge.

The financial support by the former Interest Union for Science and the later Ministry for Science and Technology of Croatia is gratefully acknowledged.

My thanks are also due to my former research assistant, Boris Cota, who provided the indices of names and subjects.

Berkeley, California B. HORVAT

List of symbols

$a_{ij} = x_{ij}/\hat{X}_j$	input (reproduction) coefficient
$A = [a_{ij}]$	matrix of input (reproduction) coefficients
$B = [b_{ij}]$	matrix of output coefficients
D	depreciation
$c = C/L$	consumption per capita
C	total consumption
g	rate of growth of labour
$G = 1 + g$	growth factor
h_j	rate of growth of output
$h = g + \gamma = G\Gamma - 1$	rate of return
$H = 1 + h$	factor of return
$i = I/K$	rate of gross investment
I	gross investment
$J = J - R$	new investment
$k = K/L$	machine–worker ratio
K_j	number of machines in sector *j* after vertical integration
$\hat{K}_j$	original number of machines in sector *j*
$\tilde{k} = \tilde{p}_2 k$	capital–worker ratio in *b*-prices
L_j	number of workers in sector *j* after vertical integration
$\hat{L}_j$	original number of workers in sector *j*
$\tilde{L} = L/X_1$	standardized productivity of workers in terms of X_1
$m = \kappa_1\lambda_2 - \kappa_2\lambda_1$	relative mechanization
n	life-span of machines
p	prices in labour time, *l*-prices
$\tilde{p} = p/p_1$	prices in terms of baskets, *b*-prices
$\bar{\bar{p}}_j = \tilde{p}_j/w^0$	standard (constant) price
$r = 1/\gamma + h$	rental rate
R	maximal *r*
	replacement
$\mathscr{R}$	total rent
t	time
T	technology matrix
v_i	rent per acre of land of quality *i*
V	maximal rent
w	wage rate

$\tilde{w}=w/p_1$	real wage
W	maximal wage
X_j	final output of sector *j*
$\hat{X}_j$	gross output of sector *j*
$y=Y/L$	social product per capita
Y	social product (GNP)
$z=Z/L$	land–labour ratio
Z	land area
$\alpha,\beta,\ldots$	combinations of techniques, usually pairs
γ	rate of technological progress
$\Gamma=1+\gamma$	factor of technological progress
$\delta=\nu^{-1}$	real depreciation rate
$\zeta_j=Z_j/X_j$	land input coefficient
$\kappa_j=K_j/X_j$	vertically integrated (full) capital coefficient
$\hat{\kappa}_j=\hat{K}_j/X_j$	original (direct) capital coefficient
$\tilde{\kappa}_j=\tilde{p}_2\kappa$	capital coefficient in *b*-prices
$\lambda_j=L_j/X_j$	vertically integrated (full) labour coefficient
$\hat{\lambda}_j=\hat{L}_j/\hat{X}_j$	original (direct) labour coefficient
m^s	rate of increase in number of machines of type *s*
$\nu^{-1}(g)$	rate of replacement when fixed assets are expanding at the rate *g*
π	rate of profit
$\xi_j=R_j/X_j=\nu^{-1}\kappa_j$	replacement coefficient
τ	vintage index
$\omega=p_2K/L=p_2k$	organic composition of resources capital–worker ratio in *l*-prices
$x=X/L$	per capita quantities
$\bar{X}$	fixed quantity
X^K	optimal or modified quantity
pX	values in terms of labour time, $w=1$
$\tilde{p}X$	values in terms of baskets, $p_j=1$
$\overline{ac}$	line connecting points *a* and *c*

PART I

INTRODUCTION

1 Methodological considerations

1.1 Why pure theory?

The present study is an exercise in pure theory. It is, therefore, desirable to start our inquiry by exploring the epistemological status and the role of pure theory in economics.

Economics is a branch of praxiology, the general theory of efficient action.[1] In fact, economics is its only branch that has been reasonably well established. Praxiology as well as economics are about optimizing. The optimization means maximizing desirable results given resources or minimizing the input of resources given a prescribed target. If praxiology is conceived as general and applied, pure economics turns out to be applied praxiology:

$$\left.\begin{array}{l}\left.\begin{array}{l}\text{use value}\\ \text{scarcity}\end{array}\right\}\text{ general praxiology}\\ \text{consumption and production as determined}\\ \text{by exchange and distribution}\end{array}\right\}\text{ economics}$$

As long as individuals contemplate dividing their labour time between cultivating flowers and playing the piano, they are acting at the level of general praxiology. If, however, they sell the flowers or play for the public in exchange for income, they engage in economic activities.

Economics as applied praxiology is a discovery of neoclassical theory. When Stanley Jevons, at the beginning of the neoclassical era, described his work as an attempt, 'to treat Economy as a Calculus of Pleasure and Pain' (1871, p. *VI*), he was undertaking an exercise in praxiology. Six decades later, when Lionel Robbins published his own definition of economics – which came to be considered as a representative neoclassical definition – he did the same: 'Economics is the science which studies human behaviour as a relationship between ends and scarce means which have alternative uses' (Robbins, 1932, p. 15).

Yet, pure economics is not the whole of economics neither is economics only praxiology. If empirical relevance is added, pure economics becomes economics proper. If production relations are included, economics becomes political economy (Horvat, 1985). The epistemological tree of economic science is depicted in Fig. 1.1.

An economic theory is either positive or normative. The former is about

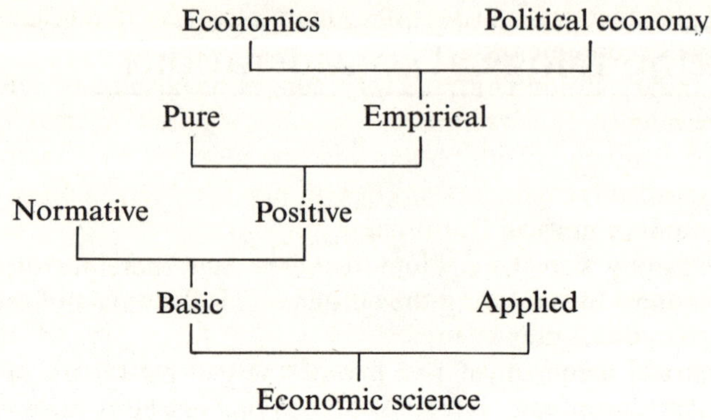

Figure 1.1 The epistemological tree of economics

what is (facts), the latter about what ought to be (values). Judgements about what ought to be are value judgements. 'More is better than less' is such a judgement. It is taken as granted in explaining economic behaviour. But it is certainly not shared by a Buddhist or a Stoic. The distribution of income is a classic field of value judgements. Arguing in favour of egalitarian income distribution on the basis of socialist, humanitarian, philosophical or other convictions is an exercise in normative economics. Every design of taxes involves value judgements. The value premiss that individuals are better off in a chosen position than they are in any other position – underlies most of welfare economics. In general, normative economics may be defined as a branch of economic theory that uses positive economics for the purpose of giving practical advice, particularly in questions of public policy.

The distinction described is substantive. There is also another, methodological distinction. Economics may be normative in a sense that is morally neutral, namely rational as opposed to behavioural. The latter may or may not be rational. The theory of consumer behaviour – to take a characteristic example of conceptual confusion – is a theory of rational choice (praxiology), not a theory of actual behaviour. Here 'rational' means a consistent pursuit of one's goals whatever they are. The often stressed self-interest is one possible such goal, but so are altruism, humanitarianism and many others. Given resources, the goals may be achieved more or less fully, i.e. efficiently. Normative economics in this sense derives the standards of efficiency that may or may not be fulfilled in the empirical world. Therefrom comes the next dichotomy between pure and empirical theory.

The pure theory uses analytical statements (whose truthfulness is determined by the meanings of words), the empirical theory uses also synthetic statements (whose truthfulness is determined by the facts of experience). A history of pure theory is a history of economic analysis that is just a part of the history of economic thought.

A pure theory, if non-contradictory, cannot be falsified by reference to empirical evidence. It is irrefutable because it is purely deductive. Even if stripped of economic or any other interpretation, its bare mathematical structure must still remain intact. The criterion for the evaluation of a pure theory is not its empirical truthfulness but its analytical usefulness. If the theory is logically correct, i.e. if logical and mathematical (also an aspect of logic) rules are satisfied – the implications follow from the premisses – the theory is true. But it may be useless.

An empirical theory must also pass the test of logical consistency. In addition, it must conform to empirical facts too. An empirical theory is thus less general, must pass two tests – logical and empirical – and may be (empirically) true or false. In fact, we can never be absolutely sure about its truth because unexpected future events may falsify it. Therefore it is useful to describe an empirical theory as being falsifiable. Further, while corroboration reveals nothing about the structure of a theory and leaves it as it stands, falsification is an instrument of scientific progress because it indicates the need and direction of improvements. Falsifiability also eliminates tautologies. An empirical theory need not be discarded if the adverse effect is non-reproducible (Popper, 1968, p. 118) or, in general, if it is of little significance. Besides, because of the stochastic nature of economic phenomena, a single adverse effect is not a sufficient reason for the rejection of a theory. As M. Blaug pointed out, an adverse result indicates an improbability that the respective hypothesis is true, not a certainty that it is false (1984, p. 362). Also, factual counter-evidence may not be reliable, or it may be misinterpreted. This happens because all facts are theory-laden, a theory is not isolated but depends on background hypotheses that may be wrong and the empirical background depends on the accepted paradigm. Therefrom the well known Duhem's thesis (1906) that an individual hypothesis cannot be conclusively falsified and discarded because we always test the particular hypothesis in conjunction with auxiliary statements and therefore we can never locate the source of a refutation. The ubiquitous *ceteris paribus* clause saves virtually any economic theory. James Conant (1947, p. 36) and Imre Lakatos (1970, p. 116) emphasize that even a falsified theory is not rejected before an alternative, better theory is formulated. A pure theory, however, must be rejected if its deductions are not logically valid. A pure theory is similar to a mathematical theory. An empirical economic theory is similar to the theory as usually understood in natural sciences.

The logical basis of a pure theory is an axiomatic system. Such a system must satisfy four basic requirements (Popper, 1968, pp. 103–4):

a. it must be free from contradictions which, as we have already noted, is the crucial test for the validity of a pure theory;
b. the axioms must be independent so that none can be deduced from the others;
c. the axioms must be sufficient for a deduction of all statements of the theory; and
d. also necessary. In economics such systems are called models, and axioms are called assumptions.

The foregoing considerations represent no more than an introduction into the field of economic methodology. The epistemological problems involved are much more complex. But, following the praxiological rule of minimizing the costs given the target, I shall not discuss them here any longer. The definitions stated suffice to eliminate the frequent confusions about the meanings of pure and empirical theories in economics.

Our goal is, no doubt, to produce empirically falsifiable theories that generate predictions about unknown future events. Why then pure theories at all? There are several reasons for that. Economic world is so complex that we need some simplification in order to be able to analyse it at all effectively. Thus, economists eliminate many details from their analysis and construct relatively simple models of the world. Such models are a classifying device. They provide standards of reference. They are substitutes for experiments, which are crucial in natural sciences and hardly possible in economics. The construction of mathematical models is an excellent device for rigorously defining the concepts used. Finally, they provide a sort of logical scaffolding for empirical economic theory. In short, the pure theory does not predict empirical events; it serves as an 'engine of analysis', as already noted by Neville Keynes (although he taught that this was the feature of economic theory as such; Blaug, 1980, p. 86).

The difference between pure and empirical theory was noted by economists a long time ago, although, as the example of Neville Keynes shows, it was differently interpreted. The nineteenth century authors such as Senior, Mill, Cairnes and Marx failed to distinguish between logical and empirical truth. Instead, they talked of theories that were obviously true and disturbing causes that accounted for the discrepances with the observed facts (Blaug, 1980, p. 81). This approach mimicked natural sciences and has had rather unfortunate consequences. Malthusian law of population and Marxian laws of increasing exploitation and the falling rate of profit have been deemed true in spite of the contradicting evidence.

A more appropriate approach is the following one. Any exact science needs mental constructs for abstract analysis (Machlup, 1978, pp. 170–96). Already Henry Poincaré studied the role of constructs in geometry and theoretical physics (1908). A couple of years earlier (1904) Max Weber designed his *ideal type* as a suitable construct for social sciences (Weber, 1922). Such constructs represent idealized objects (like rational consumer and perfectly competitive firm or ideal conductor and vacuum) or free inventions (like mathematical concepts). A model is then made up of interrelated constructs. A pure theory is a collection of interrelated models. Although pure theory is present to a certain extent in other sciences as well, it is particularly important for physics and economics. Modern physics is dominated by abstract models whose variables cannot be measured directly but that are constructed to derive the facts ascertained by experimental physicists. The evolution of the common sense Democritus's idea of the elementary particles is revealing in this sense. The first generalization of the concept occurred in the quantum physics where the location and the velocity of an electron cannot be determined simultaneously and therefore, in a collision, it cannot be distinguished from other electrons. The second generalization occurs when the energy quanta in an electromagnetic wave are described as photons with mass zero so as to be able to travel with the speed of light. Graviton, not yet experimentally confirmed, is also supposed to be a particle with the mass zero. Photons and gravitons are *particles* of their respective *fields*; the concepts were invented in order to avoid the conclusion that two objects at a distance affect each other in a vacuum. The third generalization of the concept of the particle is to be found in the concept of quarks that are components of the elementary particles but cannot exist independently (Strnad, 1989). Another example is Einstein's concept of four-dimensional manifold that cannot be physically represented. Such abstract models and concepts are neither true nor false; they are mental constructs that may be useful or not in deriving empirically verifiable consequences. Differently from natural sciences, controlled experiments are severely limited in economics, variability through time being due to activities based on memory (no counterpart for physical constants) and the number of relevant explanatory factors are great. Relatively isolated systems, allowing *ceteris paribus* assumption, are rare. Thus, it is much more difficult to formulate respectable empirical theories. Differently from other social sciences, economics – as applied praxiology – can easily use mental constructs in building exact models characteristic of pure theory. As a consequence, after mathematics and theoretical physics, pure theory plays a more important role in economics than in any other natural or social science.

1.2 The need for a new paradigm

We need, next, to distinguish clearly between analytical techniques and the theories they serve. If it is applied correctly, any technique must generate correct results. Thus, as far as the truth is concerned, the techniques are neutral. But they differ much in their usefulness depending on the subject of analysis.

Marginal analysis, which dominates in the neoclassical economics, requires the use of calculus. Algebra is more useful in neo-Ricardian economics based mostly on linear models. When great generality is required, the set theory appears an appropriate technique. But great generality often means great emptiness in terms of interesting information. I shall occasionally make use of calculus, but most of the analysis in this study will be conducted in terms of linear models. This will make possible the derivation of rather strong, substantial results.

Analytical techniques are neutral, but theories using them are not. Both Ptolemaic and Kopernikan theory can explain the movements of celestial bodies. Yet, the Kopernikan heliocentric theory is superior, gives simpler explanations and eventually (though not at first) provides more accurate predictions. The two theories reflect two different astronomical paradigms. The paradigms are 'universally recognized scientific achievements that for a time provide model problems and solutions to a community of practitioners' (Kuhn, 1962, p. x). The paradigms represent not only the basic visions of the world but also determine research programmes. Within a particular paradigm, there is a natural tendency not to research a certain class of problems. The situation may be even worse: certain problems simply cannot be studied scientifically.

There are only two fully established theoretical paradigms in economics. They are: classical and (somewhat inappropriately called) neoclassical[2] economics. Within each paradigm, there are different strands that need not detain us here. Of the four main economic processes – production, distribution, consumption and exchange – classical economists focused on the two former, neoclassical economists on the two latter. Classicists had not fully developed the idea that demand depends on prices. The use value of commodities was simply given by consumer tastes and it so determined the structure of demand but was independent of prices. Even to Cournot and Mill – who did consider prices – it never occurred that demand for any commodity must depend on prices of all commodities. (This view is not as false as it may look since modern empirical research has established that the vast majority of prices are cost-determined, which means that demand has virtually no influence, at least not directly but via costs changes.) Neoclassicals make the price-determined demand the centre of their analysis. Classical economists studied the distribution among social classes, insisted on empirical relevance and were, thus, almost exclusively concerned with positive empirical economics. Neoclassical economists made the individual, Robinson Crusoe, the main object of their analysis, insisted on exactness and developed normative (pure) theory as a theoretical tool. Classical economists, dealing with production, were primarily interested in reproducible resources. Given sufficient time, production can be increased to satisfy any social need. Scarcity of non-reproducible resources simply generated rent. Neoclassical economists were mainly interested in consumption and exchange[3] and were fascinated by the problem of scarcity. In the very short run, or if there is no production, everything is scarce. Traders endowed with resources engage in the exchange of goods in order to satisfy their preferences optimally – this pure exchange is the paradigmatic situation considered by neoclassicals. Trading reaches an end in the general equilibrium. What matters is allocational efficiency; production efficiency is simply assumed. Jevons and Menger do not even use supply curves and do not believe that cost influences price.

Subsequently also production was introduced into the model, but it was shaped according to consumption. Marginal products correspond to marginal utilities, factors of production are allocated similarly as are commodities, and their marginal productivities correspond to their prices, which are treated parametrically; commodities are subject to substitution and so are factors; like commodities, all factors of production are symmetrical. This approach produces an elegant and aesthetically pleasing theory but encounters great, occasionally insurmountable, difficulties. Some of them will be discussed in the next section.

It is clear that each of the two competing paradigms was designed to deal with only a part of the reality. This was not consciously intentional but was the result of the development of economics as a science. The world is too complex to be grasped at once. Also exact analysis is a result of a long process of methodological refinement. Thus, every science starts with some aspects of reality that seem relevant and uses the tools that are available. This is the stage of classical economics. Later the need for the refinement of the tools arises in order to make analysis more exact. Writings of Jevons, Walras, von Wieser and other late nineteenth-century economists are full of various 'laws'. Now those aspects of the real world are selected that are amenable to an exact analysis. The easiest turned out to be consumption and exchange problems. Texts on calculus accessible to non-mathematicians became generally available after 1850 and the requisite mathematical tools existed in the 1870s (Perron and Frobenius discovered their theorems – which proved indispensable for neo-Ricardian economics – only in 1907 and 1912.) This is the stage of neoclassical economics. Beside economics, in the nineteenth century a number of disciplines – including mathematics – passed through a methodological transformation that made possible analytical rigour. Such a natural methodological development is, in economics, modified by social factors. It is well known that neoclassicals shunned class analysis and the analysis of the social relations in general. Besides, the prevalent philosophical utilitarianism and political individualism provided perfect social environment for their Robinson Crusoe type of analysis. On the other hand, Marxian economists, who accepted the classical paradigm, have been not only methodological but also political antagonists to their neoclassical colleagues. Lacking tools and environment, they were also less rigorous.

There is an obvious need to overcome the inadequacies of the two partial paradigms. In other words, there is a need for a synthesis that will include all four economic processes and will take over the relevance from the classical and the analytical rigour from the neoclassical economics. Such a synthesis is impossible as a mechanical amalgamation of the two existing paradigms. What is necessary is a different theoretical paradigm. Classical economics deals with individual producers, neoclassical adds individual consumers, but neither deals with social economy. And social economy is not simply an aggregate of individual producers and consumers. It produces the system's specific synergetic effects. Some of such effects were first more thoroughly analysed in Keynesian economics. If synergetic effects exist, maximizing individual preferences in isolation is an exercise in delusion.

Since the mainstream theory today is neoclassical economics, it might be useful to look at it in some more detail. The physics analogy will be useful again. The economic space may also be visualized in four dimensions for the purpose at hand. The first dimension is technology which, in turn, depends on the state of arts and motivation, and the two are dependent on social relations and existing institutions. The next three dimensions are money, time and interdependent preferences of economic agents exercised under uncertainty and subject to a learning process (cf. Ward, 1972, Part III). The neoclassical economics takes technology as given, money assumed away by postulating 'neutral money' or 'perfect markets' (Say's law), time assumed away by considering a timeless, static economy (analytical time) and preferences taken as given, unchanging ('stable') and independent. In other words, of four dimensions two are assumed away and two are exogenized. This reduction provides a basis for the most distinguished modern theory, that of general equilibrium. However, it is clear that in this way an artificial world was created with no meaningful relation to the economic world. In physics we may assume away the time dimension (velocity) and still remain with a useful Newtonian physics. In economics too, we may assume away one or two dimensions and still have a meaningful economics. Yet the extreme reductionism of general equilibrium renders it a methodological exercise useless and irrelevant for empirically relevant and testable economic theory. The four-dimensional economic continuum represents a formidable theoretical problem, simply not tractable by the available tools. But some modest progress is still possible.

The new theoretical paradigm could perhaps be described as follows. A social economy is a system, i.e. a whole of interdependent parts. Not only two but three categories of economic agents exist: individual producers and consumers with their endowments and preferences and a social regulating agency. They participate in the four economic processes mentioned. The producers use the available technology and create new, more efficient ones. The system is mostly self-regulating because it possesses an institution that serves as an automatic regulation device. Market is that institution and it brings together producers and consumers. But market is not perfect even if prices are treated parametrically, and whenever it fails, 'hand regulation' becomes necessary. The social planning agency intervenes. The 'planning agency' is a catch name for a number of institutions, politically controlled, that help to eliminate market imperfections and keep the economy on the targeted track. One of the targets is full employment. More generally, the target is allocational *and* production efficiency. The three economic agents, when behaving rationally, maximize their preferences: (1) independent producers maximize profit, (2) notionally sovereign consumers maximize individual satisfaction, (3) by enabling (1) and (2) the planning agency maximizes the system's efficiency, i.e. social welfare. In a general case, the last target can be defined only by an appropriate political process. In a less general case, when we confine our attention to economics exclusively, the planning agency maximizes economic growth. By doing that and given preferences and income distribution it also maximizes the consumption of all consumers (Horvat, 1958b, 1965; 1968), which is the fundamental goal of economic activities.

The planning paradigm also suggests the fundamental methodological rule: start from the target of full employment (maximum growth if technological possibilities and social stimulus are exploited to the full) and let the three agents satisfy their preferences. This rule reverses the one applied in the other two paradigms when individual agents are left to maximize their preferences and the society is left to hope for the best believing in the almighty Invisible Hand. Why employment is so important that it may be considered an overriding social value – not only because it maximizes production and consumption but because it maximizes the life satisfaction too – is extensively explored in the study by Yale psychologist Robert Lane (1991).

To complete the description of the desirable traits of the new paradigm, we can also mention the received methodological difference between microeconomics and macroeconomics. They fall into two separate theoretical compartments. It is then argued that one would like to have a microeconomic foundation of macroeconomics. I have never heard of the reverse procedure – macroeconomic foundations of microeconomics – although one cannot see the logical difference between aggregation (in the former case) and disaggregation (in the latter one). Both requirements are probably inappropriate. What we need is one single economic science from which both branches – microeconomics and macroeconomics – can be derived. That will be attempted in the present study.

Since the rational behaviour of independent individuals cannot produce an optimal system – and, consequently, cannot even be rational – the correct methodological system requires that we start from the rational design of the economic system in order to make possible consistent and rational behaviour of individual agents. The systemic approach will hopefully provide a rigorous conceptual framework for the macroeconomic theory, a framework that has been lacking so far.

1.3 Neoclassical aporiae

The need for replacement of a paradigm arises when the old paradigm ceases to serve its purpose. That this is the case with mainstream economic theory, remains to be shown. Various authors observed conceptual incompatibilities in neoclassical theory. For instance, criticizing Marshall, Piero Sraffa demonstrated that internal economies were incompatible with perfect competition, external economies (occurring in historical time and being irreversible) with the static method and diminishing returns with partial equilibrium (Sylos-Labini, 1990). Such logical gaps can be repaired, at least up to a point (by imperfect competition, dynamic path-dependent analysis and general equilibrium approach). More fundamental are the following four classes of logical contradictions and empirically false basic assumptions: conceptual inadequacies, empirically false assumptions, synergetic effects and institutional inconsistencies. Some of them are well known, others are not. Let me start with *conceptual difficulties* and *false assumptions*, the two classes of errors being closely connected.

1.3.1 Conceptual difficulties and false assumptions

Value Neoclassicals explain value by reference to scarcity. That is certainly not incorrect. The trouble is that the explanation is too correct. An increase in prices is explained by greater scarcity; a decrease, by greater abundance and so 'values in exchange are proportional to the rarities' (Walras, 1874, p. 145). Thus, the theory is always true, it is true by definition. It cannot be falsified, even in principle. It is, in fact, a tautology. Economic value is simply redefined as scarcity (relative to the demand for a commodity). A good acquires economic value and the demand for it must be rationed by prices if at zero price demand exceeds supply. That is also the definition of scarcity. Tautologies may be useful theoretical constructs. They serve as economizers in the use of words. But they do not provide explanations. We still do not know what creates economic values, why is supply not forthcoming, why prices must be positive, and not negative or zero and what is the exact magnitude of optimal prices.

There is an additional issue of conceptual difficulty. What is gross national product that can only be expressed in value terms? An index of scarcity? If prices are explained in terms of utilities, is GNP an aggregation of incommensurable individual utilities, experiences of individual pleasures and pains? (Heilbroner, 1983, p. 22). The concept is obviously meaningless.

It is, of course, possible to invent an epicycle to restore meaning. Use a *numéraire*, say a pair of shoes. Then you may say that the gross national product of, say the United States, is equivalent to so many millions of pairs of shoes. That is meaningful, but not very useful. However, the main point is that GNP has no relation to scarcity or utility theory.

Leontief paradox There is one instance when scarcity may be defined non-tautologically and, characteristically, in this instance the theory fails. Namely, if instead of considering absolute quantities, we consider factor proportions, we may argue: if capital–labour ratio increases, capital is becoming more abundant; if it decreases, it becomes scarcer (under full employment and *ceteris paribus*). Relative prices are then expected to move in opposite directions. These observations provide a basis for the Heckscher–Ohlin theorem on the pattern of foreign trade. When expressed in terms of a physical definition of factor abundance, the theorem states that a country well endowed with a particular factor will produce, and hence export, the commodity that uses intensely that factor. In its value formulation, the theorem states that, i.e. capital will be relatively cheap in a capital-abundant country which will, therefore, export capital-intensive commodities. When Leontief (1953) undertook to test the theorem empirically – a rather rare event in the history of neoclassical economics – it turned out that the evidence was contradicting the prediction: the capital-abundant United States *imported* capital-intensive substitutes and *exported* labour-intensive goods. Several years later, I tested the theorem from the other side, and it was falsified again: the labour-abundant Yugoslav economy proved to have labour-intensive imports and capital-intensive exports (Horvat, 1962, pp. 154–6). Leontief was surprised and added an explanatory epicycle by scaling up labour requirements arguing that American workers were more effective than those abroad. Others involved human capital and natural resources (De Marchi, 1976, and others). Still others engaged in conceptual hair-splitting although to no avail (Bowen *et al.*, 1987). I explained the Yugoslav 'paradox' simply by the structure of demands (great share in export earnings of highly capital-intensive railway transit and maritime shipping, and in the imports of labour-intensive agricultural products). Surely, Yugloslav capital is no *more effective* than that abroad. Somewhat later the factor intensity of trade of some other countries (Japan, East Germany, Canada, India) was examined and it was found that in the first two cases the Heckscher–Ohlin hypothesis was corroborated, in the last two it was refuted (Bhagwati, 1964, p. 25). Also, the theory implies that large differences in factor endowments will generate large volume of trade. In reality, it is exactly the opposite: disproportionally large trade flows take place among industrialized countries that have similar factor endowments. And how to explain the intra-industry trade?

Apart from the misleading scarcity hypothesis, the case is generally illustrative of neoclassical theorizing. The theory is valid under certain assumptions. One of them is the international identity of production functions (the others are: non-reversibility of factor intensities, constant returns to scale, identity of consumption pattern; Bhagwati, 1964, p. 19). By definition, identical technologies will be used when the countries considered are equally developed, which drastically reduces the scope of the theory. Barring a few cases of exceptional natural resources (such as production of oil or the mining of gold), development is generally made possible by increasing capital–labour ratio. Thus, developed countries will be 'capital-abundant'. The difference in 'capital abundancy' will be determined by the mix of industries. For instance, Norway is relatively more 'capital abundant' because it has hydro-electric power stations, a large merchant fleet and produces oil from the sea bed. This abundance of capital does not make capital cheaper compared with similarly developed countries. Capital abundance is a result of a specific structure of economy, not the other way round. Greece has double the capital-intensive merchant fleet of Norway and that is certainly not due to capital abundancy in Greece. An epicycle may be added by arguing that it is natural resource intensity – not capital intensity – which must be considered. However, while it is true that water and oil are natural resources, merchant fleet and transit railways are not.

Thus, theoretical predictions appear to be refuted and the theory is empirically almost empty. That is sufficient for it to be discarded;[4] but it has the place of honour in all textbooks on foreign trade. The situation is even worse: the theory is not only empirically but also is logically false, even if all stated assumptions are accepted. Metcalfe and Steedman have shown that, with positive profits, the land–labour ratio does not determine relative prices uniquely (Steedman, 1979, pp. 25, 32) and that no prediction about pattern of trade is possible if capital is – as it really is – heterogeneous (ibid., p. 73). The value of capital depends on distribution and (in a closed economy) the same equilibrium capital–labour ratio may correspond to different interest rates, hence to different relative prices.

An offshoot of the theory is the factor price equalization theorem formulated by Samuelson (1948). The theorem says that trade leads to (complete) equalization of factor rewards (under incomplete specialization) despite the assumption of factor immobility if there are no impediments to trade and no transportation costs. However, in a world with heterogeneous capital there need not be a monotonic relation between commodity price ratio and the rate of interest and so trade between two countries need not logically necessarily establish the same interest rate and real wage (Steedman, 1979, p. 72). Besides, in the empirical world, real wage is by definition unequal if the level of development is unequal. No trade will equalize wages even if adjustment period is infinite. What is needed is investment in order to increase labour productivity by means of higher capital–labour ratios. And that has nothing to do with the greater actual scarcity of labour that may remain even abundant in the process in some sense if there is continual unemployment.

The factor–price equalization theorem may be easily derived in the way shown by John Hicks (1983, p. 226):

Suppose we have commodity one and commodity two and each of them is produced in two economies in equilibrium. Consequently, the unit costs of production must be the same in both countries:

$$\lambda_1 w + \kappa_1 r = \lambda_1 w' + \kappa_1 r'$$
$$\lambda_2 w + \kappa_2 r = \lambda_2 w' + \kappa_2 r'$$

From these two equations, we derive the condition:

$$r' - r = (\lambda_1/\kappa_1)(w - w') = (\lambda_2/\kappa_2)(w - w')$$

Since the capital–labour ratios are presumably different in the production of two commodities, the condition can only be satisfied if the factor prices are the same, $w = w'$, $r = r'$. It is here where Hicks leaves the theorem as proved. One should, however, notice that the result holds only if the technical coefficients (λ_i, κ_i) are *the same* in both countries (as Hicks cold-bloodedly assumes). But should they be equal since it is well known that they widely differ between say, developed and undeveloped countries? The interest rate is higher and wages are many times lower in an underdeveloped country and *that* requires an explanation. Unless we are back to 'disturbing causes' theory. The theorem says in fact that, if the two economies are sufficiently similar (same GNP per capita, same rate of growth, same system of taxation, etc.), the factor prices will be the same. And that is hardly very enlightening.

The assumptions of this artificial model, which are usually not spelled out and which generally underly the neoclassical reasoning are:

1. Financial and real capital are analytically identical. They are not, the former is *homogeneous*, the latter is *heterogeneous*.
2. One-commodity economy is representative of the many-commodity one. It is not because economy has its *structure*.
3. Adjustments are instantaneous. They are not but *last* in time.
4. Factors are symmetrical and their prices are equalized by trade. In reality, factors are *asymmetrical*. Financial capital is (relatively) mobile and its price, the interest rate, is made equal by international competition (except for differences reflecting risk). Labour is (relatively) immobile and differences in wages are enormous even if commodity market is perfect. They cannot be eliminated by trade.
5. Everything is predetermined. It is not, but depends on human initiative and other *stochastic* factors. An entrepreneur may start an industry because of his specific skills and other specific circumstances regardless of factor intensities. That will result in economies of experience. Innovations and technical advances play a similar role. In both cases it is the lower cost of production or simply the availability that determines the pattern of trade.

The other artificial assumptions will be mentioned later. It is important to realize that such assumptions are not first approximations (which is legitimate in science) but are counterfactual (which is illegitimate, as was geocentric assumption).

The above observations do not imply that there are no regularities in determining patterns of trade. They very likely exist, but they must be discovered by empirical research and not by a priori reasoning.

The same reasoning applies to the demand for capital (labour is fixed) as an inverse function of interest rate. Neoclassicals would argue that interest rate will diminish as capital becomes more abundant, which is the essence of the marginal productivity theory of interest. However, it will be shown later, if producer goods industries are more capital intensive, the increase of capital intensity will *increase* the rate of interest. Similarly conditions will be explored when an increase in land intensity will *increase* relative rents.

Utility This is defined to depend on independent individual choices. Like value depending on scarcity, the proposition is either a tautology or false. In the former case it is said that whatever is chosen represents maximum utility because consumers are sovereign in their choices. Thus, the assertion is always true. As Joan Robinson remarked: 'Utility is a metaphysical construct of impregnable circularity; utility is the quality in a commodity that makes individuals want to buy it, and the fact that individuals want to buy the commodities shows that they have utility' (1964, p. 48). In the latter case we know that choices are not sovereign but shaped by advertising, institutions and the behaviour of others. Consequently, it is inherently impossible to start from individual choices if we wish to maximize the utility of everybody. Our starting point must be society and its institutions designed in such a way that individual consumers are induced and enabled to maximize their utility.

Marginal productivities determine prices of factors of production Suppose the incremental capital–output ratio (labour remaining constant) is equal to three, ICOR = 3, which is close to empirical values. This implies a profit rate equal to 33%. However, we know that the actual rate of profit (gross of taxes) represents only about one-half of that magnitude or less. Why? Because profit is divided between workers and capitalists depending on the social strength of the two classes. Once wages are set, entrepreneurs proceed to allocate factors of production so as to maximize profits (or whatever goal they have). Thus, the actual causation is opposite from the one assumed.[5] Alternatively, if the causality is not assumed, the proposition that wages are equal to marginal value products (if this is possible) is a tautology. And that is not all.

The distribution of income according to marginal productivities of factors of production It is assumed that income results from the sale of factor services. Income is a reward for their productive contributions that exactly exhaust the product generated. That requires a special production function. It need not be linear homogeneous, but must satisfy the condition:

$$q = \Sigma f_i x_i$$

where $q = f(x)$ represents product as a function of productive factors. However, that makes profit equal to zero, $\pi = pq - \Sigma w_i x_i = pq - p\Sigma f_i x_i = 0$ (w_i are prices of factors' services). Since under capitalist institutions it is profit that makes economy tick, it cannot be non-existent. Distinguishing between pure, normal or natural profit provides no help. There will be a residual that is attributed to a non-measurable factor called 'entrepreneurship'. Consequently, not all factors are rewarded according to their marginal products. And if there is a residual, it may be distributed to all factors in many different ways. Thus, it may be closer to truth to interpret distribution as proceeding in accordance with property rights and other claims (Nell, 1980, p. 12).

The second best paradox In main-stream economics efficiency is treated primarily as (1) allocational efficiency: given the production possibility frontier, preferences and the initial distribution of income, allocate resources in such a way as to maximize social welfare provided that no one is made worse in the process. Technically that implies equality of marginal social benefit with marginal social cost, msb = msc, assuming that the underlying functions are properly shaped (continuous, monotonic and securing the stability of equilibrium). In the second step, (2) social costs and benefits are equated with private costs and benefits. Then two familiar theorems of welfare economics are derived: perfect competition leads to Pareto efficiency (meaning that there is no feasible allocation of goods such that all agents prefer it) and Pareto efficiency implies perfect competition. Thus, the proof is provided that we live in the best possible world.

The reasoning is misleading in all its stages. Leaving the initial distribution of income ('endowments') unproblematic, the reasoning is ideologically biased. Next, allocative efficiency is of trivial significance. The few attempts to measure welfare losses due to allocational imperfections indicate that they probably amount to considerably less than 1% of national income (Leibenstein, 1966, p. 393; in the Soviet Union about 1.5%, Whalley, 1976, p. 158). Given the production possibility set, this is once and for all loss that is likely to be repaired in one month of income growth. The much more important production efficiency (Leibenstein's *x*-efficiency) is generally left unexplored. And yet, productive efficiency is responsible for expanding production possibilities *every* year (Horvat, 1958b). A stagnant economy may be – and usually is – much more allocationally efficient than a fast growing economy. Commonsense would insist on the latter goal, but the teaching of economics deals almost exclusively with the former.

As for the step (2), monopoly (natural or market), externalities and public goods make identifications of marginal social and private calculus dubious, msb ≠ mpb, msc ≠ mpc.

The above remarks indicate that the theory described is poor or misleading or both because it is either not empirically relevant or directs teaching and research in the wrong direction. On top of that, it contains an aporia. In the ideal world postulated by the theory, all marginal equalities are satisfied and (Pareto) welfare is maximized. But we live in an imperfect world in which the established criteria of efficiency are of no use. For we do not know how to improve efficiency in order to move towards the ideal standard. As the familiar second best argument shows (Lipsey and Lancaster, 1956), if some of the necessary conditions for Pareto optimality are not satisfied, in general it is neither necessary nor desirable to satisfy the remaining conditions. Thus, either we already live in the ideal world of welfare theorems, and then no traffic signs are necessary to tell us that we are there; or we live far away, and then no traffic sign is available to tell us in which direction to move.

Individual preferences paradox Welfare theorems, mentioned in the preceding paragraph, imply another logical difficulty. If initial distribution of income and individual preferences are given, the volume and structure of output are determined for any existing technology. One of the preferences is the propensity to save, which determines the volume of saving. Saving may be increased (reduced) if interest rate (profit rate) is increased (reduced). But that implies changes in wages, i.e. a redistribution of income that will make some people worse off, and that contradicts initial assumptions. Therefore, additional adjustments are impossible. Mathematically speaking, the system would be overdetermined. Saving provides resources for investment, and investment is a precondition for the creation of new jobs. It is only by fluke that the number of new jobs offered and demanded is equal. And if some people (or capital) remain involuntarily unemployed, that cannot represent an efficient allocation of resources. Consequently, the achievement of the Pareto optimum means its destruction at the same time (even in the ideal world of perfect information and without public goods and external effects).

The contradiction may also be expressed in the following way. In the Fisherian neoclassical world, intertemporal preferences determine the rate of discount which, together with technology and profit maximization, determines the rate of investment. The latter is only by fluke equal to investment necessary to provide new jobs. And if preferences to work (i.e. full employment) are to be honoured as well, the system is overdetermined. Thus, individual preferences in a *laissez-faire* market are basically inconsistent and that is amply demonstrated by economic history.

Simple psychological analysis reveals the cause of the logical contradiction. Political liberalism dictated the view that each citizen's preference counts equally (economy of traders). But when it comes to industrial organization (economy of producers), wage earners and profit makers belong to two different classes whose preferences are opposed. Hence, two different optimalities which, in general, do not coincide.

The way out of the difficulty is rather obvious. The overriding *social* preference is full employment. It can be established by economic policy and not by *laissez-faire* market. Once established, the free play of individual choices leads to a consistent outcome. Full employment means full use of resources that will eventually make everybody better off. Thus, one would like to make full employment the focal point of the value theory and to view it as a direct precondition for the welfare optimum. Full employment (which includes technically determined frictional unemployment) is attainable, may be measured and increasing employment increases welfare.

Capital as a factor of production Every factor of production, such as labour or land, has independent existence and must be measurable in the unchanging units of measurement. Capital does not pass these tests because its value depends on the distribution of income into wages and profits. If capital, as embodied in fixed assets, remains absolutely unchanged, but the distribution parameters change, its value may change in any direction. Since capital cannot be reduced to a single quantity, it is logically impossible to calculate marginal products by varying unit-amounts.

The difficulty in dealing with capital arises from the fact that it lives a double existence: as a stock of goods and a sum of values. Productive capital, represented by producer goods *is* a factor of production. But different machines cannot be aggregated and they are being constantly created and destroyed by wear and tear.

To render it homogeneous, capital is presented in value form, as a fund that has a permanent existence. Ever since J.B. Clark capital was visualized by neoclassicals as a mythical entity that 'lives by transmigration, taking itself out of one set of bodies and putting itself into another, again and again' (Clark, 1899, pp. 9–20). In a more modern textbook formulation capital is 'regarded as a fund of abstract productive power which endures forever even though individual capital assets wear out and are replaced by different types of capital assets' (Dewey, 1965, p. 28). Capital fund yields interest like the money deposited in the bank. But this banking paradigm is ill-suited for a technologically determined production theory. A bank may reduce the demand for money by increasing the interest rate, which is a sort of price at which money is bought and sold. In the production sphere, higher interest rate is compatible with lower as well as with higher capital intensity, depending on the technology. In the market, each commodity has just one price; but the same technique may be used at a lower as well as at a higher interest rate if it happens to 'reswitch'.

Suppose interest rate in an economy is less than the rate of growth of net national product. That may happen when workers' savings are greater than capitalists' consumption (assuming no taxes and the rate of interest equal to the rate of profit). The value of national capital (representing the discounted value of infinitely expanding national income) in that economy will be infinite. Income generating assets will assume an infinite value also in the case when the interest rate is zero. To avoid such meaningless results, we must discard the definitions of a permanent productive power and make capital depend on a specific vintage of fixed and circulating assets of limited life-span.

Capital goods need not be aggregated. In the general equilibrium theory old and new machines are treated as different commodities, and dummy markets are created for contingent commodities. Now prices of the commodities can be determined for each time period and each state of nature. But in the equilibrium, profits disappear and the interest rates – linking the prices of commodities with those of their substitutes available at different points of time – have no specific connection with the prices of machines.

Capital theory is conceptually the least satisfactory part of the neoclassical theory.

Interest Neoclassical economics treats interest as a price for capital services. But any price must have a definite dimension, value per physical unit, and interest is nothing of the kind. Interest has only time dimension ($1/t$), and time is neither value nor commodity. As it cannot be explained within the theory, interest is treated metaphorically. The history of economic thought is known for a number of interest parables. Currently the most popular is the one that explains interest by time preference. This explanation is either tautological (high interest rate = high time preference, low interest rate = low time preference, whatever the reasons) or irrational (if now the cake of today is preferred to the cake of tomorrow, tomorrow the same cake will be preferred to the one eaten yesterday), or false. Namely, even if all individuals remain the same and, presumably, their time preferences do not change, the interest rate may change in any direction, depending on the rate of growth. It may even become negative and as such serve as a discount rate for evaluating investment projects. That will be illustrated in Chapter 4.

Macroeconomically, Keynes made interest primarily a monetary phenomenon; liquidity preference (given the money supply) determines interest rate and that has nothing to do with the time preference. In the neoclassical theory interest rate is determined by an interplay of the time preference (the supply of saving) and the marginal productivity of capital. The former is a metaphor and the latter is conceptually unsound, as we saw above. Substituting marginal productivity of investment for that of capital makes the proposition only slightly less meaningless.

Substitution If the price of a consumer good or of a productive input increases, they will be substituted by less expensive equivalents. Such substitution is legitimate and is empirically confirmed. But it becomes illegitimate when it is extended to the factors of production. If labour can always be substituted for capital, then, given flexible wages, labour will always be fully employed. But it is not. The empirical fact is that for any installed technology substitution possibilities are extremely limited, technical coefficients are practically fixed.[6]

Consider a simple model. In a closed economy with reproducible factors of production all costs consist of current and embodied (capital) labour. Production and consumption goods industries are assumed to have the same organic composition of resources, which is also empirically true (as an approximation capital–wage bill ratios are equal). If the relation between two components of labour does not change – because capital assets are getting cheaper in terms of labour in the same proportion in which labour is getting more productive in terms of quantities of produced capital goods – economic development means reducing *both* capital *and* labour per unit of physical output. Consequently, we may expect that there will be no substitutability between labour and capital. And, indeed, that is the case, at least for basic processes. Therefore, the general theorist is well advised to assume fixed coefficients.

This general conclusion may be modified in various ways in order to make it consistent with empirical evidence. Certain flexibility is provided by the fact that ancillary processes – handling, packaging, internal transport, storage processes, repair shops – do allow a certain amount of substitution between capital and labour. Next, an increase in the number of shifts and an increase in the size of capacity (generating economies of scale and increasing capital intensity) look like substitution activities although they are not. Also, the overall capital/labour intensity may be changed if different industries are allowed to grow at different rates, the structures of supply and demand being reconciled by exports and imports. However useful, this is not the neoclassical substitutability. It has been observed that in poor countries the labour intensive variants of certain production processes (i.e. in textiles) are used. But this is so because poor entrepreneurs cannot obtain sufficient capital to use more profitable capital-intensive processes that require larger plants. The history of the destruction of Indian cottage industry by imports of cheaper English industrial textiles is well known.

In general, for any new venture, substitution is technically possible within a large interval but is economically limited because new investment must also be profitable. Here technological progress intervenes. Modern, more mechanized, technology is usually more profitable than the older less mechanized one even if wages are lowered to a subsistence level. New technology generally reduces both capital and labour per unit of output. And even if this is not the case, the required higher quality and greater precision make capital intensive automation indispensable. Thus, the assumption of great substitution possibilities between labour and capital is misleading. Empirically feasible substitution is very modest *ex ante* and almost non-existent *ex post* (at full capacity). Economically meaningful isoquants do not exist as curves of any length. And if the capital–labour relation cannot vary very much in the short run, unemployment cannot be cured by lower wages but by greater investments (in a closed economy).

Strictly speaking, unlimited smooth substitution assumption does not generate conceptual difficulties but rather erroneous theoretical conclusions. The concept is not logically contradictory but is simply misleading being an empty box.

Analytical and historical time Analytical time belongs to static and historical time to dynamic analysis. The latter is considered more realistic but is also incomparably more complicated. Therefore, static analysis is often treated as a simple approximation to reality. This approach encounters two difficulties, one logical and one substantial. The logical difficulty may be illustrated by the concept of marginal product. In analytical time it is a legitimate concept: one variable varies while all others are kept constant and that is expressed by a partial derivative. When the concept is used in actual description of economic activities, one enters historical time. Here at least *two* variables vary, the original one *and time*, and the former partial derivative is inapplicable. One really needs the second derivative since all variables are functions of time. Thus, marginal product of labour will be $\delta Q/\delta L\delta t$, and there is no reason why the first and the second derivative should be equal. Quite the contrary, they will usually have different signs because the static marginal product is decreasing and the dynamic one is increasing (because of technological progress). One may say that in the world of no changes, the time variable may be neglected and then there are no inconsistences. The trouble is that economic theoreticians do not remain in the imaginary timeless world but they apply their conclusions to the real world. This logical jump usually leads to completely false characterization of the economy as is demonstrated by e.g. the neoclassical theory of Illyrian firm (Horvat, 1986a).

The substantial mistake simply means poor theory. The analytical time, with concomitant marginal equalities, is applicable to long-run decisions (when all variables can be varied independently of each other) or to a full use of conventional capacity. However, most of the decisions are short run and, over the business cycle, most of the time capacity is not fully used. Consequently, the theory is seldom applicable. As an illustration, take again the theory of the firm. The theory postulates that the maximization of profit requires that marginal cost be equal to price or marginal revenue. It assumes that costs can be classified into fixed and variable costs. Fixed costs, being constant, do not influence partial derivatives. However, there are two kinds of fixed costs: sunk costs and contractual costs; the former are postponable, the latter must be regularly paid whatever the use of capacity.

Now, contractual costs do *not* enter marginal costs (as usually defined) but *do* enter the price (Horvat, 1991).

It is, of course, possible to reformulate the mainstream theory so that all decisions become long-run ones. But that would destroy its simplicity, symmetry and aesthetic beauty. Therefore, that is not done and a great deal of microeconomic and general equilibrium theory remains meaningless.

False behavioural (and welfare) assumptions One of the basic assumptions of neoclassical welfare theory is that (1) money income has great utility and determines the demand for labour, (2) labour is unpleasant, represents a disutility that determines the supply of labour, and (3) the equilibrium employment and highest welfare are determined by the intersection of the two curves. Psychological and economic empirical research have falsified all three statements. Robert Lane (1991) has shown that utility of money income is modest and that it is the sense of achievement that represents the most important source of motivation. Consequently, it is not the quantity of consumption goods but social organization of production that is behaviourally important. Lane also showed that (free) work, far from being a disutility, is one of two major sources of lifetime satisfaction. Consequently, even fully compensated unemployment represents a great welfare loss. If the two fundamental assumptions are false, the conclusion cannot be right. We, therefore, witness the appearance of new employment theories that try to explain the observed facts. More importantly, the elaborate logical structure, built on two arbitrary assumptions, must be theoretically useless.

1.3.2 Synergetic effects

I shall next list several synergetic effects that do not fit the neoclassical paradigm. They are closely connected with what logicians call the fallacy of composition.

The methodological individualism contradiction If economic events may be predicted from the behaviour of individual economic agents, which is the basic methodological hypothesis of neoclassical economics, then macroeconomics is simply microeconomics aggregated. We know that this conclusion contradicts empirical evidence. We also know why: systemic effects are not accounted for. There is an interesting episode in the postwar methodological debate that illustrates the point well. How does a firm behave? The following hypotheses have been offered: the firm (1) maximizes profits, (2) maximizes the share of the market, (3) maximizes a multivariate utility function (profit, prestige, control, etc.), (4) satisfices because of information constraints, (5) uses rules-of-thumb because of uncertainty.

Methodological individualism requires that the five hypotheses be empirically tested and the one that passes the test best be taken as a basis for the theory of the firm. However, that is not done. It is proclaimed that, in order to survive under competition, firms behave *as if* they maximized profits, and that the realism of the hypotheses–assumptions is irrelevant; what matters is prediction. This is the answer given by Milton Friedman (1953) and others and it has come to be known as theoretical instrumentalism. Instrumentalism fails to provide us with complete explanation, and without the explanation, we are never sure that macroeconomics will work in the same way next time. This is the price to be paid because of the poor methodology. However, for our present purpose, the most important is the logical contradiction involved: it is proclaimed that the *behaviour of the system be derived from the behaviour of individual agents*; in fact the procedure is reversed and the consistency is achieved by deriving the *behaviour of the agents from the working of the system* (see Blaug, 1980, pp. 117–19).

Keynes's thrift paradox The more an individual saves, the better off he is (his wealth increases). The more all individuals save, the worse off they are (because aggregate demand shrinks causing unemployment). Private virtues turn out to be a public vice. In a closed household, saving provides possibility for investment. In a closed economy it is the other way round: investment generates saving. Unemployment, due to low level of business activities caused by low profitability, cannot be cured by reduction of wages but by an increase in spending. More generally, *rational* behaviour of all agents may generate cyclical downturns in which everybody is *worse off*.

The crowding effect The effect is due to the limited absorptive capacity of an economy for productive investment. For high rates of investment (around 40% of GNP) marginal social efficiency of investment is reduced to zero and even below zero. At the same time, firms will be unaware of that because the marginal efficiency of investment for individual firms will be positive and so will interest rate (Horvat, 1968).

The replacement effect Even if the technology does not change, real capital cost per unit of output for an economy varies with the rate of growth (see Chapter 4).

The employment effect While in an economy with constant technology the real capital cost per unit of output falls as the rate of growth increases, the labour cost per unit of net output increases because of demographic investment (see section 4.2).

Most of the problems enumerated above can be solved by inserting Ptolemaic epicycles into the neoclassical theory. But it is obviously more desirable to design a different theory that will generate explanations in a simpler way and straightforwardly.

1.3.3 The implicit social system assumptions

The neoclassical theory is about the efficient allocation of resources. But it fails to achieve its professed goal and, in fact, it cannot possibly achieve it given the assumptions about the social system. Thus, the *implicit social system assumptions* provide the third group of objections against the neoclassical paradigm. Using the epicycle called 'The Golden Rule' – which makes little sense in a *laissez-faire* economy and properly belongs to a planned economy – Richard Goodwin (1982, p. 171), advances the following set of arguments:

> (1) To each profit rate corresponds a rate of relative prices. A change in relative prices alters a technique of production chosen by competitive producers.
> (2) To any particular growth rate there corresponds an efficient technique ... which ... yields a greater consumption than any other technique.
> (3) This best technique will be chosen by competitive producers if the profit rate on invested capital equals the growth rate.
> (4) Any consumption by owners of produced capital goods means that a profit rate is greater than growth rate. The result is a choice of an inefficient technique, in the sense that both capitalists and workers could consume more had the technique associated with equal growth and profit rates been chosen.
> (5) All capitalist economies are inefficient in this sense, since capitalists also in fact consume part of profits.
> (6) Any profit rate greater than growth rate amounts to levying taxes on output for the benefit of a particular class. The result is ... a sub-optimal allocation of resources. This is separate from and additional to the unjustifiable distribution of consumption.
> (7) Therefore, optimality requires in effect expropriation of capitalists, since if the owners of capital can never, now or in a future, consume any of the income, the ownership of capital is nominal, its "fruits" accruing to the whole society.

Optimality also requires economic (not legal) expropriation of landowners because otherwise a perfectly competitive economy generates higher prices and an inefficient allocation of resources. The distortion of rent, due to the institution of private property, together with the allocationally correct determination of rent, will be discussed in Chapter 13.

Generally, even in the most perfect competition, pricing – and, consequently, allocation of resources – is inefficient because of institutional constraints posed by private property.

Having listed the important defects of contemporary theorizing, I focused on logical inconsistences and contradictions. As already noted, the logical consistency is the primary and necessary (though not sufficient) condition for an acceptable theory. Logically deficient theories end up – with rare exceptions – to be also empirically false theories. That is well demonstrated in Lester Thurow's (1983) analysis of the deficiencies of the modern economic theories as empirically relevant and in Alfred Eichner's (1983, pp. 210–18) analysis of empirical emptiness of the four crucial neoclassical constructs (indifference curves, isoquants, positively sloped supply curves and marginal physical product curves).

1.4 The labour theory of value

The value theory represents the core of any economic theory. In this sense it is paradigmatic for an economic theory. Or, in the words of Joseph Schumpeter: '... the problem of value must always hold the pivotal position, as the chief tool of analysis in any pure theory that works with a rational scheme' (1954, p. 588).

I shall make use of the insight of classical economists who realized that labour is not just one of the factors of production, fully symmetrical with others, but that it enjoys a unique position in the economic process being its prime mover. This is certainly true sociologically. It will prove to be true economically as well, providing so an opportunity for the design of a possible grand social science synthesis at some future date.

Assuming that giving birth to a child is determined by autonomous values not directly related to economics, the population changes will be considered exogenous. For the purpose of this study, the participation in the labour force will also be considered as exogenously motivated. (A positive theory of employment will easily relax this assumption.) Thus, labour force is given at any moment of time. What we are after is to maximize the production of consumer goods in order to maximize economic welfare of the population (given the distribution of income determined by other considerations; Horvat, 1982, ch. 9–III). Given material resources and technology, this will be achieved if the labour input in every product produced is minimized. Consequently, all we need is to determine the quantity of labour embodied in commodities in order to allocate them optimally. The commodities are evaluated in labour time, prices are determined as labour (time) prices.

The general professional opinion about labour prices is reflected in the contention that they are either impossible or that they provide false indicators of allocation. One of the standard questions in the undergraduate economics exams is to ask why is the labour theory of value false? To substantiate these observations, I shall quote four representative opinions of the authors that cover the entire spectrum of political–ideological positions, from a conservative to radical and socialist ones:

> The postulate of asymmetry – people make machines but not vice versa – is, of course, the foundation of the so called labour theory of value and the pointless activity of people who take it seriously.... The labour theory of value is an intellectual curiosity that economists have long since abandoned to theologians. (Dewey, 1965, pp. 25, 41)

> One of the conclusions of this book is that Marx's economics can acquire citizenship in contemporary economic theory by detaching it from its root, the labour theory of value and grafting it onto the von Neumann stock so as to produce Marx–von Neumann flower. (Morishima, 1973, p. 194)

> If we define *value* as the labour time required to produce a commodity and then advance the proposition that commodities normally exchange at prices proportional to their *values* in this sense, then we have to reduce it from a metaphysical statement to a hypothesis. But it is a hypothesis that it would be a waste of time to test, for we know in advance, and Marx also knows, that it is not accurate. (Robinson, 1964, p. 38)

> The labour theory of value ... while of interest for the history of economic thought, has no place in today's economic analysis because it has been overthoroughly demolished. (Lerner, 1972, p. 50)

Five standard objections are used to dismiss the labour theory of value:

1. It cannot explain prices of goods in fixed supply such as works of art, rare books and old stamps.
2. It cannot explain prices of goods in excess supply (or demand).
3. It cannot explain differences in prices due to heterogeneity of labour. In other words, wages of labour of differing skills can be explained only in terms of the value of their products.
4. It cannot handle price formation when two primary factors are involved.
5. It cannot explain relative prices because labour is not the only factor of production and simple addition of labour time spent in production gives patently wrong prices.

To refute the first four objections is not particularly difficult:

1. The labour theory attempts to explain the prices of *reproducible* goods and so it cannot be criticized for failing to do something it never intended to do.

   Already Ricardo knew that commodities in fixed supply 'form a very small part of the mass of commodities daily exchanged in the market' (Ricardo, 1821, p. 12), and as such were not particularly interesting. We saw in the preceding section that the only alternative theory, the scarcity theory, is an exercise in circular reasoning: value is explained by scarcity; scarcity is not physical but demand determined concept; and demand depends on values attributed to commodities.

Though not designed to deal with fixed supply, labour theory can nevertheless say something meaningful applying the concept of opportunity cost. When I consider the prospects of buying an old stamp, I evaluate its price in terms of labour time necessary to earn an equivalent income. The ratio of prices is equal to ratios of opportunity labour costs.

2. Labour theory is an equilibrium theory. As such it provides standards for the evaluations of non-equilibrium and non-efficient positions.
3. As noted in the preceding section, the distribution of income is institutionally determined. Strong unions and social-democratic governments make for a lot of difference in the wage structure. Labour management increases wages up to the limit of technological possibility by wiping out (excess) profits. Different countries using the same technology have different wage differentials. Long ago English economist Dickinson, a socialist by persuasion, exposed the institutional determination of the wage structure in his *Institutional Revenue* (1932). The book was simply ignored by neoclassical professional establishment. More recently, Piero Sraffa was somewhat more successful. He showed, in the words of Joan Robinson, that 'a given technical situation is compatible with any proportion of relative shares. This rules out the notion of earnings determined by productivity'. Thus, the distribution appears to depend 'upon commercial, social and political influences and the fortunes of the class war' (Bhaduri and Robinson, 1980, p. 111).

   It follows that wages are set institutionally and production is adjusted to maximize profits – which is the causation already mentioned. Wages are social weights attached to different categories of workers. In this way workers are rendered homogeneous, standard workers who can be counted. All that remains to achieve conceptual consistency is to assume perfect substitutability of standard workers at the margin of production for adjustment purposes. It also follows that wages cannot be treated symmetrically with rent and interest, which is the simple recognition of the fact that workers are not commodities. It will be shown later in the text (Section 14.2) that the heterogeneity of labour can be easily incorporated in the analysis.
4. The second primary factor is non-producible land. If land is produced – say an artificial island in the sea – it represents capital and not a primary resource. Land as a primary factor is not produced, consequently does

not incur cost and the income it generates – rent – does not enter cost of production. Rent is not the cause but the result of price formation. Land in fixed supply is a factor counterpart to commodities in fixed supply whose price is pure scarcity price, i.e. depends exclusively on demand. In a sufficiently short short run, any factor may be non-reproducible and earn rent. In the long run, rent is the difference between the (scarcity) value of demand and the labour value of supply, which is insufficient to meet demand if only the most efficient technique of production is used. Since rent is a demand generated addition to costs of production, the Ricardo solution of the problem may be applied: consider production at the margin where no rent is generated. A different aspect of land is often confused with the one just described (Buchanan, 1929). As a primary factor, land is in fixed supply. But land has many alternative uses, and for any particular use it is not in fixed supply. Thus, rent as an opportunity cost enters costs of production. This aspect will not be considered.

5. The fifth objection is a real one. The Ricardo–Marx labour theory of value is certainly not accurate. It is, however, a *non sequitur* to claim that *any* labour theory of value *must* be false in a non-stationary economy. Economic processes occur in time. Time is an intrinsic dimension of economic phenomena. It is therefore, an elementary requirement of economic analysis that all dated variables be brought to the same point of time. Ricardo and Marx committed a methodological error in adding dated labour diachronically. (Admittedly they did that because they did not know how to aggregate labour otherwise, but that is a different story.) The procedure is illegitimate because in a changing economy, dated labour is not homogeneous and cannot be added. If, however, the synchrony rule is followed and care is taken of the relevant synergetic effects, the road is opened to a rigorous labour theory of value that is also a theory of relative prices. It is the purpose of this study to explore how far we can travel along this road.

Regarding any theory of value, three questions may be asked: about the source of value, about its determinants and about the measure of value.

The first question is somewhat metaphysical and is not particularly interesting analytically. The answer, however implies quite important theoretical consequences in political economy; the proper answer permits a meaningful definition of surplus (value). As no good has an economic (exchange) value if it is not useful, it may be argued that utility is the source of value (J.B. Say). That is more than we need, notes Walras (1874, p. 201) since extremely useful goods, such as air, may have no exchange value. For this reason, since Adam Smith, economists have distinguished between use value and exchange value and have tried to explain the source of the latter. Common observation indicates that a useful thing acquires exchange value when its supply is limited relative to demand. A good that is both useful and available in limited quantitities relative to demand may be called scarce. Thus, neoclassical economists generally argue that scarcity is a proper source of value. That, however, leads to circular reasoning described above: a useful thing has exchange value when it is scarce, and we declare it scarce when we observe that it has exchange value! On the other hand, classical economists pronounced labour as the source of value (value without qualifying adjective always means exchange value). That is less than we need, notes Walras, because valuable objects, such as collectors' items, do not embody labour. Therefore Ricardo simply admitted that 'possessing utility, commodities derive their exchangeable value from two sources: from their scarcity, and from the quantity of labour required to obtain them' (1821, p. 11).

I prefer to answer the first question in the following way. In order to maximize economic welfare of individuals comprising society, an optimal allocation of resources and an optimal structure of final output (given the distribution of income) ought to be achieved. For that purpose, heterogenous goods and services must be attributed exchange values so that they can be aggregated and properly allocated. A good is produced in quantities that satisfy demand at a value depending on labour inputs technologically necessary. For reproducible goods, as noted by J.S. Mill (1848, p. 455), it is not supply and demand that determine value, it is the value that determines supply and demand. Since value depends on labour, labour is the source of value, and labour values are objectively determined. If a good with use value does not require labour input for its procurement, it is either a free good with no exchange value or a non-reproducible good with positive exchange value. The latter goods, being in *fixed* supply, do not acquire value in the process of *production*. If they are consumption goods, they can be exchanged at values that consumers subjectively choose to attribute to them (while taking account of the opportunity labour costs). If they render productive services, they merely modify the input of labour. It appears that labour value is objective and measurable and represents a production concept while scarcity value is subjective and unmeasurable and represents a consumption concept. They belong to different fields of analysis. The difference between exchange value and labour value, if it exists, represents rent. The difference between exchange value and scarcity value makes no sense and for two reasons: (a) the former is an objective and the latter a subjective quantity and (b) because the latter is defined to be always proportional to the former (at the margin).

The foregoing answer has also well-known theoretical consequence. If labour adds value to objects used in production, and the remuneration of labour (wages) is less than the value added, the difference represents a surplus appropriated by the owners. This surplus measures the rate of exploitation unless the owners are all members of the society.

As for the second question, three determinants of exchange value may be recognized: social distribution of wealth, individual subjective preferences and objective input of resources itself dependent on the available technology. Regarding the third question, labour (time) is the measure of exchange value. Unlike the scarcity theory with its unmeasurable subjective utility, the labour theory is able to use an objective measure.

Labour values serve primarily as a normative standard for efficiency comparisons. They are, therefore, long-run equilibrium values. That implies full employment of labour and full use of productive capacity. The unit value of a good or service is called price.

One last point concerns the loose talk about labour prices often found in the literature. Ever since Smith invented his measure of 'the labour which a commodity can command', real values or labour prices have been derived from market prices deflated by wages (p_j/w). The dimension is correct, labour time per unit of output (Lt/X_j), but the magnitude is not. The price is arbitrary, not optimal. No amount of competition will make such prices optimal, i.e. efficient, unless certain systemic conditions are fulfilled.

2 The model

2.1 The general model

The model to be used in the present study has the following ingredients:

I. Six classes of economic objects
   A. Two final products
      1. Heterogeneous consumer goods
      2. Heterogeneous investment goods
   B. Intermediate products
      3. Heterogeneous intermediate goods
   C. Three resources
      4. Heterogeneous labour
      5. Heterogeneous capital
      6. Heterogeneous land

Labour and land are primary, capital is a produced resource. Capital (5) and investment goods (2) are physically identical but economically different. The former is a resource, the latter are products. This 'double character' of capital is a source of confusion and analytical difficulties.

II. Investment and intermediate goods make producer goods that consist of *fixed assets* and *inventories*. Fixed assets belong to different vintages and have different durability. However, it will be assumed that they have the same rectangular time profile, i.e. the output capacity remains unchanged during the service life and the scrap value is zero. This is an analytical, not an essential simplification, and is a good approximation to reality. Fixed assets with different time profiles are analysed in Horvat (1973a). Inventories may be assumed proportional to output and as such they are absorbed in proportionally augmented technical coefficients. Even simpler is the assumption of perfect synchronization of production and consumption so that there is no need for inventories.

III. *Production.* Each commodity is produced by one or more alternative fixed-proportion activities that are additive and exhibit constant returns to scale for a given technology. Commodities can also be jointly produced. It is assumed that the production period of fixed assets is one time period called one year. By the end of the year they are installed and are ready for production from the beginning of the next year. Production periods of all other commodities are $1/n_i$ years, where n_i are integer numbers 1,2,.... The output capacity is assumed to be fully used. Labour force changes only at the beginning of the year. If an industry produces a commodity for different economic uses – e.g. refrigerators for households and for restaurants – it will be notionally separated into two industries, one producing pure consumer good and the other producing pure producer good. Everything else is left to the theory of the firm.

IV. *Consumption* depends on consumer preferences and the distribution of income, which are assumed exogenously given. Endogenization is a matter of respective empirical theories, which is left to the theory of consumer behaviour.

V. *Technological progress* is neutral or biased, embodied or unembodied, different for different industries and is exogenously given. As such it determines the rate of growth of output for a given labour force. Endogenization of technological progress is left to the theory of economic growth (see Horvat, 1972). Economy of scale as well as external economies and diseconomies, i.e. non-constant returns are included in the effects of technological progress.

VI. *Economy* is closed. Opening the economy is left to the theory of foreign trade. Next, economy is either stationary or changing. If changing, it changes (expands or contracts) at a constant rate. Variable rates of growth would require the consideration of transition from one steady state to another, which is left to the theory of planning.

VII. Since the model is *normative*, not behavioural, certainty and full information are assumed.

VIII. *Monetary* (money and banking operations) and *fiscal* (taxation) processes are left to the theory of economic policy. However, by its inherent logic, the model will generate financial flows providing, thus, a basis for an integration of real and financial processes.

The foregoing eight characteristics do not represent the full description of the model. In order to avoid repetition, the remaining characteristics will be described in the section dealing with the canonical model. Namely, if the full set of characteristics were kept all the time, the analysis would become unwieldy. For this reason we need a simpler model to start with.

2.2 The elimination of intermediate products

Consider a closed economy consisting of n industries each producing one commodity. The book of blueprints is much larger, but selected are only the most efficient techniques, one for each industry. The criteria for selection will be discussed in due course. These techniques are observed. The economy may be described by an input–output format in which the rows represent shipments of goods for intermediate and final use while the columns represent activities (processes). At the beginning of the reproduction cycle, certain quantities of resources are available: primary labour and reproducible capital. Non-producible land is neglected as inessential for the purpose at hand. Labour (workers of a standard skill) and capital (plants of a standard specification) are homogeneous and are measured in terms of numbers of identical units (worker-years and plant-years). The number of standard workers is obtained by attributing each worker its social weight (wage), assuming perfect substitutability. Standard plants are assumed to be multipurpose plants capable of producing any consumer or producer good. Admittedly, this is a heroic simplification. But it will take us very far. It follows that capital–output ratios and capital–worker ratios will differ depending on what is being produced.

	Intermediate output shipped to industries				Final output	Gross output
	1	2	...	n		
Industries: 1	x_{11}	x_{12}	...	x_{1n}	X_1	$\hat{X}_1$
2	x_{21}	x_{22}	...	x_{2n}	X_2	$\hat{X}_2$
	.	.	...	.	.	.
	.	.	...	.	.	.
	.	.	...	.	.	.
n	x_{n1}	x_{n2}	...	x_{nn}	X_n	$\hat{X}_n$
Resources:						
Labour	$\hat{L}_1$	$\hat{L}_2$	...	$\hat{L}_n$		
Capital	$\hat{K}_1$	$\hat{K}_2$	...	$\hat{K}_n$		
Gross output:	$\hat{X}_1$	$\hat{X}_2$	...	$\hat{X}_n$		

The input–output schema displays the basic economic duality of which we shall make use right from the beginning. In order to balance the economy (to achieve an equilibrium), the planner (market) must produce two sets of balance equations. Summing up across the rows, material balances will be produced with all output being distributed between intermediate and final demand and all resources being distributed among industries:

$$\begin{aligned} &\sum_j x_{ij} + X_i = \hat{X}_i \\ &\sum_j \hat{L}_j = L, \quad \sum_j \hat{K}_j = K \qquad i,j = 1, \ldots n \end{aligned} \tag{2.1}$$

In order to sum up the columns, a consistent set of prices must be used:

$$\sum p_i x_{ij} + w\hat{L}_j + rp_k^j \hat{K}_j = p_j \hat{X}_j, \quad i,j=1,\dots n \tag{2.2}$$

Here we have a dimensional problem. $\hat{X}_j$ and x_{ij} are flows, $\hat{L}_j$ and $\hat{K}_j$ are stocks. For the purpose of value balances we shall interpret L as worker-years and K as plant-years. Consequently w is the price of one worker-year and rp_k^j is the price of one plant-year. Note that r, an interest rate, has the dimension $1/t$, which represents the rate of change per unit of time.

The sets of balances do not imply behavioural equilibrium. For that, in addition, *ex ante* plans must be fulfilled. For our purpose that is irrelevant. But they do imply normative equilibrium, because resources are fully used and best techniques are applied while consumers' preferences are respected.

Since the gross output of an economy must be the same whether summation is carried across the rows or down the columns, we may write:

$$\sum_j p_i \hat{X}_i = \sum_i \sum_j p_i x_{ij} + \sum_i p_i X_i = \sum_j \sum_i p_i x_{ij} + w \sum_j \hat{L}_j + r \sum_j p_k^j \hat{K}_j = \sum_j p_j \hat{X}_j \tag{2.3}$$

Intermediate products cancel out and we get the familiar social accounting identity (in vectors):

$$\sum p_i X_i \equiv wL + rp_k\, K \tag{2.4}$$

the value of final output is equal to gross national income distributed between labour and capital. This identity holds only for the sum total, not sectorally:

$$p_i X_i \neq w\hat{L}_i + rp_k^i \hat{K}_j.$$

To establish sectoral equality we need some more computation.

Define technical coefficients of production processes:

reproduction coefficients $\quad a_{ij} = \dfrac{x_{ij}}{\hat{X}_j}$

labour coefficients $\quad \hat{\lambda}_j = \dfrac{\hat{L}_j}{\hat{X}_j}$

capital coefficients $\quad \hat{\kappa}_j = \dfrac{\hat{K}_j}{\hat{X}_j}$

In a more compact notation, technical coefficients may be expressed by a reproduction matrix $A=[a_{ij}]$ and by two row vectors of resource coefficients, $\hat{\lambda}=[\hat{\lambda}_j]$ and $\hat{\kappa}=[\hat{\kappa}_j]$. The summation across the rows gives:

$$\begin{aligned} A\hat{X}+X&=\hat{X} \\ \hat{\lambda}\hat{X}&=L \\ \hat{\kappa}\hat{X}&=K \end{aligned} \tag{2.5}$$

Since intermediate transactions may be cancelled out, it is desirable to find a linear operator that will map final, not gross, output into resources sectorally. In the terminology of input–output analysis, direct coefficients (resources per unit of gross output, $\hat{\lambda}_j$ and $\hat{\kappa}_j$) are replaced by full coefficients (resources per unit of final output, λ_j and κ_j). It follows immediately that:

$$\begin{aligned} \hat{X}&=(I-A)^{-1}X \\ \hat{\lambda}(I-A)^{-1}X&=L \\ \hat{\kappa}(I-A)^{-1}X&=K \end{aligned} \tag{2.6}$$

The required operator is the Leontief inverse and full coefficients are given by $\lambda=\hat{\lambda}(I-A)^{-1}$ and $\kappa=\hat{\kappa}(I-A)^{-1}$. In this way available labour and capital are reallocated among vertically integrated sectors, which produce final output of resources directly without the mediation of intermediate production. Total labour and total capital remain the same, $\Sigma\hat{L}_j=\hat{L}=\Sigma L_j=L$, $\Sigma\hat{K}_j=\hat{K}=\Sigma K_j=K$, but sectoral allocation of resources is different, $\hat{L}_j\neq L_j$, $\hat{K}_j\neq K_j$. Full resource coefficients are larger than the direct ones, $\lambda_j=\frac{L_j}{X_j}>\frac{\hat{L}_j}{\hat{X}_j}=\hat{\lambda}_j$ (and similarly for κ_j) because $(I-A)^{-1}>I$, A indecomposable in (2.6). The social accounting identity is given by:

$$pX=wL+rp_kK=(w\hat{\lambda}+rp_k\hat{\kappa})(I-A)^{-1}X=(w\lambda+rp_k\kappa)X \tag{2.4a}$$

It is also possible to proceed in the following way. A full labour coefficient means direct and indirect (with respect to intermediate goods) labour per unit of final output. For good j[1]:

$$\lambda_j=\hat{\lambda}_j+\sum_i a_{ij}\lambda_i \tag{2.7}$$

or in matrix notation

$$\lambda=\hat{\lambda}+\lambda A \tag{2.8}$$

from which it follows that

$$\lambda = \hat{\lambda}(I - A)^{-1} \tag{2.9}$$

and similarly for full capital coefficients.

There is yet another possibility to calculate full coefficients if duality property is taken into account. Use (2.2) to sum up the values of the columns:

$$pA + w\hat{\lambda} + rp_k\hat{\kappa} = p$$
$$p = w\hat{\lambda}(I - A)^{-1} + rp_k\hat{\kappa}(I - A)^{-1} = w\lambda + rp_k\kappa \tag{2.10}$$

Full labour and capital coefficients are the same as above. If left- and right-hand sides of (2.10) are post multiplied by the vector of final outputs X, gross national income is obtained as in (2.4a). Besides, (2.10) shows how prices of commodities resolve into the wage and rental parts. Raw material costs (pA) have been absorbed into full coefficients.

2.3 Canonical model

In designing our canonical model we might wish to follow a certain minimax procedure. We would like to have the simplest possible model with the maximum of strategic relationships preserved undistorted. If that is achieved, we shall be able to generalize the model in various directions selecting from the catalogue of the general model one feature at a time.

The structure of an economic paradigm is not unlike that of physics. Physics studies specific physical *objects* (particles) that are moved around by *forces* (four of them) and the system is governed by certain basic *principles* (of symmetry, of least action, of conservation of energy) and generates certain basic *effects* (relativity, quantum).[2] The conceptual inventory of our economic model may be described in the following way:

A. *Three economic objects*

1. *Consumer goods* in standard assortments called baskets (X_1). Consumer goods are characterized by use value which, being subjective, is not measurable. Baskets, being standard, may be counted and added. The process of producing consumer goods has three dimensions: a number of baskets of certain utility is produced within a period of time.
2. *Producer goods* of a standard specification called plants (X_2). Plants consist of structures and machine outfits. Since structures change slowly, the main attention is focused on machines and so this term is used interchangeably with plants. Plants represent the only produced resource, homogeneous fixed capital (K_j). It is

characterized by durability n ($0<n<\infty$) and efficiency $\kappa_j = K_j/X_j$. Depending on the context, K_j is the number of identical plants or of plant-years in industry j vertically integrated. Plant-time is perfectly divisible. All plants last exactly n years with constant output capacity, which is always fully used and at the end of their service life they are scrapped without cost or benefit. The production process has four dimensions: a number of plants of a certain durability and efficiency used within a period of time.

3. Homogeneous *labour* (L) is the only primary resource. It is characterized by productivity measured by labour coefficients, $\lambda_j = L_j/X_j$. Depending on the context, L_j is a number of identical workers or worker-years in the vertically integrated industry j. In the latter case there is perfect divisibility. The production process has three dimensions: a number of workers working with certain productivity within a period of time.

B. Labour and capital coefficients together with the durability of plants represent *alternative technologies of the vertically integrated economic system*, $T(\lambda, \kappa, n)$, which change in time. Before vertical integration, technology would also include separate matrix of technical coefficients (A). In the present model this matrix is implied but is not made explicit.

C. *One structural–behavioural postulate*: There are four classes of economic agents who are rational and maximize the satisfaction of their preferences: consumers maximize utility, producers and bankers profits and planners social welfare. The latter implies that the sole purpose of production is the output of consumer goods. Consequently: (a) net output consists of consumer goods only; (b) everything else represents supporting output, and (c) maximized consumption implies the application of the most efficient techniques and the full use of resources.

D. *Three principles*

1. *Duality principle.* Quantity and price relationships are simultaneously generated by the same structure of an economy.
2. *Synchrony principle.* The dimensionality of L and K in the production process (i.e. the variability in time of their various characteristics) requires that in a changing economy all inputs and outputs be evaluated at the same point of time in order to make them commensurable. It is only in the stationary economy, which remains the same through time, that diachronic and synchronic labour inputs are the same.
3. *Conservation principle.* The value of outputs is equal to the value of inputs.

E. *Two dynamic effects*

1. *Replacement effect* (K input). The effect is present only in a changing economy. Because of the durability of plants, replacement cost per unit of output capacity decreases (increases) as the rate of growth of capital stock increases (decreases).
2. *Employment effect* (L input) also appears only in a changing economy. Because of the requirement of full employment, the cost of producing net output (consumer goods) increases (decreases) as the rate of labour force growth increases (decreases). This increased (reduced) costs consist in providing jobs for new workers.

The two dynamic effects are logical consequences of the synchrony principle. And, of course, they are empirically real and measurable. The equivalence between the rate of physical change of L and K and the value change characterized by the interest rate to be demonstrated in due course, is a consequence of the duality principle.

The analysis in the preceding section suggested, and the present model incorporated this suggestion, that all industries be aggregated in two sectors. The first sector produces baskets of consumer goods and the second sector produces plants (machines). The two-sector model, pioneered by Marx in the 1860s but well developed only after the Second World War, has proved to be an extremely versatile tool in economic analysis.

3 Stationary economy

The same volume and structure of output is produced year after year. The number of workers and the number of machines do not change in time. Technology is also fixed. Input and output flows remain constant through time.

3.1 Material and value balances

As already mentioned, the economy displays a duality that has far-reaching consequences. Resources (and technology) determine output, and consistent value balances of output flows determine prices. On the other hand, given the prices, the allocation of resources follows. Accordingly, there are two sets of equations that determine output and prices respectively.

We start, as do planners in a Planning Bureau, by producing material balances of resources:

$$\text{Resource balances: } \begin{aligned} L_1 + L_2 &= L \\ K_1 + K_2 &= K \end{aligned} \qquad (3.1)$$

In order to keep the output capacity constant under stationary conditions, $1/n$ scrapped machines must be replaced every year in each sector:

$$R_j = \frac{1}{n} K_j, \quad j = 1,2$$

and so capital balance may be expressed as:

$$\text{Investment balance: } R_1 + R_2 = \frac{1}{n} K$$

Labour and capital are allocated to vertically integrated sectors 1 (production of baskets) and 2 (production of machines). The input of resources, evaluated at consistent prices, must satisfy value balances:

$$\text{Value balances: } \begin{aligned} p_2 R_1 + w L_1 &= p_1 X_1 \\ p_2 R_2 + w L_2 &= p_2 X_2 \end{aligned} \qquad (3.2)$$

Consistent with the synchrony rule, in value balances, capital input is simply equal to gross investment $p_2 R_j$. We must also observe equilibrium conditions whereby the output of machines is equal to replacement of machines and the wage bill is equal to the value of consumer goods:

$$\text{Equilibrium conditions: } R_1 + R_2 = X_2$$
$$wL = p_1 X_1 \qquad (3.3)$$

The third equilibrium condition:

$$wL_2 = p_2 R_1$$

whereby the basket sector buys p_2R_1 machines in exchange for wL_2 baskets is implied in the first two conditions:

$$p_2R_1 + p_2R_2 = p_2X_2 = p_2R_2 + wL_2 \Rightarrow p_2R_1 = wL_2$$

which makes it analytically redundant.

3.2 Quantity and price equations

Technical coefficients are full coefficients. By applying them, and taking into account the second equilibrium condition, resource balances are transformed into quantity equations.

$$\text{Quantity equations: } \lambda_1 X_1 + \lambda_2 X_2 = L$$
$$\kappa_1 X_1 + \kappa_2 X_2 = K = nX_2 \qquad (3.1a)$$

Price equations are value balances per unit of output. Taking into account that unit replacement is given by:

$$\frac{R_j}{X_j} = \frac{1}{n} K_j, \quad j = 1,2$$

the vertical summation of (3.1a), evaluated at proper prices, or simply (3.2) per unit of output gives:

$$\text{Price equations: } p_2 \frac{1}{n} \kappa_1 + w\lambda_1 = p_1 \qquad (3.2a)$$
$$p_2 \frac{1}{n} \kappa_2 + w\lambda_2 = p_2$$

The output of each sector is easily determined from (3.1a):

$$X_1 = \frac{n - \kappa_2}{\lambda_2\kappa_1 + \lambda_1(n - \kappa_2)} L, \qquad X_2 = \frac{\kappa_1}{\lambda_2\kappa_1 + \lambda_1(n - \kappa_2)} L \tag{3.4}$$

Output is determined by technology (λ, κ, n) and by the availability of the primary resource, labour (L). The produced resource (K) *does not enter* the equations. *Relative* output depends exclusively on capital coefficients and the durability of machines; the proportion in which the two goods are produced is *invariant to labour coefficients changes*:

$$\frac{X_1}{X_2} = \frac{n - \kappa_2}{\kappa_1} \tag{3.5}$$

The system (3.2a) has characteristically one degree of freedom – because of three unknowns in two equations – which means that only *relative* prices are fully determined. Absolute prices depend on the price of labour (w):

$$p_1 = \frac{\lambda_2\kappa_1 + \lambda_1(n - \kappa_2)}{n - \kappa_2} w, \qquad p_2 = \frac{n\lambda_2}{n - \kappa_2} w \tag{3.6}$$

For $w = 1$, (3.6) and (3.4) give $p_1 = \frac{L}{X_1}$, which is the labour price of baskets. The same is not true for p_2, $p_2 \neq \frac{L}{X_2}$. That is explained by the fact that *only* X_1 *is net output*. The equilibrium condition requires that the value of consumer goods (p_1X_1) be exactly equal to wage bill (wL), and so is proportional to labour, which is not true for the value of machines ($p_2X_2 \neq wL$). The equality $p_1X_1 = wL$ implies that there are no unearned incomes. Otherwise the wage rate would be smaller than the price of labour, $w < p_0$, and the net income equality would read $p_1X_1 = p_0L$. Nominal wage is real wage evaluated in consumer good price, $w = p_1\tilde{w}$, where $\tilde{w} = X_1/L$ because the entire net output is consumed by workers. By (3.4) and (3.6) the same result follows:

$$\tilde{w} = \frac{w}{p_1} = \frac{1}{p_1} \text{ for } w = 1 \tag{3.7}$$

i.e. real wage is equal to the reciprocal value of consumer good price expressed in labour time.

Since machines are used in the production of baskets, p_1 depends on all technical coefficients. But baskets are not used in the production of machines, and so p_2 depends only on the technical coefficients of the machine sector. *Relative* prices do not depend on the price of labour (wage rate) and are exclusively determined by the technology of the system:

$$\frac{p_1}{p_2}=\frac{\lambda_1}{\lambda_2}+\frac{\lambda_2\kappa_1-\lambda_1\kappa_2}{n\lambda_2} \tag{3.8}$$

Relative prices are equal to the ratio of full labour coefficients, $p_1/p_2=\lambda_1/\lambda_2$ if either:

a. machines last infinitely long, $n=\infty$, or
b. $\lambda_2\kappa_1-\kappa_2\lambda_1=0$.

The former condition implies that there are no capital costs. The latter condition implies $\kappa_1/\lambda_1=\kappa_2/\lambda_2$ which means equal degree of mechanisation in both sectors, $K_1/L_1=K_2/L_2$.

3.3 Embodied labour

By rearranging (3.6), labour prices ($w=1$) may also be expressed in the following way:

$$\begin{aligned} p_1&=\lambda_1+\frac{\lambda_2}{n-\kappa_2}\kappa_1=\lambda_1+p_2\frac{\kappa_1}{n} \\ p_2&=\frac{\lambda_2}{n-\kappa_2}n=\lambda_2+p_2\frac{\kappa_2}{n} \end{aligned} \tag{3.6a}$$

Since λ_1 and λ_2 represent the amount of current labour time (live labour) per unit of output, the quantities:

$$p_1-\lambda_1=\frac{1}{n}p_2\kappa_1, \qquad p_2-\lambda_2=\frac{1}{n}p_2\kappa_2 \tag{3.9}$$

represent embodied labour per unit of output. Embodied labour is measured by replacement coefficient (κ_j/n) evaluated at labour price of capital good (p_2). Equations (3.6a) say that labour contained in one unit of output (p_j) consists of direct (λ_j) and indirect $\left(\frac{1}{n}p_2\kappa_j\right)$ labour.

There is yet another method for the calculation of labour prices. In (3.6a), p_2 enters the equation for p_1, but not vice versa. This means that the only problem is to determine p_2, labour contained in a machine. Direct labour is given by λ_2, but indirect labour is an unknown quantity embodied in κ_2/n machines expended in the production of one new machine. To produce κ_2/n

machines, we have to expend $(\kappa_2/n)(\kappa_2/n)$ machines and for that another replacement expenditure of $(\kappa_2/n)(\kappa_2/n)^2$ machines is necessary and so on. An infinite series is obtained:

$$\kappa_2/n+(\kappa_2/n)^2+(\kappa_2/n)^3+\ldots=\frac{n}{n-\kappa_2}$$

whose sum measures the number of machines contained in κ_2/n. The series is convergent because of:

$$\frac{\kappa_2}{n}=\frac{R_2}{X_2}<1.$$

Since in the production of every machine λ_2 of direct labour is necessary, total labour contained in a machine is:

$$p_2=\lambda_2\frac{n}{n-\kappa_2} \tag{3.6b}$$

which is the same as in (3.6).

PART II

CHANGING ECONOMY I: GROWTH OR DECREASE OF LABOUR FORCE

4 Two dynamic effects

Consider an economy in which technology remains unchanged, as in the stationary economy, but labour force expands (contracts) at a constant rate g. The stock of machines must grow (diminish) at the same rate so as to ensure full employment. Growth generates two important effects that must be incorporated into our balancing equations.

4.1 Replacement effect

4.1.1 Dilatation of economic time

Let the economy grow sufficiently long so that the necessary adjustments have been carried out and the system has achieved balanced steady growth. Annual replacement will again represent a fraction of total stock of machines, yet this fraction will now depend not only on the durability of the machines but also on the rate of growth. If machines have the rectangular life-time profile – their productive capacity is fully used and remains unimpaired over n years at the end of which machines are scrapped without cost or benefit – and unit gross investment ($I_1 = 1$) has been increasing at the rate g (by factor $G = 1 + g$), then at time t replacement amounts to:

$$R_t = I_{t-n} = G^{t-n-1}, \qquad G = 1 + g \tag{4.1}$$

The number of machines in operation is equal to the number of all machines installed in the last n years:

$$K_t = \sum_{t-n+1}^{t} I_t = G^{t-n} \frac{G^{n-1}}{g} \tag{4.2}$$

From (4.1) and (4.2) we derive the relation between current replacement and the stock of machines:

$$\frac{1}{v} = \frac{R_t}{K_{t-1}} = \frac{g}{G^{n-1}} \tag{4.3}$$

where $1/v$ represents a diminishing function of the rate of growth, which follows from the properties of the geometric series:

$$v = \frac{G^{n-1}}{g} = 1 + G + G^2 + \ldots + G^{n-1}$$

$$\frac{\delta}{\delta_g}\left(\frac{1}{v}\right) = \frac{\delta}{\delta_g}(1 + G + \ldots + G^{n-1})^{-1} < 0, \qquad g > -1$$

$1/v$ represents dynamic replacement cost, which corresponds to replacement cost in the stationary economy:

$$\frac{1}{n} = \frac{R^0}{K^0} \tag{4.5}$$

Indeed, when the rate of growth is reduced to zero, (4.3) becomes (4.4):

$$\lim_{g \to 0} \frac{1}{v} = \frac{1}{n} \tag{4.6}$$

For positive rates of growth $\frac{1}{v} < \frac{1}{n}\left(\text{for } g < 0, \frac{1}{v} > \frac{1}{n}\right)$ and the difference is the greater the higher the rate of growth (contraction). Both v and n have the dimension of time. We, thus, encounter an economic relativity effect whereby n static years are lengthened into v dynamic years.[1] To contraction of capital cost corresponds the dilatation of economic time.

The effect varies quantitatively very little if time profiles of output capacity are different. The rectangular time profile has been chosen because of mathematical convenience and also because there is some evidence that it approximates the average case better than the other pure profiles. If it is compared with linear and proportional decay profiles (for $g = 5\%$ and $n = 30$), dynamic replacement as a fraction of static replacement for the three profiles appears to be 0.43 as against 0.35 and 0.38 (Horvat, 1973a, p. 102). These figures also indicate that the effect is rather strong. For high rates of growth, replacement costs practically disappear (n/v is between 0.03 and 0.05 for $g = 15\%$, i.e. 30 static years are lengthened into more than 600 dynamic years, which means that for all practical purposes fixed assets last forever).

Two other cases merit some attention. If an asset is fully expended in one production cycle, which means that the service life is reduced to $n = 1$, then also $v = 1$ whatever g, and the asset is really an intermediate good, i.e. raw material or semi-finished product. An intermediate good is an asset whose service life is one production period. If the service life is extended into infinity, $n = v = \infty$, replacement disappears. In both cases there is no replacement effect. Thus, the frequent assumption in economic models that capital is circulating or that its duration is infinite implies neglecting an essential dynamic effect.

We may now systematize our findings. If the rate of growth is different from zero, dynamic capital cost (R_t) will diverge from the static capital cost (R_t^0). The transformation factor β:

$$\beta = \frac{R_t}{R_t^0} = \frac{1/v}{1/n} = \frac{n}{v} = \frac{ng}{G^{n-1}} \tag{4.7}$$

transforms greater static cost into smaller dynamic cost or, what is the same, longer dynamic time into shorter static time (assuming $g > 0$). The characteristics of β are:

$$\begin{array}{llll} \lim_{g \to 0} \beta = 1 & \frac{\delta\beta}{\delta g} < 0 & \lim_{g \to \infty} \beta = 0 & \lim_{g = -1} \beta = n \\ \lim_{n = 1} \beta = 1 & \frac{\delta\beta}{\delta n} < 0 & \lim_{n \to \infty} \beta = 0 & - \end{array} \tag{4.8}$$

There is no transformation and, consequently, no replacement effect in stationary economy ($g = 0$) and for intermediate goods ($n = 1$), which do not last in time. Faster growth and longer durability reduce capital cost below its stationary value of the base period. Very high rates of growth and very long service life of fixed assets eliminate capital cost. Finally, for negative rates of growth ($g < 0$), capital cost increases above the stationary level ($\beta > 1$) up to the limit of full amount of the existing capital (nR^0 for $g = -1$).

The replacement effect is portrayed in Fig. 4.1 in which discrete analysis, used so far, is replaced by continuous analysis to make the explanation simpler.

Fixed capital consists of n yearly gross investments and is represented by the area under the investment curves. In a stationary economy $I_t = R_t$ = constant. The higher g, the larger will be K_t. But R_t does not change. Therefore, $\frac{1}{v} = \frac{R_t}{K_t}$ will diminish as the rate of growth increases. Alternatively, for $R_t = I_{t-n} = 1$, it is simply the case $v = K_t$ and v will increase the faster the rate of growth of K. For $g \to \infty$, the 'mass' of capital tends to infinity and economic time becomes infinitely long, $K \to \infty$, $v \to \infty$. R_t and K_t are compared at the same point of time, which is an application of the synchrony principle. The resulting replacement curve is shown in Fig. 4.2.

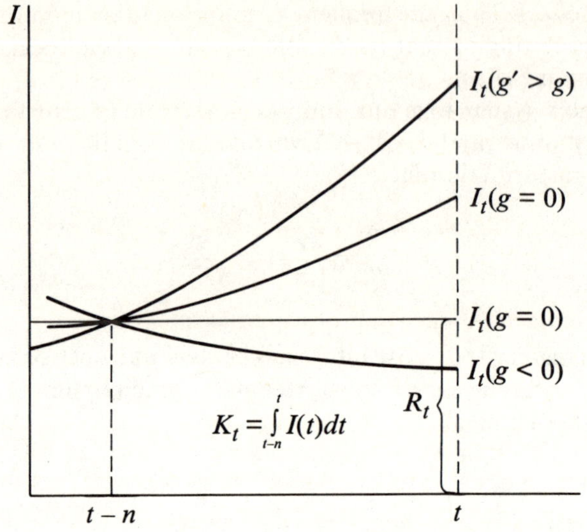

Figure 4.1 *Replacement effect (rectangular time profile of assets)*

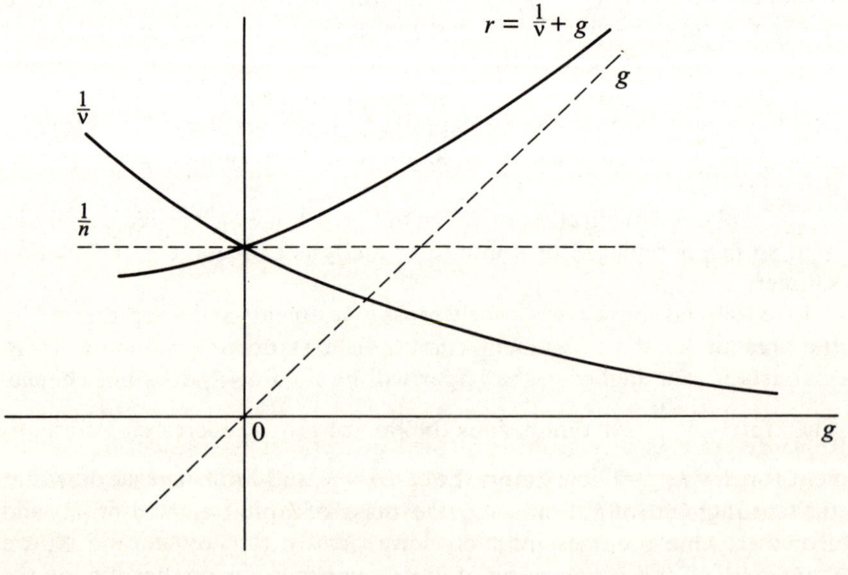

Figure 4.2 *Replacement and rental curves*

4.1.2 *The meaning of depreciation*

Consider now the relation between replacement and depreciation. Equal annual depreciation amounts (D) must over the service life of an asset be accumulated at the interest rate i to provide for K_t exactly equal to the acquisition value of the asset K_0:

$$\sum_1^n D(1+i)^{n-1} = D\frac{(1+i)^{n-1}}{i} = K$$

The annual depreciation per unit of capital is equal to:

$$\frac{D}{K} = \frac{i}{(1+i)^{n-1}} \qquad (4.3a)$$

which, of course, is equal to unit replacement in (4.3) with i interpreted as g. Interest rate turns out to be generated by the rate of growth of capital assets.

The result can be generalized. But before I do that, let me draw attention to another frequent methodological error. The favourite assumption about the type of depreciation/replacement is the so called radioactive decay. However, that has nothing to do with capital depreciation. Annual wear and tear generate maintenance costs – either maintaining an old machine or investing in a new one that will keep total capacity constant – and these are costs without time dimension like any other cost. The crucial test for the existence of a capital good is limited durability, $1 < n < \infty$. Since radioactive decay goes on forever, $n = \infty$, capital cost is reduced to zero and replacement effect disappears. If n is limited, what remains of a fixed asset after n years must be scrapped and replaced, and we may generalize the relation between depreciation and replacement under constant rates of growth as follows.

Depreciation is a cost of fixed assets that are assumed used at the capacity. Thus, depreciation per unit capacity must be constant:

$$D_t = \frac{1}{m} K_t$$

Replacement is clearly growing at the same rate as investment. If investment is growing at a constant rate and fixed assets are also decaying at a constant rate, the output capacity, consisting of the last n investments, will also be growing at a constant rate. Consequently, replacement will represent a constant proportion $\frac{1}{\mu}$ of fixed capital:

$$R_t = \frac{1}{\mu} K_t$$

and the magnitude of μ will depend on the rate of growth, rate of decay and the durability of assets. As two capitals must be equal, we may write:

$$\mathrm{m}D_t = \mu R_t \tag{4.9}$$

Since m and μ are constants, D and R grow at the same constant rate, which equals the rate of growth of capital. At that rate depreciation is capitalized, $i = g$.

$$\int_0^n D(t)\, e^{gt}\, dt = K_0 \tag{4.10}$$

Replacement is equal to investment made n years earlier reduced for the decay in the intervening n years:

$$R_n = I_0 e^{-gn}$$

and capital is the sum of all gross investments taking into account decay:

$$K_n = \int_0^n I_0 e^{-g(n-t)} e^{gt}\, dt$$

But we need capital n years earlier because these are the assets whose replacement today must be financed out of accumulated depreciations. Since investments n years earlier are replacements today, we may write:

$$K_n = \int_0^n R(t) e^{gt}\, dt \tag{4.11}$$

Comparing (4.10) and (4.11) we find that depreciation and replacement must be the same, $D(t) = R(t)$.

The concept of depreciation provides a link between micro- and macroeconomics. Also, it introduces financial flows into the analysis in a natural way as will be shown in Chapter 16.

4.2 Employment effect

The other of our two resources, labour, will also generate a dynamic effect in a changing economy. If labour force is growing, output capacity must be increased in order to keep labour employed and per capita consumption constant. Planners call this additional investment *demographic investment* since it does not increase the level of living but represents the cost of new jobs. It is the cost of necessary growth. I propose to investigate the problem in three stages.

4.2.1 The Austrian technology: labour alone as a factor of production
Let us first consider the Austrian world of roundabout processes in which labour is the only input. Production is of distributed-inputs-point-output type. Suppose all processes last two years and use identical technology with one unit of labour input each year per unit of final output called B (basket).

In two years one unit of commodity B (baskets) is produced by total input of labour of two units, one per year. Suppose labour expands by factor $G=1+g$ and economy consists of two processes operating simultaneously.

		Processes				Employment
Years	0	1				1
	1	1	G			$1+G$
	2	B	G	G^2		$G(1+G)$
	3		GB	G^2	G^3	$G^2(1+G)$

The columns indicate diachronic summation of labour inputs, which is always 2 labour units per unit of commodity B. The rows indicate synchronic summation of labour inputs, which is $G(1+G)=G(2+g)$ per unit of B. The synchronic input is greater than the diachronic one, $G(2+g)>2$, because of the growth of labour force. The reverse is true for a declining labour force. If employment expands at the rate g, each dated labour input must be expanded at the same rate in order to evaluate all inputs in 'present', synchronic labour values. In year zero labour input is 1. By the time output B is delivered in year two, it will expand to G^2. In year one labour input in the same process is also 1, and since it is frozen in the production only one year, by the time B is delivered it will have expanded to G. For this reason, while diachronic costs are 2 labour units, the synchronic costs amount to $G+G^2=G(1+G)$ labour units. The rate g plays the role of interest rate. No fixed assets are around and so this time interest is generated by the growth of labour. Therefrom the appellation 'employment effect'.

The synchronic summation of labour inputs represents systemic costs of producing net output in any given year. We still have to show why this is relevant for price formation. The Ricardo–Marx labour price of commodity B is $p=2$. That is not a correct price because, by violating the principle of synchrony, it leads to a misallocation of resources. The allocationally efficient price is $p=G\,(2+g)$. For example, for $g=10\%$ the correct labour price is $p=2.31$.[2]

The problem of allocational efficiency is encountered when more techniques are available for the production of a commodity. Suppose that apart from the already applied technique, two others are discovered successively and the commodity is divisible:

Commodity		B	
Techniques	α	β	γ
Labour input at $t=0$	1	2	0.95
$t=1$	1		0.95

It always pays to switch from α to β because output in the current year can be increased by basket B without reducing any of the outputs in the future years. It is also obvious that γ will be preferable to α. But what about β and γ? It all depends on the growth of labour force. If labour does not expand, γ is preferable because at any time 1.90 workers will produce B in a year while the technique β always requires 2 workers. But if the work force grows at the rate g, the number of workers delivering the same quantity of finished B will increase to $G(1+G)$. The society will be indifferent between β and γ if $G(1+G)0.95=2$, which gives $G=1.035$. Thus, if labour force expands at a rate greater than 3.5%, it pays to apply technique β because the available workers will produce more of B than by using γ. For that reason (and for $g>3.5\%$, say $g=0.04$) labour price must not be the diachronic sum of labour inputs $(0.95+0.95=1.90)$ but its synchronic sum $p_\gamma=1.04\times 2.04\times 0.95=2.1$ and this price must be compared with $p_\beta=2$ in order to choose the correct technique. In this example p_β turns out to be 5% lower than p_γ and so technique β will be chosen.

4.2.2 Technology with labour and circulating capital

In the next stage of approximation, let us consider the popular model of circulating capital. It has been popular since the days of Marxian schemata because of its easy generalizations and because economists did not know how to handle more complex cases. Though simple, this model is also treacherous.[3] It is an intermediate case, in terms of complexities, between Austrian labour-alone approach and the most difficult and complex case of durable capital. In the context of our analysis, circulating capital or intermediate goods may be considered as machines lasting one year.

Therefore, $a_{ij}=\kappa_j$, $n=1$, and replacement effect is absent. Machine industry may now be brought into A matrix. It produces intermediate goods for both industries. The basket industry produces no intermediate goods, $X_1=\hat{X}_1$. Labour force grows at the rate g ($G=1+g$). Matrix A may be used in two versions, one standard (A) and the other equivalent (GA).

Technology	Final output	Gross output and employment
$A=\begin{bmatrix} 0 & 0 \\ \hat{\kappa}_1 & \hat{\kappa}_2 \end{bmatrix}$	X_1 $g(\hat{\kappa}_1\hat{X}_1+\hat{\kappa}_2\hat{X}_2)$	$\hat{X}_1$ $\hat{X}_2$
$GA=\begin{bmatrix} 0 & 0 \\ G\hat{\kappa}_1 & G\hat{\kappa}_2 \end{bmatrix}$	X_1 0	$\hat{X}_1$ $\hat{X}_2$
$\hat{\lambda}_1 \quad \hat{\lambda}_2$		L

In order to employ additional, gL, labour next year, output of X_2 must increase above its last year level. This accumulation is equal to $g(\hat{\kappa}_1\hat{X}_1 + \hat{\kappa}_2\hat{X}_2)$. Alternatively, we may expand the input matrix by factor G, GA, and eliminate the final output of machine industry, $X_2=0$. The two approaches are equivalent; the former being conceptually more adequate, the latter more elegant. The rest of the story is straightforward. Sum up across the rows:

$$G\hat{\kappa}_1\hat{X}_1+G\hat{\kappa}_2\hat{X}_2=\hat{X}_2$$
$$\hat{X}_2=\frac{G\hat{\kappa}_1}{1-G\hat{\kappa}_2}\hat{X}_1 \tag{4.12}$$

$$\mathrm{L}=\hat{\lambda}_1\hat{X}_1+\hat{\lambda}_2\hat{X}_2=\hat{\lambda}_1\hat{X}_1+\hat{\lambda}_2\frac{G\hat{\kappa}_1}{1-G\hat{\kappa}_2}\hat{X}_1 \tag{4.13}$$

Since $p_1X_1=p_1\hat{X}_1=L$, it follows that

$$p_1=\frac{L}{X_1}=\hat{\lambda}_1+\hat{\lambda}_2\frac{G\hat{\kappa}_1}{1-G\hat{\kappa}_2} \tag{4.14}$$

The second price may be derived directly from the summation down the column:

$$p_2=\hat{\lambda}_2+p_2G\hat{\kappa}_2$$
$$p_2=\frac{\hat{\lambda}_2}{1-G\hat{\kappa}_2} \tag{4.15}$$

If we remember that $w=n=1$, the price formulae compared with the stationary conditions in (3.6) demonstrate that growth increases capital cost by G. In other words, inputs are expanded at the rate of labour force growth.

The third and final approximation is dealt with in Chapter 5.

5 Quantity and price equations

5.1 Real capital cost

Real capital cost is equal to the number of machines necessary to replace scrapped machines in order to keep the output capacity constant. In a stationary economy this number remains constant and so does replacement per unit of output capacity. Because of replacement effect, in a growing economy unit replacement diminishes as the rate of growth increases. This implies that an increasing proportion of gross investment can gratuitously be used for net additions to capacity. For very high rates of growth – say beyond 15% – almost all of the gross investment (99% at the growth rate of 15%) can be used for the expansion of output capacity.

If employment grows at the rate g, machine industry must produce sufficient number of machines to cover both replacement and accumulation needs. The second equilibrium condition remains the same as in (3.3) in the stationary economy, while the first now reads:

$$\mathrm{R}+\Delta K=X_2, \qquad \Delta K=gK$$

which may be written as:

$$\frac{1}{v}K+gK=rK=X_2, \qquad r=\frac{1}{v}+g \tag{5.1}$$

where r, called rental rate (rental per physical machine is rp_2, where p_2 is its price) is in fact rate of gross investment. Gross investment, consisting of replacement and accumulation, per unit of capital appears to be unit real capital cost necessary to keep per capita consumption constant. Note the difference between replacement ($1/v$) and capital (r) costs; the two are equal only in a stationary economy.

Replacement effect $\left(\frac{1}{n}-\frac{1}{v}\right)$ reduces capital cost while employment effect (g) increases capital cost of producing net output and these two effects partially offset each other. In a stationary economy gross investment is, of course, equal to replacement and so the difference between rental rate and stationary replacement rate is zero, $(r-1/n)=0$. In a changing economy, this difference may be positive or negative:

$$\frac{\delta}{\delta g}\left(r-\frac{1}{n}\right)=\frac{G^{n-1}+ngG^{n-1}}{(G^{n-1})^2}+1\gtreqless 0$$

By means of binomial series we find:

$$\frac{\delta v}{\delta g}\gtreqless 0\Rightarrow 1\gtreqless(1+g)^{-1},\quad g\gtreqless 0$$

In a growing economy ($g>0$) the difference between gross investment and stationary replacement increases, in a declining economy ($g<0$) decreases (but absolutely increases). It follows that

$$r=\left(\frac{1}{v}+g\right)\gtreqless\frac{1}{n}\qquad\text{for } g\gtreqless 0 \tag{5.2}$$

For positive rates of growth, rental rate is greater than stationary cost, for negative rates it is smaller. In both cases absolute difference increases (see also Fig. 4.2).

5.2 Quantity equations

We are now ready to consider the familiar dual system of equations. Balances of resources are the same as before (3.1). The second of the quantity equations is different and the set will be spelled out fully.

$$\text{Quantity equations: } \lambda_1X_1+\lambda_2X_2=L$$

$$\kappa_1X_1+\kappa_2X_2=K=\frac{1}{r}X_2 \tag{5.3}$$

By solving the equations, one easily finds outputs of baskets and machines and their ratio:

$$X_1=\frac{1-r\kappa_2}{\lambda_2r\kappa_1+\lambda_1(1-r\kappa_2)}L,\qquad X_2=\frac{r\kappa_1}{\lambda_2r\kappa_1+\lambda_1(1-r\kappa_2)}L \tag{5.4}$$

$$\frac{X_1}{X_2}=\frac{1-r\kappa_2}{r\kappa_1} \tag{5.5}$$

The solution has the same general characteristics as (3.4) and (3.5) and for $g=0\left(r=\frac{1}{n}\right)$ they are, of course, identical. Outputs depend on all technical coefficients (and g), but their ratio is independent of labour coefficients. Given L, the output of machines increases, and, as a consequence, the output of baskets decreases compared with the stationary economy (for $g>0$). This is due to the fact that dynamic capital cost is larger than the static one, $r>\frac{1}{n}$. Comparing (5.5) and (3.5), we see that a smaller number of baskets is produced per machine in a growing economy.

5.3 Price equations

Summing up down the columns of resource balances (3.1) we obtain value balances similar to those in (3.2):

$$\text{Value balances: } p_2R_1^*+wL_1=p_1X_1$$
$$p_2R_2^*+wL_2=p_2X_2 \qquad (5.6)$$

In the light of preceding discussion, replacement R may be interpreted as absolute static rental, $r=\frac{1}{n}$ being rental per unit of capital or the rental rate. Similarly R^* is dynamic rental and both R and R^* represent gross investment:

$$R^*=I=rK, \qquad r=\frac{1}{v}+g \qquad (5.7)$$

As already observed, part of gross investment $\left(\frac{1}{v}K\right)$ is used to keep absolute output constant, while the other part (gK) matches increasing employment and that part planners call demographic investment. Together $\left(\left(\frac{1}{v}+g\right)K=rK=I\right)$, they ensure that per capita output does not decline, e.g. that real wage ($\tilde{w}=X_1/L$) does not change.

The derivation of price equations is now straightforward:

$$\text{Price equations: } p_2r\kappa_1+w\lambda_1=p_1$$
$$p_2r\kappa_2+w\lambda_2=p_2 \qquad (5.8)$$

Growth (decline) simply augments (reduces) capital coefficients κ_j into $r\kappa_j$, as compared with the stationary $\frac{1}{n}\kappa_j$. The same substitution appears in the solution of the equations.

$$p_1 = \left(\lambda_1 + \frac{r\kappa_1}{1 - r\kappa_2}\lambda_2\right)w = w\lambda_1 + p_2 r\kappa_1$$

$$p_2 = \frac{\lambda_2}{1 - r\kappa_2}w = w\lambda_2 + p_2 r\kappa_2 \tag{5.9}$$

$$\frac{p_1}{p_2} = \frac{\lambda_1}{\lambda_2} + r\frac{\lambda_2\kappa_1 - \lambda_1\kappa_2}{\lambda_2} \tag{5.10}$$

Again labour prices consist of live labour (λ_j) and embodied labour ($p_2 r\kappa_j$). The wage rate (w) determines the absolute level of prices and does not enter relative prices. For $w = 1$ absolute prices are expressed in labour time. Since growth augments capital coefficients, while labour coefficients remain the same, both prices are higher than in a stationary economy. In an economy with diminishing population $\left(g < 0, r < \frac{1}{n}\right)$ it is the other way round. Thus, *the same technology generates different labour prices depending on how the economy changes.* This is a consequence of two dynamic effects and of the application of the synchrony principle.

Again relative prices are equal to ratios of labour coefficients when the degree of mechanization is the same in the two sectors, or for $r = 0$. The latter condition requires that $r = 1/v - g = 0$ or $g = -1$ (cf. 4.3).

Finally, the value of net output is exactly equal to currently expended labour measured in worker-years:

$$p_1 X_1 = L, \qquad w = 1$$

which is simply the second equilibrium condition of (3.3) for value balances (5.6).

5.4 Social accounting concepts

We are now in a position to tidy up part of the inherited conceptual inventory.

Social accounting uses the concepts of gross and net product and gross and net investment. The same concepts are used in model building. But the concepts are confused and misleading, as the schematic representation in Figure 5.1 will make evident (for $g > 0$).

The difference between the two schemes is primarily due to different treatment of capital cost. Only in a stationary economy does depreciation (accumulated at zero interest rate) equal replacement, D = R. In a changing economy they differ, and so do other aggregates, NI ≠ J, NNP ≠ N. In particular, net investment is *not* a net addition to output capacity, NI ≠ ΔK.

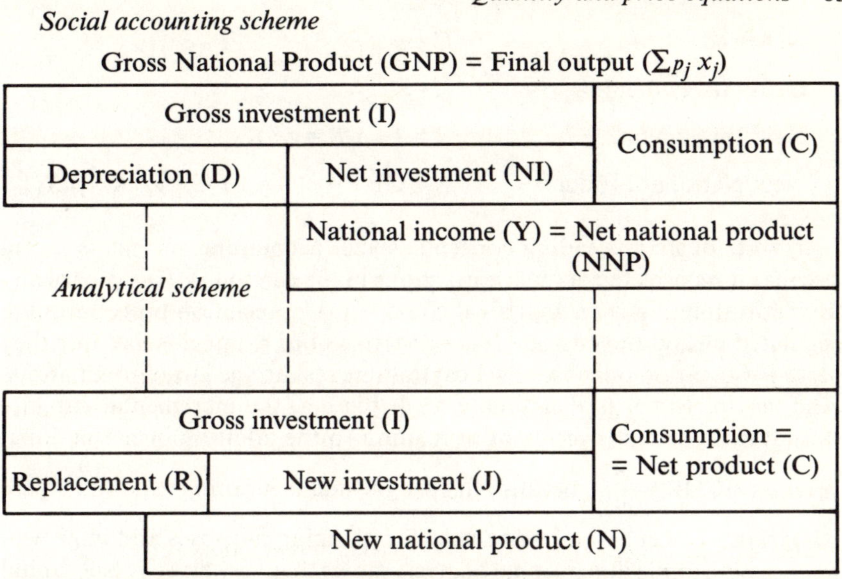

Figure 5.1 *Social accounting and analytical schemes*

If that is required, we need new investment, $J = \Delta K$. Similarly, national income is not new value over and above capital costs incurred to keep the output capacity unimpaired. The aggregate that has this property is new product. Also, D, NI and Y are *accounting* items. R, I and N are bundles of *commodities*.

The second difference lies in the treatment of net output. One must distinguish between net and supporting output. Both – machine and basket – industries produce final output. But since the purpose of production is output of consumer goods, basket industry must be considered as producing net output and machine industry as producing supporting output. The latter covers replacement and growth requirements (costs). That X_1 ought to be considered net product, was already pointed out by Oscar Lange (1936), but the lead was not followed. Note that inclusion of part of investment (net or new) in net product produces double counting: first in the year when capital goods are produced and then in subsequent years when they help to produce – and consequently transfer their value – to product.

Applying the symbols of our canonical model, the aggregates to be used in analysis are the following ones:

Gross National Product: $\quad GNP = p_1X_1 + p_2X_2$

Replacement: $\quad p_2R = \frac{1}{v}p_2K$

Net Product:	$C=p_1X_1$
Gross Investment:	$I=p_2X_2$
New Investment:	$J=I-p_2R=gp_2K$
New National Product:	$N=GNP-p_2R=J+C=gp_2K+p_1X_1$

In spite of its misleading concepts, social accounting scheme is useful because it records the actual transactions in the economy. This is basically an institutional, not an analytical construct. Depreciation procedures are regulated by law and custom. It is useful to record net profits, because they serve for taxation purposes. Net capital reflects the age structure of assets. And so on. But it is illegitimate to define e.g. the incremental capital–output ratio as net investment in relation to the addition of net national product, $ICOR=\frac{NI}{\Delta Y}$, because this magnitude is meaningless. And so are all variants of net capital when used for planning purposes and in growth analysis. A simple dimensional analysis shows that very clearly. Net capital measures capital along two dimensions simultaneously – quantity (which is reflected in output capacity) and age distribution – and therefore provides no direct information about either. Net capital may increase and output capacity diminish and vice versa. Therefore the magnitude of ICOR on the net capital basis expresses no technological relation – it may even be negative – and provides no information on the efficiency of investment. The correct definition reads $ICOR=\frac{J}{\Delta GNP}$.

5.5 Interest parables

Interest has always been puzzling for economists. Unable to offer a scientific explanation, they took to inventing parables. Besides, interest and profit have often been used interchangeably.

Nasau Senior invented the first of the popular parables: that of *abstinence*. He treated abstinence as a factor of production. In the same way as labour is rewarded by wages so is abstaining from spending one's capital rewarded by profit (1836, p. 89). The parable was taken over by J.S. Mill, Stanley Jevons and others and became an established theory. Socialists (Lasalle, Marx and others) ridiculed it by comparing the 'abstinence' of Rotschild with the profligacy of a labourer who spends his entire income. Neoclassical authors answered the critique by quite seriously arguing that savings of a millionaire were intramarginal and their rewards benefit from saver's surplus! In fact, what Senior was doing was to extol the virtue of frugality, which is the precondition for capital to emerge. But even that triviality is not free from logical contradiction. As argued by Joan Robinson (1956, p. 393): '... since saving is mainly out of profit, and real wages tend to be lower the higher the rate of profit, the abstinence associated with saving is mainly done by the workers, who do not receive any share in the reward'.

The concept of abstinence was not particularly attractive for obvious reasons. In an article in 1887 MacVane replaced it by *waiting*. Marshall and Cassel popularized the new term. Marshall equated waiting with the 'postponement of enjoyment' (1920, p. 233) or with saving (1920, p. 830). Production, if it takes time, requires waiting. The exertions and sacrifices involved in waiting represent real cost of production. Cassel identified the 'supply of waiting' with saving. All this was hardly more than a change of words. No one knew how to measure abstinence or waiting.

Nevertheless, the ground was prepared for the next parable, that of *time preference*. The concept has a several century old history. But its modern history begins with Böhm-Bawerk. He argued that interest was caused by the smaller marginal utility of future larger wealth and by an underestimation of future wants. To these two psychological reasons, he subsequently added a third one: the greater productivity of roundabout processes (Böhm-Bawerk, 1889, chs. II–IV). Later, however, Schumpeter demonstrated that in a stationary economy interest disappears, whatever the length of the production period. Competitive entrepreneurs bid up input prices and the entire product is imputed to labour and land. Competition and imputation destroy a possible surplus (Schumpeter, 1912, p. 326). Alternatively, with a spectrum of techniques available, positive interest is simply irrational: it would lead to the choice of a less productive technology and would forever lower consumption below the level technologically possible. In spite of that, the theory was developed into the most popular neoclassical theory: interest arises from the interaction of psychological time preference with the physical *productivity* of investment, the rate of return over cost. Irving Fisher (1907, 1930) took that theory over and produced his known triple equality: rate of interest equals rate of time preference (which he called impatience) equals rate of profit. Most of standard neoclassical theory is Fisherian today. The aporiae regarding the time preference part of that theory were exposed in Chapter 1. Now we turn attention to the productivity part.

To illustrate their theories, economists designed colourful examples. The main problem was to prove positive marginal productivity of capital. Böhm-Bawerk and Wicksell considered costless maturing of wine and the growth of trees to show the productivity of time. But time is compatible with any positive interest rate which, being assumed, is not explained. Frank Knight (1944) invented crusonia plant that grows without limits like a capital fund. D. Dewey very seriously uses the crusonia parable to explain 'modern' capital theory and adds a parable of his own: the taste for investment as willingness of an individual to exchange present consumption for capital assets (1965, pp. 59, 60). The usual textbook example is, of course, Robinson Crusoe. He faces an alternative of either catching fish by hand or postponing consumption, making a net and catching more fish thereafter. The foregone consumption is investment and excess fish to be consumed in the future is interest on invested capital. However, the example is misleading. It is not the productivity of capital as such that is responsible for more fish. It is the superior technique that produces the surplus over product of an obsolete technique (catching by hand). If a method is discovered whereby the same net catches more fish, then a surplus is produced without any additional investment. If the net is produced by half the time compared with the old method, then capital can be disinvested without reducing the catch, or even increasing it. At the macroeconomic level the sacrifice theory encounters additional logical difficulties: the groups of people who make sacrifices and reap benefits are overlapping, but are not the same.

Following the Fisherian trail, Robert Solow made valiant efforts to salvage neoclassical capital theory. In his view, the central concept in a capital theory is the rate of return on investment. His basic model is depicted in Fig. 5.2 (Solow, 1963, pp. 16–25; interpretation and symbols are mine).

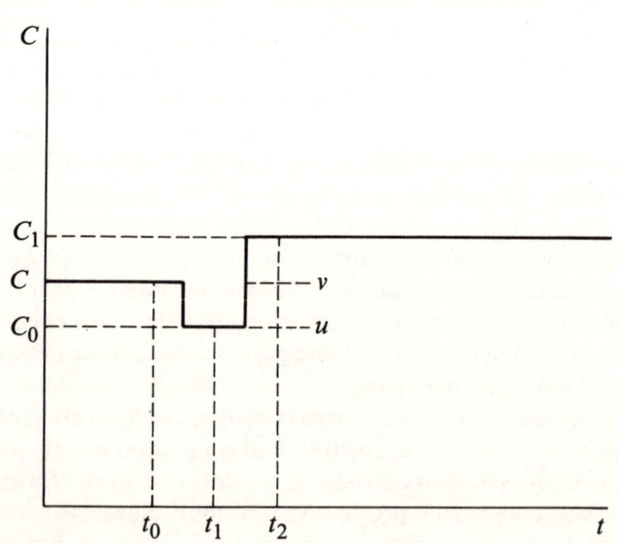

Figure 5.2 The rate of return, v/u

Consider a stationary economy that expects a group of immigrants to be fully employed at t_2 and thereafter the population will no longer change. In order to avoid complications caused by the replacement effect, assume infinite durability of assets, n=infinity. Consequently, there is no replacement in the system; the entire production cost consists of living labour. The economy has at its disposal K machines that are used to produce $C=X_1$ baskets. At t_1 a part of the machine stock is used to produce additional machines to provide jobs for the immigrants at t_2. As a consequence, C will decline by u at t_1 and increase to $C+v$ at t_2, when additional workers, equipped with additional machines will produce additional v baskets. Thus, u appears to be investment and v is return in perpetuity. Consequently, the social rate of return on investment is $i=\frac{v}{u}$. It is true that v is not 'marginal' physical product of investment because labour input also increases. On the other hand, unemployed labour has zero value and so socially v *is* the marginal value product.

The explanation just given encounters various difficulties. Suppose u is being invested every year in quantities uniformly expanding. Consequently, consumption and fixed capital grow at a rate g forever. The discount rate is clearly $i=g$. But Solow's formula indicates no relation between i and g, $i=Gv/Gu>v/C=g$. Next, let labour and capital remain unchanged while output grows at the rate g due to technological progress. In this case consumption increases without any previous reduction in consumption and the Fisher–Solow rate of return is infinite, $v/u=gC/0=\infty$. If there is no technological progress $v/u>0$ for the society but $v/u=0$ for every individual since per capita consumption does not change. There are no price signals that would indicate to an individual that it is worthwhile to reduce present consumption to reap future gains. Even if individuals were omniscient and knew about coming immigrants, they would not move as they face a peculiar Fisherian investment opportunity schedule that makes possible reduction of present consumption but no increase in future consumption. And if they increase their future consumption, that implies exploitation and an irrational choice of techniques. It is possible that an increase in total output will activate economies of scale and, thus, decrease unit costs and increase per capita consumption. But this is a consequence not the cause (motive) of the investment undertaken, the motive being preserving full employment, which implies social rationality. In conclusion: the rate of return may move between zero and infinity and that is not very enlightening. Fisherian notions simply cannot explain macroeconomic phenomena.

Finally, why exactly u and v? Neoclassicals would answer that the ratio is determined by somehow (this 'somehow' is called time preference) established interest rate and u and v are determined by marginal productivity of capital or by efficiency of investment. The answer is vacuous because we still do not know why exactly i and what is the efficiency of investment in an economy with unchanged technology.

The systemic answer is straightforward and consistent. Assume that machine–worker ratio is the same in both sectors ($\kappa_1\lambda_2=\kappa_2\lambda_1$) so that workers remain fully employed during the transition. Otherwise workers would be temporarily unemployed or different techniques would have to be chosen during transition or both. To employ new g workers with unchanged technology it is necessary to produce and install $X_2=gK$ machines. In order to produce these machines, $K_2=\kappa_2 X_2$ machines must be transferred from the basket to the machine sector where so far no machines existed because only consumer goods were being produced. The output of baskets lost is equal to:

$$u=\frac{K_2}{\kappa_1}=\frac{\kappa_2 X_2}{\kappa_1}=\frac{\kappa_2 gK}{\kappa_1}=\kappa_2 gX_1$$

Since per capita consumption remains the same, the additional output of baskets is equal to $v=gX_1$. The rate of return appears to be:

$$\frac{v}{u}=\frac{gX_1}{\kappa_2 gX_1}=\frac{1}{\kappa_2}$$

That looks familiar: the rate of return as the reciprocal value of incremental capital output ratio (ICOR). The novel feature is that only capital coefficient of the machine industry appears relevant and not (value) capital–output ratio pertaining to the entire economy.

So much about the quantities that Solow used in order to avoid even mentioning the controversial term capital. However, equipped with the labour theory of value, we can equally easily look at the dual side, to see what happens to prices. This is the preferred approach in the general equilibrium theory. In fact, unable to make sense of the interest rate, general equilibrium theorists try to substitute it with an intertemporal price system.[1]

> For example, a sacrifice of one unit of commodity of type s at a date t releases p_{st} units of account, and this enables the purchase of an additional $(p_{st}/p_{s(t+1)})$ units of the same commodity type to be delivered at date $(t+1)$. It is then natural to define:
>
> $$i_{st}=\frac{p_{st}}{p_{s(t+1)}}-1$$

as the own rate of return for commodity type s between the dates t and $(t+1)$. Note that i_{st} will typically differ for different commodity types as well as date pairs. (Dixit, 1977, p. 14; symbols are mine)

The price of consumer good follows straightforwardly from the second equilibrium condition for value balances $p_1C=L(w=1)$. Labour force is constant until t_1, increases at t_2 and is constant afterwards. Consumption is constant until t_0, decreases at t_1, increases at t_2 and is constant afterwards. The number of baskets produced at t_1 is:

$$X_1-g\kappa_2X_1=X_1(1-g\kappa_2)$$

and the evolution of prices is given in the table below:

Year	t_0	t_1	t_2
Labour employed	L	L	$L(1+g)$
Consumption	C	$C(1-g\kappa_2)$	$C(1+g)$
Prices: $p_1^t=L^t/C^t$	λ_1	$\lambda_1(1-g\kappa_2)^{-1}$	λ_1
p_2^t	λ_2	$\lambda_2(1-g\kappa_2)^{-1}$	λ_2

Somewhat different considerations led to the establishment of the machine price. Because of $n=\infty$ and no growth at t_0 and t_2, capital cost is zero $(r=1/n+g=0)$ and price is determined exclusively by labour coefficient, $p_2^0=p_2^2=\lambda_2$. At t_1 price is different: synchronic capital cost is now positive and amounts to gross investment necessary to employ additional labour, $X_2=gK$. That is in fact, the first equilibrium condition for value balances. Consequently $r=g$. Solving price equations as in (5.9):

$$rp_2\kappa_1+\lambda_1=p_1, \qquad r=1/n+g=g, \qquad 1/n=0$$
$$rp_2\kappa_2+\lambda_2=p_2, \qquad \kappa_1\lambda_2=\kappa_2\lambda_1, \qquad w=1$$

we obtain prices shown in the table, and the basket price is, of course, the same as computed above.

Two *different* own rates of return (interest) may be ascertained during the transition period, one *negative* and the other positive

$$i_1^1=i_2^1=\frac{p^0}{p^1}-1=-g\kappa_2$$

$$i_1^2 = i_2^2 = \frac{p^1}{p^2} - 1 = g\kappa_2(1 - g\kappa_2)^{-1}$$

They happen to be the same for both commodities (because of the same organic composition of the two industries). Yet they differ both from Solow's type rate of return (v/u) and from my rental rate (g). It is only the latter that plays the role of interest rate and ought to be used in price formation.

It has already been mentioned that labour force may remain constant but investment of u triggers technological progress (embodied) that will increase output permanently by amount v. After the change, the prices will obviously be lower than before. Since $L(t_2) = L$ and $C(t_2) = C + v = C(1 + g)$, the price of the basket will be lowered to $p_1(t_2) = L(t_2)/C(t_2) = L/C(1 + g) = \lambda_1(1+g)^{-1}$. The change of price p_2 depends on the type of technological progress. After t_2 the economy remains stationary and $g =$ interest rate $= 0$ as in a stationary economy ought to be.

This brief historical sketch demonstrates the futility of all efforts of the received theory to treat the phenomenon of interest. It is, of course, possible to invent an epicycle that will accommodate the preference theory. Assume that consumers act under 'the veil of ignorance' about their status in life. Then they will strongly distinguish between existential preferences (concerning life and employment) and all other preferences (concerning the structure of consumption). They will first choose to be employed because otherwise they cannot consume. But it is simpler to apply the systemic approach which gives clear and straightforward answers. Whatever the impatience or time preference, all workers have to be employed in a rationally organized economy. If the market automatism fails to produce that result, the planning authority must intervene with hand regulation. Whatever productivity and marginal productivity of capital, interest rate must be equal to the rate of growth of labour force. Thus, one source of interest is to be found in the interaction of employment and replacement effects that produces the required 'marginal productivity.' The other source is provided by technological progress, which is the next item on our study agenda.

PART III

CHANGING ECONOMY II: TECHNOLOGICAL PROGRESS

6 Once-and-for-all technological change

6.1 Some conceptual issues

Technological progress is a very complex phenomenon that can analytically be only approximated and hardly exactly described. Technological change implies (1) new ways of making old goods and (2) making new goods. The latter implies (a) improved versions of old goods, which goes under the heading of quality change, and (b) completely new goods. Next, the production of new goods implies the change of own cost structure (in case of consumer goods) or also the change of the cost structure of industries using new goods (in case of producer goods). The cost structure may change because (1) the material elements of production change (embodied change) or (2) non-material elements of production change (unembodied change). Finally, technological progress may be endogeneously or exogeneously determined. In reality, of course, we encounter a mixture of all changes enumerated. It is not intended to give a complete theory of technological change here; that would require a separate treatise. Instead, I shall try to demonstrate how the labour theory solves some of the problems in a more natural way.

Our economy is characterized by five technical coefficients: two labour coefficients, two capital coefficients and the durability of machines. The change of any of these coefficients has a definite economic meaning.

If κ_2 is reduced, one *old* machine (and proportionally more labour) will produce more *new* machines. The new machines may be the same as the old ones but be running longer per year due to improved repair. Or the design of the machines may be changed. As soon as new machines are installed, *new* machines will begin to produce *new* machines. In the transition period technology will be mixed. After all old machines have been scrapped, there will be again a pure technology of identical machines. Even if these machines are different from old machines, they may be equally well counted as the old ones. If κ_1 is reduced, one machine produces more baskets. And if n is increased, for given output, replacement cost (the number of machines scrapped) in both industries decreases.

An increase in labour productivity – λ_1 and λ_2 decline – implies less living labour per unit of output (labour is now equipped with more machines since κ_j remain intact). Whether λ's are reduced or κ's are reduced and n increased, the change always implies an increase in the productivity of labour. In the former case of direct labour, in the latter of indirect labour. Consequently, technological progress is always labour saving.

Reduction of capital coefficients (given n) implies an economy in embodied labour, of labour coefficients an economy of living labour. Yet, this distinction is different from the distinction between embodied and unembodied[1] technological progress. Embodied technological progress implies a new design of machines; new machines are different. Under unembodied progress machines remain the same but are used more efficiently (because of an improved organization, greater experience of the workers, better repair, and the like) and also the productivity of living labour may increase. Consequently, embodied TP affects only the last vintage of machines, unembodied TP affects the entire capital stock. It is, of course, possible to treat workers as machines and to consider any change in labour productivity (machines remaining the same) as a change in human capital. I do not find this latter approach particularly enlightening for the purpose at hand. Both embodied and unembodied progress may change any of the five technical coefficients.

Machines may be more efficient or less costly or both. This may be called the double character of fixed assets (fixed capital), which has important analytical consequences. Since machines produce machines, the two effects cannot be easily disentangled. That presents a nightmare for social accountants trying to measure machine output or the stock of machines in constant prices. A possibility of precise distinction is relatively simple in consumer goods industry. If a machine produces more baskets, it is more efficient (κ_1 reduced). If at the same time it embodies less labour, it is less costly (p_2 is reduced). The combined effect is measured by the reduction of engaged embodied labour per unit of physical output ($p_2\kappa_1$). The combined effect may remain the same (κ_1 and p_2 need not) even if machine is changed physically as long as the basket remains the same. Thus, a change in design does not represent a special problem. Per analogiam, in machine industry κ_2 measures efficiency, and p_2 cost and $p_2\kappa_2$ the combined effect *if the machine remains unchanged.* If it changes, $\kappa_2 = K_2/X_2$ still measures efficiency because the same new machines are in the numerator (after the old capital stock has been replaced) and in the denominator and so the machine dimension cancels out. But p_2 is no longer comparable and neither is $p_2\kappa_2$. Thus, while $p_2\kappa_1/n$ has a straightforward interpretation as embodied labour expended per unit of consumer good, $p_2\kappa_2/n$ does not have such an interpretation. This indicates that we have to take into account yet another effect of price changes.

A changed machine may require a changed amount of labour time for its production. It follows that in order to be able to count machines, we must measure our machines in invariant units. We may take the standard basket of consumer goods as a *numéraire* that implies dividing all prices by p_1. Or we may simply measure value in labour time, the result is the same. The two value capital coefficients are:

$$\tilde{\kappa}_1 = \frac{p_2/p_1 \cdot K_1}{p_1/p_1 \cdot X_1} = \frac{p_2 K_1}{p_1 X_1} = \frac{p_2}{p_1}\kappa_1$$

$$\tilde{\kappa}_2 = \frac{p_2/p_1 \cdot K_2}{p_2/p_2 \cdot X_2} = \kappa_2$$

In other words, machines of constant efficiency in terms of baskets – which is the same as labour embodied in the machine per unit of labour embodied in output it produces – are measured simply by value capital coefficients with baskets as a *numéraire*. For the machine industry value and physical capital coefficients are, obviously, the same (when K_2 and X_2 represent machines of the same vintage).

The foregoing considerations indicate that technical coefficients fall into two groups which should be sharply distinguished: λ_1 and κ_2 are comparable across techniques, λ_2 and κ_1 depend on how machines are measured. But the product $\lambda_2\kappa_1$, which often occurs in the equations, is also comparable across techniques since L and X_1 are homogeneous (and $\lambda_2\kappa_1$ has dimensions L/X_1).

If labour force is growing, $\frac{1}{n}$ will be replaced by $r = \frac{1}{v} + g$. Since $r > \frac{1}{n}$, this will have the same effect as an *increase* in κ_j (or a reduction in n), which is equivalent to technological regress, as already mentioned before. The faster growth, the more 'adverse' its effect on technological progress, *ceteris paribus*. However, since growth tends to speed up TP, which is known as the Verdoorn Law (Verdoorn, 1980), the overall effect is not known in advance. If the employment and Verdoorn effect cancel out, we have accumulation and consumption increasing simultaneously – something considered contradictory in the neoclassical interest theory.

In general, the accumulation of capital in value terms (embodied labour time) and in physical terms (expansion of output capacity) need not move together under the conditions of technological change. It is impossible for the value of an identical machine to increase while its output does not (labour productivity remaining unchanged) because that would imply technological regress and the respective production technology will simply not be used. But it is entirely possible that a decumulation of value capital be accompanied by an accumulation of physical capital. Besides, a reduced value of capital stock may make possible not only larger physical output but also larger value output. This will happen if total labour force is growing, but labour employed in the machine industry is sufficiently reduced.

As far as equipment is concerned, its changing shape is of no special concern. We must only be aware of implications. However, unless explicitly specified, I shall assume unembodied TP, i.e. unchanged design of machines. Also, for the time being, baskets will be assumed to remain identical in terms of quantities, proportions, and qualities of consumer goods.

6.2 Output and price changes

If in a stationary economy positive technological change occurs, the output will begin to increase. After a transitional period, during which necessary adjustments will be made, economy will reach a new, higher, stationary level. We then compare the old and the new stationary level. Since two stationary levels are compared, we may use equations characterizing simple reproduction ($g=0, \nu=n$).

As already mentioned, the technology of our economy is described by three sets of parameters, κ_j, λ_j, and n. If any of these parameters change, both production and prices must change. For two industries and three parameters, of which two are specific for each industry, there will be $2\times 2\times 2+2=10$ effects on output and the same number of effects concerning prices. It will be useful to systematize these effects. For this we use equations (3.4) and (3.6).

Output changes (6.1)

Reduction of labour coefficients:

$$-\frac{\delta X_1}{\delta\lambda_1}<0, \quad -\frac{\delta X_1}{\delta\lambda_2}<0; \quad -\frac{\delta X_2}{\delta\lambda_1}>0, \quad -\frac{\delta X_2}{\delta\lambda_2}>0$$

Reduction of capital coefficients:

$$-\frac{\delta X_1}{\delta\kappa_1}<0, \quad -\frac{\delta X_1}{\delta\kappa_2}<0; \quad -\frac{\delta X_2}{\delta\kappa_1}<0, \quad -\frac{\delta X_2}{\delta\kappa_2}<0$$

Increase in durability:

$$\frac{\delta X_1}{\delta n}>0; \quad \frac{\delta X_2}{\delta n}<0.$$

Price changes (6.2)

Reduction of labour coefficients:

$$-\frac{\delta p_1}{\delta\lambda_1}<0, \quad -\frac{\delta p_1}{\delta\lambda_2}<0; \quad -\frac{\delta p_2}{\delta\lambda_1}=0, \quad -\frac{\delta p_2}{\delta\lambda_2}<0$$

Reduction of capital coefficients:

$$-\frac{\delta p_1}{\delta \kappa_1}<0, \quad -\frac{\delta p_1}{\delta \kappa_2}<0; \quad -\frac{\delta p_2}{\delta \kappa_1}=0, \quad -\frac{\delta p_2}{\delta \kappa_2}<0$$

Increase in durability:

$$\frac{\delta p_1}{\delta n}<0; \quad \frac{\delta p_2}{\delta n}<0.$$

As far as production is concerned, an increase in labour productivity (reduction of labour coefficients) leads to an increase in all outputs, given the labour force L. An increase in the efficiency of machines (reduction of capital coefficients) increases output of consumer goods but, understandably, reduces output of capital goods. The same is the effect of an increase in the durability of machines.

Price effects are independent from the availability of the primary resource L and depend exclusively on technological changes. Improvements in productivity of labour and machines and increased durability of machines diminish labour–time prices. Since sector No. 1 does not participate in the production of machines, technological improvements in that sector (reduced λ_1 and κ_1) have no impact on prices of machines. Thus, prices of machines are determined exclusively by technological changes in sector No. 2 that produces machines.

6.3 Three measures of capital intensity

Technological progress will affect differently various structural parameters used in economic analysis. The three are relevant here:

1. *Capital coefficients in value terms* (capital–product ratios):

$$\tilde{\kappa}_1=\frac{p_2K_1}{p_1X_1}=\kappa_1\frac{p_2}{p_1}, \quad \tilde{\kappa}_2=\kappa_2, \tag{6.3}$$

$$\tilde{\kappa}=\frac{p_2K}{p_1X_1+p_2X_2}=\frac{np_2X_2}{p_1X_1+p_2X_2}=\kappa$$

2. *Technical composition of resources* (machine–worker ratios, degree of mechanisation):

$$k_1=\frac{K_1}{L_1}=\frac{\kappa_1}{\lambda_1}, \quad k_2=\frac{\kappa_2}{\lambda_2}, \quad k=\frac{K}{L}=\frac{\kappa_1X_1+\kappa_2X_2}{\lambda_1X_1+\lambda_2X_2} \tag{6.4}$$

3. *Organic composition of resources* (capital–labour ratios):

Table 6.1 Effects of a single technological change ($w=1$)

Variables	Technological progress: Pure Neutral I	Pure Neutral II	Mixed: Capital saving I	Capital saving II	Neutral capital using	I	II	III	Technological change without TP: Capital saving I	Capital saving II	Neutral capital using I	II	I	II
	$\lambda_j\Gamma^{-1}$	$\lambda_1\Gamma^{-1}$ $\kappa_1\Gamma^{-1}$	$\lambda_j\Gamma^{-1}$ $\kappa_j\Gamma^{-1}$ $n\Gamma^{-1}$	$\lambda_j\Gamma_\lambda^{-1}$ $\kappa_j\Gamma_\kappa^{-1}$ $n\Gamma_\kappa^{-1}$	$\lambda_1\Gamma^{-1}$ $\lambda_2\Gamma^{-2}$ $\kappa_1\Gamma$	$\lambda_j\Gamma^{-1}$ $\kappa_j\Gamma$ $n\Gamma$	$\lambda_1\Gamma^{-1}$ $\kappa_2\Gamma$ $n\Gamma$	$\lambda_j\Gamma_\lambda^{-1}$ $\kappa_j\Gamma_\kappa$ $n\Gamma_\kappa$	$\kappa_j\Gamma^{-1}$ $n\Gamma^{-1}$	$\lambda_2\Gamma^{-1}$ $\kappa_2\Gamma^{-1}$ $n\Gamma^{-1}$	$\lambda_2\Gamma^{-1}$ $\kappa_1\Gamma$	$\lambda_2\Gamma$ $\kappa_1\Gamma^{-1}$	$\lambda_2\Gamma$ $\kappa_2\Gamma$ $n\Gamma$	$\kappa_j\Gamma$ $n\Gamma$
X_1	$X_1\Gamma$	$X_1\Gamma$	$X_1\Gamma$	$X_1\Gamma_\lambda$	$X_1\Gamma$	$X_1\Gamma$	$X_1\Gamma$	$X_1\Gamma_\lambda$	same	same	same	same	same	same
X_2	$X_2\Gamma$	same	$X_2\Gamma$	$X_2\Gamma_\lambda$	$X_2\Gamma^2$	$X_2\Gamma$	same	$X_2\Gamma_\lambda$	same	$X_2\Gamma$	$X_2\Gamma$	$X_2\Gamma^{-1}$	$X_2\Gamma^{-1}$	same
p_1	$p_1\Gamma^{-1}$	$p_1\Gamma^{-1}$	$p_1\Gamma^{-1}$	$p_1\Gamma_\lambda^{-1}$	$p_1\Gamma^{-1}$	$p_1\Gamma^{-1}$	$p_1\Gamma^{-1}$	$p_1\Gamma^{-1}$	same	same	same	same	same	same
p_2	$p_2\Gamma^{-1}$	same	$p_2\Gamma^{-1}$	$p_2\Gamma_\lambda^{-1}$	$p_2\Gamma^{-2}$	$p_2\Gamma^{-1}$	same	$p_2\Gamma^{-1}$	same	$p_2\Gamma^{-1}$	$p_2\Gamma^{-1}$	$p_2\Gamma$	$p_2\Gamma$	same
p_1X_1	same	same	same	same	same	same	same	same	same	same	same	same	same	same
p_2X_2	same	same	same	same	same	same	same	same	same	same	same	same	same	same
$\tilde{\kappa}_1$	same	same	$\tilde{\kappa}_1\Gamma^{-1}$	$\tilde{\kappa}_1\Gamma_\kappa^{-1}$	same	$\tilde{\kappa}_1\Gamma$	$\tilde{\kappa}_1\Gamma$	$\tilde{\kappa}_1\Gamma_\kappa$	$\tilde{\kappa}_1\Gamma^{-1}$	$\tilde{\kappa}_1\Gamma^{-1}$	same	same	$\tilde{\kappa}_1\Gamma$	$\tilde{\kappa}_1\Gamma$
$\tilde{\kappa}_2$	same	same	$\tilde{\kappa}_2\Gamma^{-1}$	$\tilde{\kappa}_2\Gamma_\kappa^{-1}$	same	$\tilde{\kappa}_2\Gamma$	$\tilde{\kappa}_2\Gamma$	$\tilde{\kappa}_2\Gamma_\kappa$	$\tilde{\kappa}_2\Gamma^{-1}$	$\tilde{\kappa}_2\Gamma^{-1}$	same	same	$\tilde{\kappa}_2\Gamma$	$\tilde{\kappa}_2\Gamma$
k_1	$k_1\Gamma$	same	same	$k_1\Gamma_\lambda\Gamma_\kappa^{-1}$	$k_1\Gamma^2$	$k_1\Gamma^2$	$k_1\Gamma$	$k_1\Gamma_\kappa\Gamma_\lambda$	$k_1\Gamma^{-1}$	same	$k_1\Gamma$	$k_1\Gamma^{-1}$	same	$k_1\Gamma$
k_2	$k_2\Gamma$	same	same	$k_2\Gamma_\lambda\Gamma_\kappa^{-1}$	$k_2\Gamma^2$	$k_2\Gamma^2$	$k_2\Gamma$	$k_2\Gamma_\kappa\Gamma_\lambda$	$k_2\Gamma^{-1}$	same	$k_2\Gamma$	$k_2\Gamma^{-1}$	same	$k_2\Gamma$
ω_1	same	same	$\omega_1\Gamma^{-1}$	$\omega_1\Gamma_\kappa^{-1}$	same	$\omega_1\Gamma$	$\omega_1\Gamma$	$\omega_1\Gamma_\kappa$	$\omega_1\Gamma^{-1}$	$\omega_1\Gamma^{-1}$	same	same	$\omega_1\Gamma$	$\omega_1\Gamma$
ω_2	same	same	$\omega_2\Gamma^{-1}$	$\omega_2\Gamma_\kappa^{-1}$	same	$\omega_2\Gamma$	$\omega_2\Gamma$	$\omega_2\Gamma_\kappa$	$\omega_2\Gamma^{-1}$	$\omega_2\Gamma^{-1}$	same	same	$\omega_2\Gamma$	$\omega_2\Gamma$

$$X_1=\frac{n-\kappa_2}{\lambda_2\kappa_1+\lambda_1(n-\kappa_2)}L, \quad p_1=\frac{\lambda_2\kappa_1+\lambda_1(n-\kappa_2)}{n-\kappa_2}, \quad \Gamma=1+\gamma$$

$$X_2=\frac{\kappa_1}{\lambda_2\kappa_1+\lambda_1(n-\kappa_2)}L, \quad p_2=\frac{n\lambda_2}{n-\kappa_2}, \quad L=\text{const} \tag{3.4}$$

$$\tilde{\kappa}_1=\kappa_1\frac{p_2}{p_1}, \quad k_1=\frac{\kappa_1}{\lambda_1}, \quad \omega_1=p_2k_1$$

$$\tilde{\kappa}_2=\kappa_2, \quad k_2=\frac{\kappa_2}{\lambda_2}, \quad \omega_2=p_2k_2 \tag{6.3}$$

$$\omega_1 = \frac{p_2 K_1}{L_1} = p_2 k_1, \quad \omega_2 = p_2 k_2, \quad \omega = \frac{p_2 K}{L} = p_2 k \tag{6.5}$$

Prices used are, of course, exact labour prices and therefore, $w=1$. Expression (6.5) needs a slight elaboration. Using (6.3) and remembering $p_1 X_1 = L$, $nX_2 = K$, we obtain organic composition as a function of value capital coefficients and durability:

$$\omega = \frac{n\kappa}{n-\kappa} \tag{6.5a}$$

For sufficiently large n – the average life-span of fixed assets in the modern economy is 30 years or more – the magnitude of organic composition is approximately equal to that of capital coefficient in value terms, $\omega = \kappa$.

It is of some interest to note the difference between Marx's 'organic composition of capital' and my 'organic composition of resources'. Marx defined his concepts for an analysis of specific, capitalist, institutions. Thus, his organic composition is a ratio between constant capital (C= fixed and circulating capital) and variable capital (V= wages advanced).

$$\omega_M = \frac{C}{V} = \frac{C}{wL}$$

Since wL are wages paid out for the period before the product was finished and ready for sale, wL is a flow. Consequently, ω_M has time dimension and represents stock/flow ratio. My concepts are designed to analyse conditions for optimal use of resources and are not institutionally restricted. Thus, my organic composition is a ratio of embodied and living labour:

$$\omega = \frac{C}{L}$$

Constant capital is evaluated in labour prices, C and L are both stocks, ω is a pure number. The two ratios are numerically equal, $\omega_M = \omega$, if $w=1$, i.e. if the turnover period of variable capital is defined as a time unit. Note also that an alternative definition of the organic composition for the entire economy is capital–net output ratio, $\omega = p_2 K / p_1 X_1$, since $p_1 X_1 = L$.

6.4 Patterns of technological change

There are several special patterns of technological change worthwhile exploring (see Table 6.1).

1. *Neutral technological progress of type one*. Let both labour coefficients decrease at the rate γ, $\lambda_j=(1+\gamma)^{-1}\ \lambda_j^0$, which means that labour productivity increases $(1+\gamma)=\Gamma$ times. It follows from (3.6) that prices of both commodities will also be reduced Γ times. It follows from (3.4) that output of both industries will increase Γ times. Thus, value of output will remain unchanged, $p_jX_j=p_j^0X_j^0$. This is the consequence of labour prices ($w=1$), while labour is kept constant. Real wage will increase in the same proportion as output, $\tilde{w}=\Gamma X_1^0/L=\Gamma\tilde{w}^0$. Since technical change has not affected capital coefficients, after an adjustment period the old structural relationship will be re-established. It follows from (6.3)–(6.5) that capital coefficients in value terms will remain unchanged, technical composition of resources will be doubled (if machines remain physically unchanged), while organic composition of resources also remains invariant to change. Because of the last effect, this pattern of technological progress may be called Marx-neutral. It may be also called labour-augmenting TP. Since capital–output ratio remains unchanged, it may also be considered Harrod-neutral TP if γ is interpreted as interest rate. Finally, in labour prices capital–labour ratio is equal to organic composition. Thus, it is also Hicks-neutral because the rate of technical substitution remains constant along p_2K/L ray (and is equal to zero). Since in real world economies, rapid increases in labour productivity are accompanied by relatively slow changes in capital–output ratios in value terms, Marx-neutral technological progress of type one may be taken as a reasonable approximation of reality.[2]
2. *Neutral technological progress of type two*. If technological change occurs in consumer goods industry, that will leave prices of machines unchanged. Let the change be such that both technical coefficients in consumer goods industry be reduced in the same proportion, $\lambda_1=\Gamma^{-1}\lambda_1^0$, $\kappa_1=\Gamma^{-1}\kappa_1^0$. As a result X_1 will increase and p_1 decrease Γ times leaving the value of consumer goods unchanged, $p_1X_1=p_1^0X_1^0$. The output of machines and their prices remain unaffected. Consequently, structural characteristics of the system $\tilde{\kappa}_j$, k_j and ω_j remain unchanged. As the stock of machines remains constant through time, the growth of net output occurs without any new investment.
3. *Capital saving technological progress I and II*. In the first variant all technical coefficients (λ_j, κ_j, and n) are reduced by the same factor Γ, which leaves relative prices unchanged. Both outputs are increased by Γ, which leaves relative outputs unchanged. Values of sectoral outputs remain unchanged. However, value capital coefficients are reduced. Since κ_j and λ_j are reduced in the same proportion, machine–labour ratios, $k_j=\kappa_j/\lambda_j$, also remain unchanged. But the organic composition

of capital is reduced by factor $\Gamma = (1+\gamma)$: $\omega = \Gamma^{-1} p_2^0 k = \Gamma^{-1} \omega^0$. In the second variant labour coefficients decrease by factor Γ_λ, capital coefficients and durability by Γ_κ. It turns out that Γ_λ affects both outputs and prices, Γ_κ affects value capital coefficients and organic composition, while machine–worker ratios are affected by both TP factors. A reduction in n may be justified by the effects of strong TP in λ_j and κ_j, which make for an earlier scrapping of machines. Shorter n makes this type of TP mixed.

4. *Mixed technological progress generally*. If labour productivity increases while machine efficiency decreases (or vice versa), but gains outweigh losses, TP is mixed. In general, whenever TP is resource-using it must also be (other) resource-saving. TP may be interdependent (what happens in one industry depends on changes in the other) or independent. In the latter case each industry must improve its own efficiency otherwise the change will not be undertaken. This condition is satisfied by the patterns of TP shown in Table 6.1: prices in each industry either fall or remain unchanged. Independent technological progress will be assumed throughout this book.
5. *Technological change without technological progress*. Technological progress implies increasing real wages (X_1 for fixed labour). If an alternative technology leaves X_1 unchanged, there is no progress but simply a technological change. Such a change may be neutral, capital saving or capital using and it is always mixed. Several such patterns are shown in Table 6.1. At any one time a book of blueprints may contain a number of such alternative technologies. They are equally eligible if they make possible the same per capita output of consumer goods with the same input of living and embodied labour. Note that under the condition of independence of changes in the two industries, Neutral II and Capital Using I change will never be undertaken because they generate higher machine prices.

6.5 Final comments

Table 6.1 does not exhaust the list of all possible simple patterns of TP. Yet, it is sufficiently inclusive to make possible some generalizations. A change in X_1 (L = constant) determines whether there is technological progress or not:

$$\frac{\Delta X_1}{\Delta t} \begin{cases} >0, & \text{technological progress} \\ =0, & \text{technological change without TP} \\ <0, & \text{technological regress} \end{cases}$$

By its very definition, TP implies that net output increases without any increase of total labour input. There may be no new investment, as in

Neutral II TP, or new investment may be even negative, if efficiency of machine production sufficiently increases.

A change in X_2 does not indicate anything about changes in capital intensity. Increased output of machines, with *unchanged durability* and capital coefficients, will, of course, increase machine–worker ratios (k_j). If also capital coefficients improve, organic composition may fall while k_j remain unchanged, as in Capital Saving I TP. If the life-span of machines is lengthened, even k_j, may be reduced.

Value capital coefficients and organic composition change in the same direction, which also follows from (6.5a). It is, therefore, sufficient to consider only changes in the organic composition:

$$\frac{\Delta\omega}{\Delta t}\begin{cases} >0, \text{ capital using TP,} \\ =0, \text{ neutral TP,} \\ <0, \text{ capital saving TP,} \end{cases} \qquad \begin{matrix} \omega = p_2 k \\ g = \text{constant} \end{matrix}$$

If technological progress occurs only in the production of consumer goods (Neutral II), all indicators of capital intensity remain unchanged. If it occurs in the production of machines, the pattern is not so simple. If at the same time the durability of machines is shortened to $n\Gamma^{-1}$, there will be no progress, but simply a capital saving change. If n remains unchanged, with TP affecting only the production of machines ($\lambda_2\Gamma^{-1}$ and $\kappa_2\Gamma^{-1}$), it follows from (6.1) and (6.2) that all prices decrease, X_1 increases while X_2 may change either way. Next, k_1 and k_2 remain unchanged, while $\omega = p_2 k$ decreases. Thus in both cases capital–worker ratios remain unchanged, but TP in consumer goods production leaves ω undisturbed, while if it occurs in machine production, TP is capital saving.

A similar analysis may be conducted with respect to changes of technical coefficients. Improvements in both λ_j increase outputs and reduce prices. Improvements in both κ_j reduce prices, increase output of X_1 but reduce output of X_2. On the other hand improvements in λ's increase k's but leave ω's undetermined. Reductions in κ's diminish both k's and ω's. As a general orientation, it may be said that improvements in labour coefficients reduce prices and increase outputs, while improvements in capital coefficients reduce capital intensity measured either by k_1 or ω_j. Effects of individual changes in technical coefficients are given in (6.1) and (6.2).

In Table 6.1 the value of sectoral outputs remains the same. This is not necessarily so but is a result of implied assumptions. Net product is always the same, $p_1 x_1 = 1$, $x_1 = X_1/L$ but the value of machine output per capita:

$$p_2 x_2 = \frac{n\lambda_2\kappa_1}{(n-\kappa_2)[\lambda_2\kappa_1 + \lambda_1(n-\kappa_2)]}, \qquad x_2 = X_2/L$$

need not remain the same, as is easily seen if only one of technical coefficients is changed. It will remain the same only if the shares of direct and indirect labour in gross national product do not change. As all sixteen patterns of technological change satisfy this condition, it does not appear very strong and it also approximates empirical world. In particular, organic composition may change in any way and leave the 'factor' shares constant.

In terms of structural coefficients, constant sectoral shares in the value of final output require that technological progress proceeds so as to keep:

$$\frac{p_1X_1}{p_2X_2}=\frac{\tilde{\kappa}_2}{\tilde{\kappa}_1}\frac{K_1}{K_2}=\frac{\tilde{\kappa}_2 b_1}{\tilde{\kappa}_1 b_2}=\text{constant,} \qquad b_j=\frac{K_j}{K}$$

i.e. the ratio of value capital coefficients weighted by the shares of other sector's capital in total capital remain constant. In case of equal mechanization in both sectors ($\lambda_2\kappa_1=\lambda_1\kappa_2$) the condition reduces to:

$$\frac{p_1X_1}{p_2X_2}=\frac{\lambda_1X_1}{\lambda_2X_2}=\frac{L_1}{L_2}=\frac{a_1}{a_2}=\text{constant,} \qquad a_j=\frac{L_j}{L},\ \lambda_2\kappa_1=\lambda_1\kappa_2$$

i.e. labour shares remain constant. Per capita value of machine output remains unchanged if:

$$\frac{p_2X_2}{p_1X_1}=p_2x_2=\frac{\omega_2}{\kappa_2}a_2=\text{constant, } a_2=\frac{L_2}{L},\ p_1X_1=L,\ x_2=\frac{X_2}{L}$$

i.e. the ratio of organic composition (capital–labour ratio) to capital coefficient (machine–output ratio) in machine industry weighted by the share of machine industry labour in total labour remains constant.

7 Continuous unembodied technological progress

7.1 Changes in rental rate

Continuous technological progress generates growth. Labour productivity increases which, given L, increases output. The patterns of technological progress will remain the same, except that now formulae for growing economies must be applied (Table 7.1).

Because of higher productivity, some of the workers will be displaced. In order to re-employ them, gross investment must increase. Thus, in general, stationary n will be lengthened into dynamic v.

The first equilibrium condition requires:

$$X_2 = \left(\frac{1}{v} + g_k\right) K$$

The rate of growth of X_2 is equal to the rate of growth of capital (v and g_k being constants):

$$\frac{dX_2/dt}{X_2} = \frac{dK/dt}{K}$$

Labour productivity growth in the machine sector is reflected in the price change:

$$\frac{p_2^0}{p_2} = (1 + \gamma_2)$$

Since $p_2^0 X_2^0 = p_2 X_2 =$ constant by assumption, prices decline at the same rate at which output increases. Consequently, $g_k = \gamma_2$ and so

$$r = \frac{1}{v} + \gamma_2$$

where γ_2 determines the number of machines ($\gamma_2 K$) necessary to equip the displaced workers. It is important to note that γ_2 depends on the technological progress in the machine industry and not on the average technological progress. If technological progress is Mixed Neutral, γ_2 will be $\gamma_2=\Gamma^2-1=(1+\gamma)^2-1=\gamma(2+\gamma)$, while the average productivity growth rate will lie between that rate and γ.

The essential precondition for technological progress is that X_1 increases (L=constant). This means that X_2 may remain unchanged or even decrease. Suppose TP is Neutral II. Then TP in the two sectors amounts to (Table 7.1):

$$\frac{p_1^0}{p_1}=1+\gamma_1, \quad \frac{p_2^0}{p_2}=1, \quad \gamma_2=0$$

Quantity equations are:

$$\begin{aligned}(\lambda_1\Gamma^{-1})\,(X_1\Gamma)+\lambda_2X_2&=L\\(\kappa_1\Gamma^{-1})\,(X_1\Gamma)+\kappa_2X_2&=K\end{aligned} \tag{7.1}$$

Labour ($=L_1\Gamma^{-1}$) and machines ($=K_1\Gamma^{-1}$) become redundant at the same rate in the first sector and do not change in the second. Full employment is achieved when redundant workers are equipped with redundant machines and then produce additional γ_1X_1. Prices of baskets fall, prices of machines remain unchanged. Since total capital stock does not change, there are no costs over and above stationary replacement

$$r=\frac{1}{n}$$

In terms of machines, the economy is stationary and $\gamma_2=0$. In terms of consumer goods the economy is growing and $\gamma_1>0$. If γ_2 is interpreted as interest rate, we have the case where interest rate is zero in a growing economy.

To measure technological change, a simple device was suggested by J.E. Woods (1990, p. 318). As noted above, every technological progress must increase consumer goods. Thus, technological progress will be measured by an increase of real wage. This is shown in Figure 7.1.

Technological progress shifts wage curve outwards. In most patterns of technological progress it was assumed that the rental rate remains unchanged, r_0=constant, and this was also a part of definition of neutral change. In neutral change the organic composition of resources remains unchanged, ω=constant, and real wage in all patterns shown changes exactly by the amount of technological progress involved, $\tilde{w}_1=\Gamma\tilde{w}_0$. Naturally, the same is the change of X_1 (given L). The difference between two wages is $\tilde{w}_1-\tilde{w}_0=\gamma w_0$.

Table 7.1 Effects of continuous technological progress

		Technological Progress				
		Pure	Neutral	Capital	Saving	Mixed
		I	II	I	II	Neutral
		$\lambda_j\Gamma^{-1}$	$\lambda_1\Gamma^{-1}$ $\kappa_1\Gamma^{-1}$	$\lambda_j\Gamma^{-1}$ $\kappa_j\Gamma^{-1}$ $r\Gamma$	$\lambda_j\Gamma_\lambda^{-1}$ $\kappa_j\Gamma_\kappa^{-1}$ $r\Gamma_\kappa$	$\lambda_1\Gamma^{-1}$ $\lambda_2\Gamma^{-2}$ $\kappa_1\Gamma$
Outputs						
Baskets	X_1	$X_1\Gamma$	$X_1\Gamma$	$X_1\Gamma$	$X_1\Gamma_\lambda$	$X_1\Gamma$
Machines	X_2	$X_2\Gamma$	same	$X_2\Gamma$	$X_2\Gamma_\lambda$	$X_2\Gamma^2$
Labour prices: w=1						
Baskets	p_1	$p_1\Gamma^{-1}$	$p_1\Gamma^{-1}$	$p_1\Gamma^{-1}$	$p_1\Gamma_\lambda^{-1}$	$p_1\Gamma^{-1}$
Machines	p_2	$p_2\Gamma^{-1}$	same	$p_2\Gamma^{-1}$	$p_2\Gamma_\lambda^{-1}$	$p_2\Gamma^{-2}$
Capital intensity						
Machine-worker	k_1	$k_1\Gamma$	same	same	$k_1\frac{\Gamma_\lambda}{\Gamma_\kappa}$	$k_1\Gamma^2$
ratios	k_2	$k_2\Gamma$	same	same	$k_2\frac{\Gamma_\lambda}{\Gamma_\kappa}$	$k_2\Gamma^2$
Organic composition	ω_1	same	same	$\omega_1\Gamma^{-1}$	$\omega_1\Gamma_\kappa^{-1}$	same
of resources	ω_2	same	same	$\omega_2\Gamma^{-1}$	$\omega_2\Gamma_\kappa^{-1}$	same
Basket prices: $p_1=1$						
Real wage	$\tilde{w}=\frac{w}{p_1}$	$\tilde{w}\Gamma$	$\tilde{w}\Gamma$	$\tilde{w}\Gamma$	$\tilde{w}\Gamma_\lambda$	$\tilde{w}\Gamma$
Machine price	$\tilde{p}_2=\frac{p_2}{p_1}$	same	$\tilde{p}_2\Gamma$	same	same	$\tilde{p}_2\Gamma^{-1}$

$$X_1=\frac{1-r\kappa_2}{\lambda_2 r\kappa_1+\lambda_1(1-r\kappa_2)}L,\qquad X_2=\frac{r\kappa_1}{\lambda_2 r\kappa_1+\lambda_1(1-r\kappa_2)}L,\quad L=\text{const.}\qquad(5.4)$$

$$p_1=\frac{\lambda_2 r\kappa_1+\lambda_1(1-r\kappa_2)}{1-r\kappa_2}w,\qquad p_2=\frac{\lambda_2}{1-r\kappa_2}w,\qquad w=1\qquad(5.9)$$

$$\tilde{w}=\frac{X_1}{L}=\frac{1-r\kappa_2}{\lambda_2 r\kappa_1+\lambda_1(1-r\kappa_2)},\ \tilde{p}_2=\frac{\lambda_2}{\lambda_2 r\kappa_1+\lambda_1(1-r\kappa_2)},\quad p_1=\tilde{p}_1=1$$

$$k_1=\frac{\kappa_1}{\lambda_1},\qquad k_2=\frac{\kappa_2}{\lambda_2},\qquad \omega_1=p_2k_1,\qquad \omega_2=p_2k_2$$

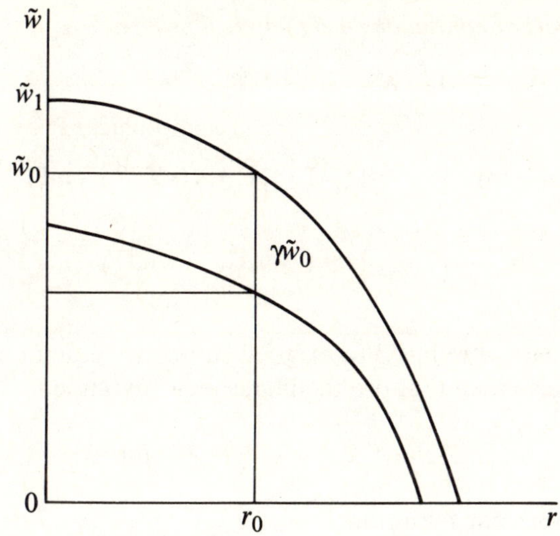

Figure 7.1 *The measure of neutral technological progress*

7.2 The formation of prices if both technological progress and growth of labour force occur simultaneously

It will be useful to revert to our duality generating input–output scheme similar to the one resulting in (4.10). The basic scheme will apply to stationary economy and subsequently I shall introduce technological progress and labour growth:

$$\begin{array}{llllll}
p_1 & \left[\begin{array}{cc} 0 & 0 \\ \frac{1}{n}\kappa_1 & \frac{1}{n}\kappa_2 \end{array}\right] & & X_1 & X_1 \\
p_2 & & & 0 & X_2 \\
\gamma & [0 & 0] & & \\
w & [\lambda_1 & \lambda_2] & & \\
 & p_1 & p_2 & &
\end{array}$$

Since it is a stationary economy, replacement costs reduce to $1/n$ and the rate of growth to $\gamma = 0$ rendering rental rate equal to $r = 1/n + 0$.

Introduce TP. Now X_1 must increase and X_2 may change at the same rate or at a different rate, say remain constant. These two basic types of TP are shown in Table 7.1 as Neutral TP I and II. Under Neutral TP I both labour coefficients decrease, as a consequence prices decrease as well, while both outputs increase. That generates the following equations:

Row summations: $$0+\Gamma X_1=\Gamma X_1$$

$$\Gamma\left(\frac{1}{v}K+\gamma K\right)=\Gamma X_2$$

Column summations: $$\left(\frac{1}{v}+\gamma\right)(p_2\Gamma^{-1})\kappa_1+w(\lambda_1\Gamma^{-1})=p_1\Gamma^{-1}$$

$$\left(\frac{1}{v}+\gamma\right)(p_2\Gamma^{-1})\kappa_2+w(\lambda_2\Gamma^{-1})=p_2\Gamma^{-1}$$

All equations can be reduced to original stationary equations with $\gamma=0$, $1/v=1/n$. It is also seen that profits finance new investment:

$$\gamma p_2\Gamma^{-1}(\kappa_1\Gamma X_1+\kappa_2\Gamma X_2)=\Gamma^{-1}p_2\Gamma X_2$$

and wages finance consumption:

$$w\Gamma^{-1}(\lambda_1\Gamma X_1+\lambda_2\Gamma X_2)=\Gamma^{-1}p_1\Gamma X_1$$

Next consider TP II. Labour and capital coefficients in the basket industry decrease, and so does the price p_1, while everything else in the machine industry remains the same:

Row summations: $$0 \quad +\Gamma X_1=\Gamma X_1$$

$$\frac{1}{n}(\Gamma^{-1}\kappa_1)(\Gamma X_1)+\frac{1}{n}\kappa_2X_2+0 \quad =X_2$$

Column summations: $$\frac{1}{n}p_2(\Gamma^{-1}\kappa_1)+w(\lambda_1\Gamma^{-1})=p_1\Gamma^{-1}$$

$$\frac{1}{n}p_2\kappa_2 \quad +w\lambda_2 \quad =p_2$$

Profit–investment and wages–consumption equalities hold. In the second price equation $\gamma=0$ because there is no technological progress and the number of machines remains constant. In the first price equation we may write:

$$\frac{1}{n}p_2\Gamma^{-1}\kappa_1=p_2\Gamma^{-1}\kappa_1\left(\frac{1}{n}+0\right)$$

Consequently, the interest rate relevant for the price formation is $\gamma=0$ as well and replacement costs are $1/n$. In the general case the rental rate is, of course, equal to $r = 1/v + \gamma$. We may confirm our previous finding: *interest rate* $i = \gamma$ *is always determined by the rate of TP in the machine industry.* Prices may fall, and then the interest rate is different from the discount rate. In constant basket prices, they are equal.

If now the labour force also grows at the rate g, the rental rate will obviously increase to $r = 1/v + \gamma + g$ with the corresponding increase of v.

7.3 Measuring technological change

When technology, i.e. technical coefficients, change, that affects output and prices in different ways. So far we have been examining the consequences of specified changes of technical coefficients. In practical statistical work the task is usually defined in the reverse fashion. The changes of technology are not specified but we have data on quantities and prices. The task is to derive a measure of technological progress from such data (assuming unembodied TP).

We start from the familiar social accounting identity of values of outputs and inputs being the same:

$$p_1 X_1 + p_2 X_2 \equiv wL + rp_2 K \tag{7.2}$$

If $w = 1$, the value of final output (GNP) is exactly equal to the labour time embodied in the commodities at the current productivity of labour.

Increase in productivity means higher output given the resources or smaller expenditure of resources given the output. The increase in aggregate output is established if physical products are evaluated at last year prices. Thus, the overall rate of technological progress in our economy is given by:

$$\frac{p_1^0 X_1 + p_2^0 X_2}{wL + rp_2 K} = 1 + \gamma \tag{7.3}$$

Note the difference in treatment of labour and capital. Labour, being primary factor, represents no problem. Capital, being produced factor, must be evaluated at p_2^0 when output and at p_2 when input. It would be inadmissible to add together labour input at current productivity and capital input at past productivity.

If exact labour prices are used, (7.3) has an interesting interpretation. Since p_2^0 means labour of last year productivity contained in the unit of X_j, the numerator represents labour time of last year labour productivity and the denominator represents labour time of this year productivity, both contained in the same this year final physical output. In this way $(1 + \gamma)$ measures the ratio between past and present labour time necessary to produce the same bill of goods and so is a natural and direct measure of labour productivity changes.

Technological progress may proceed at different pace in the two industries. Define the sectoral measures and some auxiliary relationships as follows:

$$\frac{p_1^0 X_1}{Y_1} = 1 + \gamma_1 \qquad \frac{p_2^0 X_2}{Y_2} = 1 + \gamma_2 \tag{7.4}$$

$$Y_1 = wL_1 + rp_2K_1 = wL, \qquad Y_2 = wL_2 + rp_2K_2 = rp_2K$$
$$Y = Y_1 + Y_2 = wL + rp_2K, \quad Y_1/Y = A_1, \quad Y_2/Y = A_2 = 1 - A_1 \tag{7.5}$$

and insert (7.4) and (7.5) into (7.3):

$$A_1(1+\gamma_1) + A_2(1+\gamma_2) = 1 + \gamma \tag{7.6}$$

the aggregate factor of TP is equal to the sum of sectoral factors weighted by the shares of labour and capital input in GNP. These shares represent also the shares of basket and machine industries in GNP.

The most popular production function in measuring technological progress is the Cobb–Douglas function

$$Q = L^\alpha K^\beta e^{\gamma * t}$$

If we apply Divisia indexes, we get a neat expression for the rate of TP:

$$\gamma^* = \frac{\dot{Q}}{Q} - \alpha \frac{\dot{L}}{L} - \beta \frac{\dot{K}}{K} \tag{7.7}$$

I use starred gamma in order to indicate that this neoclassical measure of TP is logically inconsistent and, therefore, theoretically false. The mistake made is to treat K and L in the same fashion as given resources.

Since K underwent a technological change, K as an input is different from K as an output and part of Q. The logically consistent function will look as follows:

$$Q = L^\alpha (Ke^{-\gamma t})^\beta e^{\gamma t}$$

which generates a consistent measure of TP:

$$\gamma(1-\beta) = \frac{\dot{Q}}{Q} - \alpha\frac{\dot{L}}{L} - \beta\frac{\dot{K}}{K} \tag{7.8}$$

The relation between the two measures is given by:

$$\gamma^* = \gamma(1-\beta) = \alpha\gamma \text{ if } \alpha+\beta=1 \tag{7.9}$$

The neoclassical measure is substantially lower.[1]

If the economy is decomposed into two or more industries, capital input-evaluated at constant prices must be reduced at the rate of TP in capital good industry (or industries).

From (7.5) $\quad Y_2 = rp_2K = p_2X_2$

and from (7.4) $\quad \dfrac{p_2^0X_2}{Y_2} = \dfrac{p_2^0X_2}{p_2X_2} = \dfrac{p_2^0}{p_2} = 1+\gamma_2 \qquad (7.10)$

Consequently, if labour–time prices are used, capital input rp_2^0K must be reduced at the rate $\gamma_2 = p_2^0p_2 - 1$.

7.4 Constant index of nominal price

Since all values represent labour values, the shares A_1 and A_2 represent also the shares of living and embodied labour in final output. These shares can change in time. Consequently, average γ may change even if sectoral γ_i remain constant and also, γ may remain constant even if sectoral γ_i change.

As prices are determined by two multiplicative terms, of which the first is conditioned exclusively by technology and r, while the second consists of nominal wage rate, it is easy to see how prices can be kept stable. Sectoral prices will be stabilized, i.e. the inflation index will remain equal to one if labour–time prices are inflated for the increase of sectoral labour productivity, $p_i^* = p_i\Gamma_i$. It follows from (7.4)

$$\frac{p_1^0X_i}{\Gamma_iY_i} = 1$$

If all prices are inflated by the average productivity factor Γ, $p_i^* = p_i\Gamma$, (7.3) gives

$$\frac{p_i^0X_i + p_2^0X_2}{\Gamma Y} = 1$$

and the general price level will be stabilized.

8 Embodied technological progress

8.1 Embodied and unembodied technological progress compared

If the design of machines and the composition of plants change in time, technological progress is embodied and we encounter new difficulties. Each vintage of plants will have different efficiency. For aggregation we need plants of equal efficiency.

The quantity of capital can be measured in two ways: by the costs of production of machines in the labour of unchanged productivity or by the output capacity. I shall call the former the *value* capital at constant prices and the latter the *size* of capital. Since X_1 is the target output and X_2 merely the supporting output, the size of capital will be measured in terms of *net output capacity*, i.e. in output of X_1. In our model the change of value in constant prices is given by $p_2^0 X_2^1 / p_2^0 X_2^0$. If the machines were physically the same, the increase in capital (the number of machines at the base prices) would be represented by X_2^1/X_2^0. But the whole point about technological progress is that machines change and this change can be decomposed into the change in number (M) and the change in size cum efficiency (Γ_κ). Since the size cannot be measured unequivocally, the latter change cannot be decomposed. Therefore $X_2^1/X_2^0 = M\Gamma_\kappa$. The change in net output capacity is simply $X_1^1/X_1^0 = \Gamma_{X_1}$. It is obvious that the two ratios need not be the same, $M\Gamma_\kappa \neq \Gamma_{X_1}$, and then we may have two different quantities of capital. To simplify the analysis, and because this is not far from reality (the share of investment in GNP stays approximately constant over one or two business cycles), I shall assume that the two ratios are equal, which means that output in each of the sectors grows at the same rate.

Consider the case when, with *constant* labour force, the output of (standard) baskets expands by factor Γ and the number of (changing) plants constructed by factor M. We assume that the life-span of plants of all vintages is the same. All plants of a given vintage are physically identical but produce two different outputs, baskets in sector one and new plants in sector two. The net output capacity of the economy (X_1) is related to the number of plants ($K = K_1 + K_2$) by a proportionality constant ($\bar{\bar{\kappa}}$):

$$K = \bar{\bar{\kappa}} X, \tag{8.1}$$

If net output expands by factor Γ, so must capital stock (K) in terms of *net output capacity* (NOC):

$$K\Gamma = K(M\Gamma_\kappa) = \bar{\bar{\kappa}} X_1 \Gamma \tag{8.2}$$

where Γ_κ is capacity factor that measures simultaneously changes in the size of plants and their efficiency. Since all plants are identical, Γ_κ must be the same for all of them. It would be desirable if Γ_κ could be decomposed into two components of size and efficiency. But that would be arbitrary. It follows from (8.1) and (8.2):

$$M\Gamma_\kappa = \Gamma, \quad \Gamma_\kappa \lesseqgtr \Gamma \text{ if } M \gtreqless 1 \tag{8.3}$$

The same number of workers operating M times more (less) machines produce Γ times more baskets. A plant of vintage τ may be substituted for Γ_κ plants of vintage $\tau - 1$ without changing the net output capacity.

Since labour remains unchanged, efficiency factor Γ measures global technological progress: increase in output of consumer goods per unit of labour, which is at the same time an increase in the real wage, $\Delta\tilde{w} = \gamma X_1/L$. If also the shares of living and embodied labour in final output do not change, i.e. the value of output of machine industry remains constant, $p_2X_2 =$ const, Γ is also the efficiency factor for each of the two industries.

We shall now compare capital stocks and new investments measured in NOC units for embodied and unembodied TP. In both cases *the number* of plants is assumed the same but the capacity will be different. Plant efficiency and size increases by the constant factor Γ_κ.

8.1.1 Capital stock

Embodied TP: $$\hat{K}_n = 1 + M\Gamma_\kappa + \ldots + M^{n-1}\Gamma_\kappa^{n-1} = \frac{(M\Gamma_\kappa)^n - 1}{M\Gamma_\kappa - 1} \tag{8.4e}$$

Unembodied TP: $$\hat{K}_n = \Gamma_\kappa^{n-1} + M\Gamma_\kappa^{n-1} + \ldots + M^{n-1}\Gamma_\kappa^{n-1} = \Gamma_\kappa^{n-1}\frac{M^n - 1}{M - 1} \tag{8.4u}$$

Capital stock consists of all gross investments in the last n years. Initial unit investment will by the nth year increase to M^{n-1} units and their unit NOC to Γ_κ^{n-1}. In the embodied case each vintage of plants has its own efficiency, while in the unembodied case all vintages have the same, last year, efficiency. Clearly, under unembodied case capital stock, measured in NOC units, is larger for the same $M\Gamma_\kappa$. (If capitals are the same, $M\Gamma_\kappa$ must be smaller).

For $M = 1$, each vintage consists of one plant and capital stock consists of n plants. At $t = n$, average net output capacity per plant is equal to:

$$\frac{\hat{K}(n)}{K}=\frac{\Gamma^n-1}{n(\Gamma-1)}=\frac{v}{n}$$

After that date K remains constant and $\hat{K}(t)$ expands by factor Γ, so that output per plant increases by the same factor.

We next consider new investment, which is the difference between gross investment and replacement. Alternatively, it is the difference between two successive capital stocks.

8.1.2 *New investment*

$$\text{Embodied TP:} \quad \hat{J}_n=(M\Gamma_\kappa)^n-1 \tag{8.5e}$$

$$\text{Unembodied TP:} \quad \hat{K}_{n+1}-\hat{K}_n=\left(\frac{M^{n-1}}{M-1}\right)(M\Gamma_\kappa^n-\Gamma_\kappa^{n-1}) \tag{8.5u}$$

Under embodied TP gross investment at $t=n+1$ is $M^n\Gamma_\kappa^n$, and scrapped plant is 1, i.e. gross investment at $t=1$. Under unembodied TP gross investment is $M^n\Gamma_\kappa^n$ augmented for the increase in efficiency of the entire capital stock. Scrapped output capacity is Γ_κ^{n-1}. Alternatively it is the difference $K_{n+1}-K_n$ as computed in (8.5u).

Since capital stock measured in NOC units expands at the same rate as X_1, growth rates under both types of TP must be the same: the rate of growth of net output (g_{x1}) is equal to the rate of growth of effective capital stock ($g_{\hat{\kappa}}$).

8.1.3 *Rate of growth*

$$\text{Embodied TP:} \quad g_{x1}=\frac{(M\Gamma_\kappa)^{n-1}}{\dfrac{(M\Gamma_\kappa)^{n-1}}{M\Gamma_\kappa-1}}=M\Gamma_\kappa-1 \tag{8.6}$$

$$\text{Unembodied TP:} \quad g_{x1}=\frac{\dfrac{M^n-1}{M-1}(M\Gamma_\kappa^n-\Gamma_\kappa^{n-1})}{\Gamma_\kappa^{n-1}\dfrac{M^n-1}{M-1}}=M\Gamma_\kappa-1$$

The rate of growth is, of course, given by the ratio of new investment and capital stock. The rate of growth of net output is the *same* under both types of technological progress, but absolute net output and its absolute increments are higher under unembodied TP because $\Gamma_\kappa > 1$ (for the same $M\Gamma_\kappa$). The same rates of growth (if the age structure of fixed assets does not change) and very slow changes in empirical world make the much simpler unembodiment hypothesis very useful.

It remains to illustrate our results by TP patterns in Table 7.1. Neutral I TP implies $M = \Gamma$ and $\Gamma_\kappa = 1$. The rate of growth of net output is $g_{x_1} = \Gamma - 1$. Under ETP new investment is $e\hat{J} = \Gamma^n - 1$, under UTP it is $u\hat{J} = \frac{\Gamma^n - 1}{\Gamma - 1}(\Gamma - 1) = \Gamma^{n-1}$ and $u\hat{J} = e\hat{J}$. That should be obvious since NOC of plants does not change. For neutral II TP we have $M = 1$ and $\Gamma_\kappa = \Gamma$ giving the same rate of growth. The two types of new investments are $e\hat{J} = \Gamma^n - 1$ and $u\hat{J} = n(\Gamma^n - \Gamma^n - 1)$ giving $u\hat{J} > e\hat{J}$ and the two investments become equal at the limit when the rate of TP is reduced to $\gamma = 0$. In the case of Mixed Neutral TP, $M = \Gamma^2$ and so $\Gamma_\kappa = \Gamma^{-1}$. New investment with ETP is the same as under Neutral I and II TP, $e\hat{J} = \Gamma^n - 1$, while UTP gives $u\hat{J} = \frac{\Gamma^{2n} - 1}{\Gamma^2 - 1}(\Gamma^{2-n} - \Gamma^{1-n})$, and $u\hat{J} > e\hat{J}$. Generally, as long as $\Gamma_\kappa \geq 1$, new investment cannot be smaller under unembodied as compared with embodied TP, $u\hat{J} \geq e\hat{J}$. It is equal when the capitals are equal and grow at the same rate.

8.2 Replacement

All three quantities – baskets, plants and productivity – may change at different rates. Which one is relevant for price formation and investment evaluation? How are current prices determined?

Labour prices are cost prices. The two cost components are labour costs and capital costs. Labour costs are determined by technology exclusively (λ_j). Capital costs consist of two items: replacement and new investment necessary to maintain full employment. Both items depend on technology (κ_j, n) and the rate of growth of employment (g). For $g = 0$, capital costs depend exclusively on technology. If technology does not change, economy is stationary and capital costs reduce to $\frac{1}{n}K$.

If $g = 0$ and technology changes, replacement is still $R_t = I_{t-n}$ and so its current rate depends on the rate of growth of capital. But the efficiency of machines changes in time and so replacement depends also on technological progress. What has to be replaced is not physical machines but output capacity. If the stock of physical machines expands at the rate m, and their efficiency cum size at the rate γ_κ, output capacity expands at combined rate $M\Gamma_\kappa - 1$. Consequently, current replacement under embodied and unembodied TP will amount to

8.2.1 *Replacement*

$$\text{Embodied TP:} \quad e\hat{R}_{t+1} = \hat{I}_{t+1-n} = (M\Gamma_\kappa)^{t-n}, \qquad I_1 = 1 \tag{8.7e}$$

$$\text{Unembodied TP:} \quad u\hat{R}_{t+1} = M^{t-n}\Gamma_\kappa^{t-1}, \tag{8.7u}$$

where the cap denotes output capacity and the series of investments now starts at some arbitrary point of time. Current output capacity is equal to all investment in the last n years:

$$e\hat{K}_t = \sum_{t-n+1}^{t} (M\Gamma_\kappa)^{\tau} = (M\Gamma_\kappa)^{t-n} \frac{(M\Gamma_\kappa)^n - 1}{M\Gamma_\kappa - 1} \tag{8.8e}$$

$$u\hat{K}_t = \sum_{t-n+1}^{t} M^{\tau}\Gamma_\kappa^{\tau} = M^{t-n}\Gamma_\kappa^{t-1} \frac{M^n - 1}{M - 1} \tag{8.8u}$$

For $\Gamma_\kappa = 1$, $\hat{K}_t$ is the number of currently operating plants of equal efficiency.

Replacement per unit of capital is:

$$\frac{1}{ev} = \frac{e\hat{R}_{t+1}}{e\hat{K}_t} = \frac{M\Gamma_\kappa - 1}{(M\Gamma_\kappa)^n - 1} \tag{8.9e}$$

$$\frac{1}{uv} = \frac{u\hat{R}_{t+1}}{u\hat{K}_t} = \frac{M - 1}{M^n - 1} \tag{8.9u}$$

Under ETP the variable v is a function of both: increasing number of plants (M) and changes in their efficiency and size (Γ_κ). Under UTP, dynamic years uv depend exclusively on the growing number of physical plants – because the efficiency of plants of all vintages in a given year is the same – and so expression (8.9u) is the same as (4.3). ETP replacement ratio is smaller, and in general the following relation holds (L = const.):

$$ev \geq uv \geq n$$

where the equality sign applies only when there is no technological progress, $\Gamma = 1$.

Note that under ETP, n need not be equal to physical durability of machines but may be shorter. If life-span is truncated, more machines will have to be replaced by new, more efficient ones. That will increase total output. If it happens that net output also increases, truncation becomes worthwhile. Shorter n means greater replacement ratio (which increases cost) and smaller ev.

If also labour force is growing, the stock of capital will have to expand further in order to provide employment for new workers. In our formulae every M will have to be replaced by GM, where $G=1+g$ is the growth factor of labour input.

8.3 Price formation

In order to derive price equations, we must start by considering resource balances under ETP at the beginning of the current year. If labour coefficients improve, some workers will be displaced. In order to employ them, the stock of machines must increase. If also capital coefficients improve, the increase of the capital stock will be modified. If also the size of plants changes, capital stock will be modified for the third time. As already noted, changes in size and in design cannot be distinguished. Unrestricted changes make the analysis unmanageable and we need some simplification. Empirical data suggest that the proportions of living and embodied labour remain approximately constant. In a closed economy with constant L that implies that sectoral employments remain unchanged. (The labour value of p_2X_2 depends exclusively on L_2; if L is constant, so must be L_2). Initial unit gross investment is made at $t-n+1$ and these plants are of vintage $\tau=1$. Let A_1 and A_2, $(A_1+A_2=1)$, be the constant shares of sectoral gross investments. Resource balances at the beginning of $n+1$ are as follows (8.4e):

$$L_1 \quad + \quad L_2 \quad = \quad L$$

$$A_1\frac{(M\Gamma_\kappa)^n-1}{M\Gamma_\kappa-1}+A_2\frac{(M\Gamma_\kappa)^n-1}{M\Gamma_\kappa-1}=\frac{(M\Gamma_\kappa)^n-1}{M\Gamma_\kappa-1}=\hat{K}$$

The rate of gross investment (r) is the same in both sectors and so investment balance appears to be:

$$r\hat{K}_1+r\hat{K}_2=(M\Gamma_\kappa)^n=\hat{X}_2, \quad \hat{K}_j=A_j\frac{(M\Gamma_\kappa)^n-1}{M\Gamma_\kappa-1}, \quad r=\frac{1}{ev}+(M\Gamma_\kappa-1)$$

Define technical coefficients:

$$\bar{\lambda}_j=\frac{L_j}{\hat{X}_j}, \; \bar{\kappa}_j=A_j\frac{(M\Gamma_\kappa)^n-1}{M\Gamma_\kappa-1}/\hat{X}_j$$

where bars denote averages over all vintages. The usual vertical summation of the evaluated components of quantity equations produces the required price equations:

$$r\bar{p}_2\bar{\kappa}_1 + w\bar{\lambda}_1 = p_1$$
$$r\bar{p}_2\bar{\kappa}_2 + w\bar{\lambda}_2 = p_2 \qquad (8.10e)$$

The equations have the following characteristics:

1. $\bar{\lambda}_j$ are not technical coefficients of any specific vintage of plants; they represent averages calculated with respect to all vintages of plants in existence. This is in a way Marx's socially necessary labour.
2. The number of plants constructed annually increases by M, their efficiency cum size by Γ_κ. Since both factors are constant, and so is A_2, the stock of K_2 must increase equally as gross investment. Consequently, capital coefficient in the second sector does not change:

$$\bar{\kappa}_2 = \frac{K_2 M\Gamma_\kappa}{X_2 M\Gamma_\kappa} = \kappa_2 = \text{const.}$$

   and the bar is not necessary. In the first sector output increases by $\Gamma = M\Gamma_\kappa$ and so does capital stock in NOC units leaving:

$$\bar{\kappa}_1 = \frac{K_1 M\Gamma_\kappa}{X_1 M\Gamma_\kappa} = \kappa_1$$

   Technological progress implied here is such that one machine of any vintage produces the same number of machines of the next vintage but successive vintages of machines produce increasing number of baskets if $\Gamma_\kappa > 1$, or the same number of baskets if $\Gamma_\kappa = 1$.
3. The number of plants is measured in NOC units and so $\bar{p}_2$ is the price of the plant having NOC of the current vintage but produced by the capital stock of the last n vintages.
4. By definition, standard baskets do not change and so $\bar{p}_1$ represents the price of the actual basket of wage goods, $\bar{p}_1 = p_1$.
5. More recent vintages of plants have λ_j and $p_2\kappa$, smaller than are those in (8.10e) and will, therefore, earn extra profits that will be used to cover depreciation charges. Since prices are falling and technology of any vintage remains constant, depreciation must be concentrated in early years.

We are still left with the task of finding the price of the plant of the current vintage. The number of plants constructed currently ($t = n+1$) is $\hat{X}_2 = (M\Gamma_\kappa)^n$ in NOC units and $X_2 = M^n$ in physical units. The value of these plants remains the same however are they counted, $\bar{p}_2\hat{X}_2 = p_2X_2$. Consequently:

$$p_2 = \frac{\bar{p}_2 \hat{X}_2}{X_2} = \bar{p}_2 \Gamma_\kappa^n$$

If also changes in λ_j are known, we may say more about price equations. Suppose technological progress is Neutral I: capital coefficients remain unchanged, while labour coefficients decrease by Γ. With respect to the foregoing pattern of TP, that implies $\Gamma_\kappa = 1$, $M = \Gamma$. Rentals in NOC and physical units are equal. From one vintage to the next the number of plants increases by Γ and so do outputs X_1 and X_2. Since labour productivity also increases by Γ, the number of workers employed remains constant. Thus, labour is equally distributed among vintages, L/n workers operating machines of each vintage. It follows that:

$$\bar{\lambda}_j = \frac{L_j}{\hat{X}_j} = \frac{nL_j/n}{x_j(\Gamma^{1-n} + \ldots + \Gamma^{-1} + 1)} = \lambda_j(t)\,\frac{n(\Gamma^{-1} - 1)}{\Gamma^{-n} - 1}$$

$$\bar{\lambda}_j = \lambda_j(t)\,\frac{n\gamma\Gamma^{n-1}}{\Gamma^n - 1}, \qquad \lambda_j(t) = \frac{L_j}{nx_j}$$

where x_j is the output of the last vintage which employs L_j/n workers and $\lambda_j(t)$ is labour coefficient of the last vintage. Price equations (8.10e) for the *last* vintage under Neutral I TP are:

$$\begin{aligned} rp_2\kappa_1 + w\lambda_1 \frac{n\gamma\Gamma^{n-1}}{\Gamma^n - 1} &= p_1 \\ rp_2\kappa_2 + w\lambda_2 \frac{n\gamma\Gamma^{n-1}}{\Gamma^n - 1} &= p_2 \end{aligned} \tag{8.11e}$$

In these equations $w\lambda_j$ represent wages, while:

$$w\lambda_j\left(\frac{n\gamma\Gamma^{n-1}}{\Gamma^n - 1} - 1\right)$$

indicates how much average replacement cost $1/e\nu$ must be augmented to provide an appropriate depreciation for the last vintage. For older vintages replacement will have to be reduced to avoid losses and keep the same wage rate w for each vintage of plants. In a firm with a balanced distribution of plants over all vintages, the corrective items will cancel out and the price equations at the firm level will reduce to:

$$p_j = rp_2\kappa_j + w\lambda_j.$$

The equation will also apply to certain middle vintages. Note that λ_j is full (vertically integrated) and not direct ($\hat{\lambda}_j$) labour coefficient. The difference ($\lambda_j - \hat{\lambda}_j$) represents labour contained in material costs. The other component of material costs, their machine content, is given by the difference of full and direct capital coefficients ($\kappa_j - \hat{\kappa}_j$).

With unembodied technological progress no such complications arise. Plants of all vintages are equally efficient, and κ_j are ordinary capital coefficients (the number of physical plants per unit of output), same for all vintages so that depreciation rates do not change.

$$rp_2\kappa_j + w\lambda_j = p_j, \; r = 1/v + (GM_\kappa - 1), j = 1, 2 \qquad (8.11u)$$

The interpretation is as follows:

1. Under UTP all plants and, of course, all workers are equally efficient at the last year level. Consequently, κ_j and λ_j represent ratios of physical quantities. In the current year their efficiency increases further and that affects the necessary volume of investment.
2. The profit rate $\pi = GM\Gamma_\kappa - 1$ is the same for both types of TP.
3. The replacement ratio is different for each type of TP as shown in (8.9). Under ETP, v is a function of efficiency factor too, while under UTP it is not.

The difference between replacements is relatively great but absolutely not so important. For $n = 30$, $M = \Gamma_\kappa = 1.03$ and $G = 1.01$, the respective replacement ratios are $1/ev = 0.009$, $1/u = 0.018$. With capital coefficient equal to three, replacement amounts to respectively 2.7% and 5.4% of GNP. Since in reality technological progress is both embodied and unembodied, the actual difference is somewhere between the two figures.[1] Note that $M\Gamma_\kappa - 1 = g_{x_1}$($GM\Gamma_\kappa - 1$ if labour also expands) is the rate of growth of output (8.6). The same rate of growth appears in (8.9e). Consequently, if output rate of growth is used in calculating replacement ratio, that implies assuming embodied technological progress.

8.4 Obsolescence

Older technology is less efficient and, therefore, less profitable. In order to avoid losses, technical life-span of plants might have to be truncated and the obsolete machines scrapped at an earlier date.

Whatever the pattern of technological progress, production will become unprofitable when prices – which are the same for all vintages – will no longer cover material and wage costs:

$$p < pA^{\tau} + w\hat{\lambda}^{\tau} = w\lambda^{\tau}, \qquad \lambda^{\tau} = \hat{\lambda}^{\tau}(I - A^{\tau})^{-1} \tag{8.12}$$

where A^{τ} and $\hat{\lambda}^{\tau}$ are respectively reproduction matrix and direct coefficients vector of labour coefficients belonging to vintage τ. If labour coefficients decrease by Γ_{λ} and λ belongs to the latest vintage, the inequality:

$$p < w\lambda\Gamma_{\lambda}^{n} \tag{8.13}$$

determine the service life of plants (n). Γ_{λ}^{n} represents the factor by which real wages have increased in the last n years.

We know that an increase in the rate of growth of labour force increases r and therefore p_j. Taking that into account, (8.12) and (8.13) make possible six generalizations. The economic life of capital assets will be reduced in relation to its technological life if (1) technological progress is fast (large Γ_{λ}); (2) labour costs ($w\hat{\lambda}_j$) are high, which implies that cost of producer goods is low (given p_j); (3) technical durability of assets is long (n is large); (4) growth rate of labour is low (and, consequently, p is small).[2] Besides, (5) by reducing n, truncation increases replacement and prices; (6) by increasing Γ_{κ}, TP reduces the relative size of X_2 (embodied labour) and so reduces prices.

9 Evaluation of investment projects

9.1 Conceptual issues again

Before we proceed, some clarification is necessary. What does it mean when we say that capital coefficients have been reduced? One possible interpretation is that machines are still physically identical so that we can measure capital stock by simply counting the machines, old as well as new. Then an increased productivity of machines, with unchanged productivity of labour, implies a decrease in technical composition of resources, more workers per machine:

$$\frac{(1+\gamma)^{-1}\kappa^0}{\lambda^0}=k<k^0, \qquad \gamma>0$$

Such an effect is perfectly possible if, due to improved repair services, machine runs more hours per year while the crew of operators is enlarged by including repairmen. But the possibilities of such improvements must soon be exhausted. An opposite change, improvement in labour productivity with κ's constant, implies more machines per worker. Although specialization, division of labour and a better organization of work may make it possible that one worker operates two machines instead of one, such possibilities are also soon exhausted and after every worker will have been equipped with three, or five or ten machines further technological progress will have to come to a standstill. Thus, a continuous reduction of κ's is only slightly less unrealistic than a continuous improvement of λ's.

The two changes can be simultaneous: both labour and capital coefficients may decrease. If they decrease at the same proportional rate, machine–labour ratio will not change but output will increase. The proportional decrease of λ's will increase outputs and reduce prices in the same proportion, leaving relative outputs and relative prices unchanged. If a proportional decrease of κ's is superimposed, X_1 will increase further still – and X_2 will be somewhat reduced. Both prices will decrease even more with the price of the more capital intensive good being reduced more than the other. However, it is again unrealistic to expect that workers equipped with the same physical machines can indefinitely produce more and more output. Thus, eventually we must assume that machines change as well and that an unembodied technological progress is supplemented by technological progress embodied in new machines.

If machines change, we can still continue our physical count due to synchrony principles, but the comparison of most of the characteristic coefficients before and after the change loses economic meaning. This raises the problem of a definition of a new unit of measurement. The unit must be invariant itself. I shall take the basket of consumer goods in the base period as such a standard. This will be the *standard basket* and we shall measure changing machines in terms of the standard basket. When consumer goods change, we are in trouble again. To price statisticians the problem is known as the problem of new products and of quality change. I shall assume that at the time new products are introduced, both old and new products are produced by the same machines and labour. Thus, cost ratios will determine price ratios, and new baskets will be expressed in terms of standard baskets. Long-run equilibrium is assumed throughout, and so extra profits do not arise. It is always possible to select as a *numéraire* a consumer good – such as unavoidable corn – whose quality can be standardized and which is not likely to disappear from the market.

As for quality changes, we leave the evaluation to the consumer who will equalize the marginal utility of dinar (labour day) spent in any line of consumption.

The evaluation of investment projects requires that two different problems be solved: (a) *heterogeneous* machines and net output they produce must be compared and (b) inputs and outputs at *different points of time* must be compared. We first have to determine constant prices.

9.2 Labour time, basket and standard prices

If the wage rate is taken as a *numéraire*, $w=1$, absolute prices are expressed labour–time (p_j/w, $=l$-prices). If the basket of consumer goods is taken as a *numéraire*, $p_1=1$, prices are expressed in terms of baskets (p_j/p_1, b-prices) and nominal wage is transformed into real wage ($w/p_1=\tilde{w}$). Baskets have standard size and composition of commodities and in this sense they are standard baskets. The wage basket is the basket of some base period when one wage buys one basket and so $w=p_1^0$. In this period the number of baskets produced is equal to the number of workers, $X_1=L\,(p_1=w)$. In later periods L remains constant, but X_1 increases and so labour productivity increases.

Bearing in mind that by assumption baskets remain identical, a change in labour productivity may be expressed in three different ways:

$$\Gamma_1=\frac{p_1(0)X_1(t)}{p_1(t)X_1(t)}=\frac{p_1(0)}{p_1(t)} \tag{9.1a}$$

$$\Gamma_1=\frac{p_1(0)X_1(t)}{p_1(0)X_1(0)}=\frac{X_1(t)/L}{X_1(0)/L}=\frac{\tilde{w}(t)}{\tilde{w}(0)} \tag{9.1b}$$

$$\Gamma_1 = \frac{p_1(0)X_1(t)}{p_1(0)X_1(0)} = \frac{p_1(0)X_1(t)}{w(0)L} = \frac{X_1(t)}{L}, \; p_1(0) = w(0) \tag{9.1c}$$

Γ_1 in (9.1a) is Paasche index of prices, and in (9.1b) is its dual, Laspeyres index of quantities. The latter is also a ratio of real wages. If in the base period a basket is calibrated so that one wage buys one basket ($w = p_1$), then $\Gamma_1(0) = 1$ and so $\Gamma_1(t) = X_1(t)/L$ represents the current labour productivity in terms of baskets, and also an increase of labour productivity over the base period. Γ_1 is defined so as to measure changes in labour productivity in the *consumer good sector*, i.e. it measures changes in direct and indirect labour expended in the production of one basket. At the same time it also measures *systemic changes* in labour productivity, i.e. it measures changes in the volume of living labour (employed in both sectors) per unit of net output. In this section (9.1b) will be of primary interest.

If the standard basket is used as a *numéraire* of the system, we have an invariant unit of account. Prices in terms of baskets (b-prices) are

$$\tilde{w} = \frac{w}{p_1} = \frac{X_1}{L} = \frac{1 - r\kappa_2}{\lambda_2 r\kappa_1 + \lambda_1(1 - r\kappa_2)} \tag{9.2a}$$

$$\tilde{p}_1 = \tilde{w}p_1 = 1, \qquad w = 1 \tag{9.2b}$$

$$\tilde{p}_2 = \frac{p_2}{p_1} = \tilde{w}p_2 = \frac{\lambda_2}{\lambda_2 r\kappa_1 + \lambda_1(1 - r\kappa_2)} \tag{9.2c}$$

The real wage $\tilde{w}$ represents at the same time current productivity of labour. It indicates how many baskets can be produced by expending one worker-year. The basket-price of a plant, $\tilde{p}_2$, shows the number of baskets that can be produced by the labour embodied in a plant. The machines may change, but plants still can be counted in terms of labour embodied in baskets.

The remarkable property of prices in terms of consumer goods baskets is that they can be derived as products of ordinary labour–time prices and the real wage, $\tilde{p}_j = \tilde{w}p_j$. If labour productivity increases equally in both sectors, as under Neutral I and Capital Saving TP, relative prices will not change and basket-prices will remain constant:

$$\tilde{p}_j(t) = \tilde{w}(t)p_j(t) = \tilde{w}(0)\Gamma^t p_j(0)\Gamma^{-t} = \tilde{w}(0)p_j(0) = \tilde{p}_j(0)$$

The basket-price of a plant, $\tilde{p}_2$, depends on all technical coefficients and not only on the state of technology in the machine sector as under labour–time. A proportional increase in labour productivity (Neutral I TP), $\lambda_j = \lambda_j^0\Gamma^{-1}$, leaves $\tilde{p}_2$ unchanged. A decrease of κ_1 increases relative efficiency of machines, and $\tilde{p}_2$ increases. A decrease of κ_2, reduces $\tilde{p}_2$, which means that one physical machine now contains a smaller number of equivalent (in terms of labour) baskets. A neutral TP of type II increases $\tilde{p}_2$, while Mixed Neutral TP reduces $\tilde{p}_2$. In general, changes in $\tilde{p}_2$ indicate how TP changes the basket content of machines under new productivity of labour. (See Table 7.1, p. 86.)

If we have the following relation between two stocks of machines produced in current and base years:

$$\tilde{p}_2 K = A\tilde{p}_2^0 K^0$$

then the quantity of machines in terms of baskets in the current period is A times larger than the stock of the base period. K/K^0 represents a change in the actual number of machines, but that has no economic meaning because machines of different efficiency are not commensurable. Only if $p_2 = p_2^0$ – when labour productivity increases equally in both sectors – the relation between physically counted machines may have an economic meaning, namely $K = AK^0$ (in terms of labour costs, not in terms of capacity).

We may standardize basket-prices in terms of real wage of some base period productivity:

$$\bar{\tilde{p}}_j = \frac{\tilde{p}_j}{\tilde{w}^0} = \frac{\tilde{w}}{\tilde{w}^0} p_j = \Gamma_1 p_j \tag{9.3}$$

Such prices will prove to have some interesting properties. They will be called *standard prices*.

9.3 Present values

When individual investment projects are evaluated, inputs and outputs are dated and the rule has to be discovered that aggregates them diachronically.

In a stationary economy no problem arises because time does not matter – although even here alternative techniques with the same labour inputs but shorter production periods are preferable (see section 4.2).

Presumably a rational consumer prefers more consumption forever to less consumption forever and the use of techniques involving dated inputs is determined by the composition of demand. It is important to realize that stationariness is analytically timeless because neither of the two dimensions of labour – the number of workers and their productivity – is subject to change. As soon as the number of workers changes – either positively or negatively – time dimension is activated directly: the available labour *time* changes. When productivity changes, time dimension is implied since change means an effect per unit of *time*. It is, therefore, obvious on *a priori* grounds that the two time effects must be properly accounted for if two diachronically different streams of inputs and outputs are to be compared.

The conventional textbook rule for calculating the present value of a stream of past inputs says that they should be compounded at the ruling interest rate. But we are never given precise instructions on how to find the appropriate interest rate nor at what prices inputs ought to be evaluated. As to the prices, presumably they must be constant prices since otherwise inputs are not commensurable. Yet, how do we establish constant prices for machines whose costs and productivities vary?

Suppose a long-term social plan envisages the rate of full employment expansion of consumer goods output to be π. By the end of the planning horizon the present output of baskets will have increased to:

$$X_1(t) = X_1(0)(1+\pi)^t \tag{9.4}$$

In this system the two dated batches of consumer goods, $X_1(0)$ and $X_1(t)$, are equivalent only if (9.4) is satisfied. The expression (9.4) describes the state of the system within the planning period, it identifies the system.

In describing the system we simply apply the synchrony rule by reducing future (t) and past ($-t$) outputs to present time in order to make them comparable. The weights used are $(1+\pi)^t$. A future output will be equivalent to the present output if the following relation is satisfied:

$$X_1(0) = X_1(t)(1+\pi)^{-t} \tag{9.5a}$$

and similarly for a past output:

$$X_1(0) = X_1(-t)(1+\pi)^t \tag{9.5b}$$

We call the former procedure discounting, and the latter compounding. The discount and the compound rate is the same (π).

A system may also change unevenly. In that case it will be identified by applying dated discount rates $\pi(t)$. We shall mostly consider regularly growing systems with constant discount rates.

There are two possible causes of growth: technological progress and the growth of labour force. Thus the discount factor will be structured

$$1+\pi = G\Gamma_1, \quad G = 1+g, \quad \Gamma_1 = 1+\gamma_1$$

γ_1 is positive by definition, while g may also be negative. It is, therefore, possible that $G\Gamma < 1$ which makes π negative, $\pi < 0$. It is possible, but not likely empirically.

An investment project consists of two parts, of investment outlays and of a stream of net outputs. The two streams may partly overlap. In our system investment outlays consist of plants constructed and net outputs consist of consumer baskets. The two composite commodities cannot be compared directly, and so we compare their values whereby plants are measured in standard baskets. A plant is worth while constructing if its cost in terms of baskets is not greater than its output of equivalent baskets over its lifetime. The construction of the plant may take more than one year. To simplify matters at this stage of analysis, I shall assume that the plant was constructed in one year, and that year will be considered the base year. Then our investment rule says that the project will be eligible if the present value of the stream of future net value is not greater than investment outlays:

$$\tilde{p}_2(0)X_2(0) \leq \sum_{t=1}^{n} X_1(t)\,(1+\pi)^{-t} \tag{9.6}$$

The rule is quite orthodox, only the garb is somewhat novel. First, prices are constant prices in terms of standard baskets of wage goods so that the expression on both sides of the inequality have the same dimension, namely baskets. Secondly, the discount rate is not an anonymous market rate of interest, but a very definite $\pi = G\Gamma_1^{-1}$.

In which way is all this related to the labour theory of prices?

9.4 Alternative values of investment projects

Nothing is changed in (9.5) if the same price is used to evaluate both outputs. We only assume that $g=0$ and so $\pi=\Gamma_1$. Consequently,

$$p_1(0)X_1(0) = p_1(0)X_1(t)\,(1+\gamma_1)^{-t} \tag{9.7}$$

We know that the labour value of net output is equal to living labour and so does not change when labour does not change

$$p_1(0)X_1(0) = p_1(t)X_1(t) = L \tag{9.8}$$

It follows from (9.7) and (9.8) that

$$p_1(t) = p_1(0)\,(1+\gamma_1)^{-t} \tag{9.9}$$

and we can derive the first theorem.[1]

Theorem I. If employment does not change, L=constant, while labour productivity increases at the rate γ_1; this rate functions also as a discount rate and the present value of future consumer baskets is equal to their historical costs:

$$p_1(0)X_1(t)\ (1+\gamma_1)^{-t}=p_1(t)X_1(t).$$

Similar reasoning applies to the investment rule as well. Multiply both sides of (9.6) by $p_1(0)$:

$$p_1(0)\tilde{p}_2(0)X_2(0)=p_1(0)[\tilde{w}(0)p_2(0)]X_2(0)\leq p_1(0)\sum_t X_1(t)\ (1+\gamma_1)^{-t}$$

Since $p_1(0)\ \tilde{w}(0)=1$, it follows that:

$$p_2(0)\ X_2(0)\leq\sum_j p_1(t)X_1(t) \tag{9.10a}$$

which means that labour expended on the construction of a plant must at least be recuperated in its output.

If the plant will be constructed over τ years, the present value of future investment outlays in basket prices is:

$$\sum_\tau \tilde{p}_2(\tau)X_2(\tau)(1+\gamma_1)^{-\tau}=\sum_\tau \tilde{w}(\tau)p_2(\tau)X_2(\tau)(1+\gamma_1)^{-\tau}=\tilde{w}(0)\sum_\tau p_2(\tau)X_2(\tau)$$

and similarly for baskets:

$$\sum_t \tilde{p}_1(t)X_1(t)(1+\gamma_1)^{-t}=\sum_t \tilde{w}(t)p_1(t)X_1(t)(1+\gamma_1)^{-t}=\tilde{w}(0)\sum_\tau p_1(t)X_1(t)$$

and the general investment rule is simply:

$$\sum_\tau p_2(\tau)X_2(\tau)\leq\sum_t p_1(t)X_1(t) \tag{9.10b}$$

which leads to the next theorem.

Theorem II. If employment does not change, while labour productivity increases, investment outlays and net products are made comparable by being evaluated in historical labour prices. Alternatively, any two dated products are equivalent if their historical labour values are equal. Ricardo–Marx diachronic addition of labour time makes sense when labour force does not change.

For an investment project to be eligible, the present value of Marshallian quasi rents must be at least equal to the present value of investment according to the orthodox rule. This criterion yields the following.

Corollary I. Labour time expended in investment activities must at least be recuperated in net output.

Yet another consequence follows from Theorem II. Suppose projects are evaluated in standard prices, which are clearly also constant prices. From (9.3), $\bar{\bar{p}}_j\Gamma_1^{-t} = p_j(t)$. It follows that:

Corollary II. Discounted standard values are equal to historical labour values. The rate of growth of labour productivity is the discount rate. Since $\bar{\bar{p}}_1(t) = p_1(t)\Gamma_1^t = p_1(0)$, the own interest rate of the composite commodity represented by the standard basket of consumer goods is the universal rate of discount if labour does not expand ($g = 0$).

That ought to be obvious. Instead of measuring output in terms of baskets, output is measured in labour time of equal productivity. Effective labour time expands at the rate γ_1 – the rate of expansion of output – and must be discounted at the same rate in order to be comparable with the present size of labour time.

If labour force also increases, physical labour time increases at the rate g, and global labour time – labour of equal productivity – at the combined rate $\pi = \Gamma_1 G - 1$, which is also the discount rate.

Theorem III. If physical labour expands by factor G and effective labour by factor Γ_1, global labour of equal productivity will expand by the combined factor $1 + \pi = G\Gamma_1$. In order to achieve comparability with the presently available labour, the synchrony rule requires that global labour be compressed into present size. In order to reduce global labour to the size of presently available labour, discount factor $G\Gamma_1$ must be applied. If values are expressed in standard prices, the discount factor is $G\Gamma_1$, if they are expressed in labour prices the discount factor is G.

9.5 Comparisons of investment projects

A simple investment criterion emerges: labour expended must be recuperated.

If investment outlays are treated as negative outputs, the present value of an investment project must be non-negative, $V \geq 0$, if the project is to be acceptable. Let a project have a life-span of n years and involve s different investment and consumption goods, then the present value of the project is given as follows:

$$\text{Standard prices: } V_s = \sum_{t=1}^{n} (1+\pi)^{-t} \sum_{j=1}^{s} \bar{\bar{p}}_j(t) X_j(t) \qquad (9.11a)$$

$$\text{Labour prices:}\quad V_L = \sum_{t=1}^{n}(1+g)^{-t}\sum_{j=1}^{s} p_j(t)X_j(t) \qquad (9.11b)$$

$$V_s = V_L,\ (1+\pi) = (1+g)(1+\gamma_1)$$

The economic labour time expands at the rate π and is composed of calendar labour time expanding at g and efficiency labour time expanding at γ_1. The discount rate π reduces economic labour time to its base period equivalent satisfying thus the synchrony rule. If g and γ_1 change over time and changes compensate each other so that π remains constant, (9.11a) still applies. If π itself changes, $(1+\pi)^{-t}$ ought to be replaced by:

$$\prod_t [1+\pi(t)]^{-1} \text{ and } (1+g)^{-t} \text{ by } \prod_t [1+g(t)]^{-1}.$$

Investment projects are compared by means of V: the higher is the present value of a project the more is it profitable.

Before we conclude, a curious case may be mentioned again. If labour shrinks by the same factor by which labour productivity expands, $G=\Gamma_1$, net output will be stagnant, $G^{-1}\Gamma_1=1$, but per capita net output (=real wage) will grow at the rate γ_1. Real wage will always increase at the rate of technological progress (regardless of what happens to G), because technological progress is the only source of economic progress. Stationariness means that there is no discounting because effective labour does not change.

In general there are four possible states of economy that are described by four different discount rates:

1. *Stationary conditions*: $\pi=g=\gamma_1=0$ or $\pi=(1-g)(1+\gamma_1)-1=0$. The value of an investment project is expressed in labour or in standard prices. Global labour–time either does not change, or the changes cancel out.
2. *Constant calendar labour time and technological progress*: $g=0, \gamma_1>0$, $\pi=\gamma_1$. The value of an investment project is expressed in historical labour prices (diachronic labour time).
3. *Changes in calendar labour time and constant technology*: $g\neq 0, \gamma_1=0$, $\pi=g$. The value of an investment project is expressed in synchronic labour prices, i.e. in labour prices corrected for the change in the socially available labour time (labour force).
4. *Changes in calendar labour time and technological progress*: $g\neq 0, \gamma_1>0$, $1+\pi=(1+g)\ (1+\gamma_1)$. Historical labour time is increased or reduced for the change in the socially available labour time.

PART IV

THE CHOICE OF TECHNIQUES

10 Price–quantity duality

10.1 Output and price curves

A convenient starting point for the study of the choice of techniques is to examine the geometry of the solutions of the dual system of quantity and price equations (5.3) and (5.8). The solutions, given by (5.4), (5.5), (5.9) and (5.10), are:

$$X_1=\frac{(1-r\kappa_2)L}{\lambda_1+rm},\qquad X_2=\frac{r\kappa_1 L}{\lambda_1+rm},\qquad \frac{X_1}{X_2}=\frac{1-r\kappa_2}{r\kappa_1} \tag{10.1}$$

$$p_1=\frac{(\lambda_1+rm)w}{1-r\kappa_2},\qquad p_2=\frac{\lambda_2 w}{1-r\kappa_2},\qquad \frac{p_2}{p_1}=\frac{\lambda_2}{\lambda_1+rm} \tag{10.2}$$

$$m=\kappa_1\lambda_2-\kappa_2\lambda_1,\qquad \lambda_1+rm>0,\qquad 1-r\kappa_2>0$$

The expressions are somewhat simplified by the use of the term $m=\kappa_1\lambda_2-\kappa_2\lambda_1$, which may be called the *relative mechanization* of the two industries. Recall that $m \gtreqless 0$ implies $k_1 \gtreqless k_2$. The conditions for output and prices to be finite and positive are $-rm<\lambda_1$ and $r\kappa_2<1$.

10.1.1 Properties of the curves

The properties of the functions (10.1) and (10.2) are systematized in a table and two groups of diagrams.

Table 10.1 Properties of Output and Price Functions

		X_1	X_2	X_1/X_2	p_1	p_2	p_2/p_1
d/dr,	$m\gtreqless 0$	<0	>0	<0	>0	>0	$\lesseqgtr 0$
d^2/dr^2,	$m\gtreqless 0$	$\gtreqless 0$	$\gtreqless 0$	>0	>0	>0	$\gtreqless 0$

The rental rate may vary between zero and a certain maximum R. This maximum is reached when the output of X_1 is reduced to zero, $R=1/\kappa_2$ for $X_1=0$. The intersection of the curves is arbitrary (depends on the choice of units) and has no meaning. In order to draw two curves on the same graph I shall arbitrarily assume $\lambda_2>\lambda_1$.

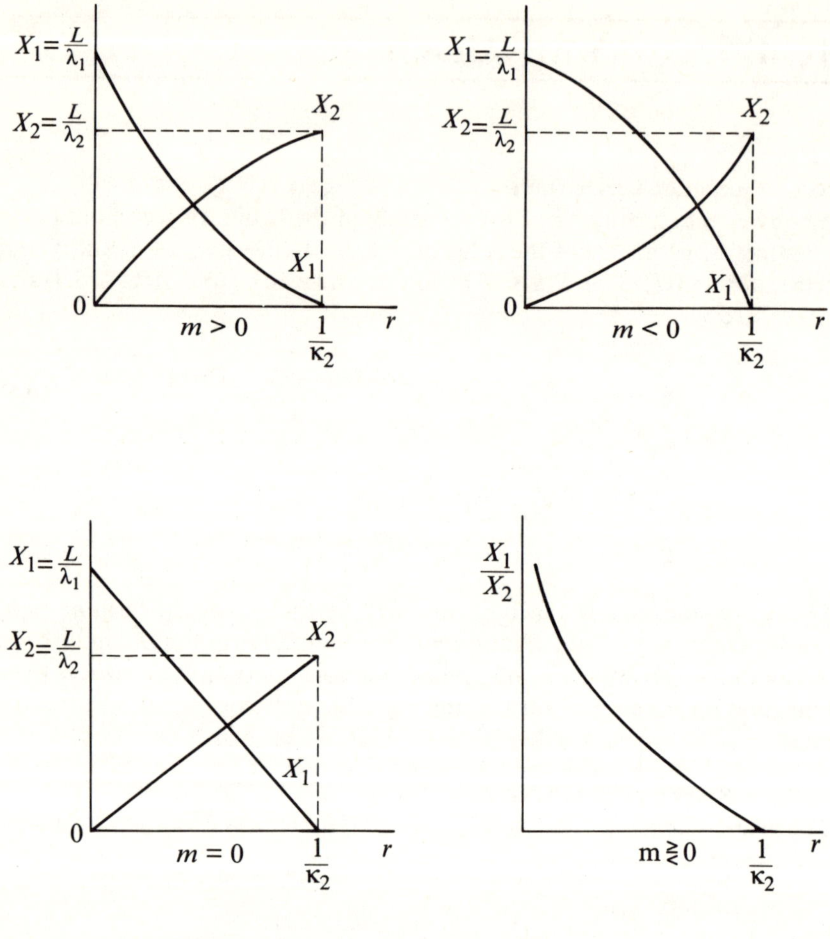

Figure 10.1 *Output curves*

When relative mechanization varies, output curves change their shapes from convex to concave and vice versa and for $m = 0$ they become straight lines. For obvious reasons the output ratio curve is always convex towards the origin.

Increasing r implies increasing labour cost of net output. Consequently, both prices are increasing functions of r whatever m. The first of the two diagrams in Fig. 10.2 is drawn on the assumption $m \leq 0$ in order to exclude the possibility of crossing of the functions (for $\lambda_2 > \lambda_1$). The ratio of prices is an increasing (decreasing) function of r depending on $m \gtrless 0$. In other words, the price of the more mechanized output increases faster. If both industries are equally mechanized, relative prices do not change and are equal to the ratio of direct labour coefficients. Note that relative price represents the basket price of machine, $\tilde{p}_2 = p_2/p_1$.

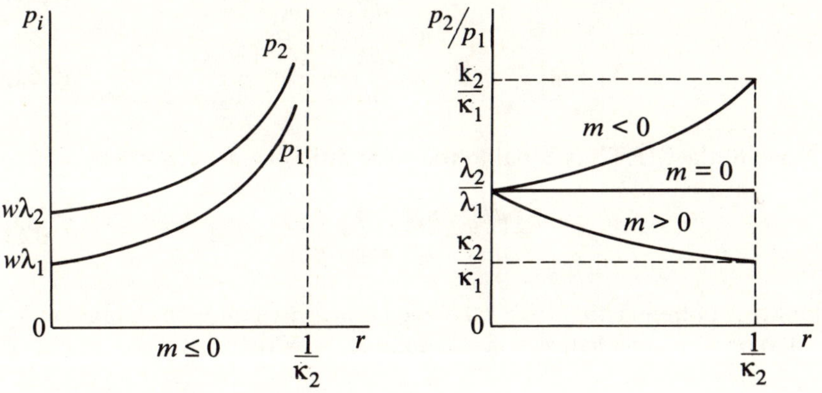

Figure 10.2 Price curves

10.1.2 Marginal rate of product transformation and relative prices

Marginal rate of transformation (MRT) of X_1 into X_2 will be different depending on what restrictions we impose on resources and rental rate. If L is fixed and $X_1 = X_1(r)$, MRT is negative:

$$MRT_1 = \frac{dX_1/dr}{dX_2/dr} = -\frac{\lambda_2}{\lambda_1} \tag{10.3}$$

If we consider price changes, we get a dual formulation of (10.3) for w fixed:

$$MRT_2 = -\frac{dp_2/dr}{dp_1/dr} = -\frac{\kappa_2}{\kappa_1} \tag{10.4}$$

If r is fixed and $X_1 = X_1(L)$, MRT is positive because L, being the only primary resource, is not limited:

$$MRT_3 = \frac{dX_1/dL}{dX_2/dL} = \frac{X_1}{X_2} = \frac{1 - r\kappa_2}{r\kappa_1} \tag{10.5}$$

The three marginal rates of transformation may also be directly obtained from quantity equations:

$$\lambda_1 X_1 + \lambda_2 X_2 = \bar{L}, \ \frac{dX_1}{dX_2} = -\frac{\lambda_2}{\lambda_1} \tag{10.3a}$$

$$\kappa_1 X_1 + \kappa_2 X_2 = \bar{K}, \ \frac{dX_1}{dX_2} = -\frac{\kappa_2}{\kappa_1} \tag{10.4a}$$

$$r\kappa_1 X_1 + r\kappa_2 X_2 = rK = X_2, \ \frac{dX_1}{dX_2} = \frac{X_1}{X_2} = \frac{1 - r\kappa_2}{r\kappa_1} \tag{10.5a}$$

None of the MRT's is equal to the price ratio in a general case:

$$-\frac{dX_1}{dX_2} \neq \frac{p_2}{p_1} = \frac{\lambda_2}{\lambda_1 + rm} \tag{10.6}$$

Equality is obtained only for $r=0$ (which is inconsistent with changes in X_2 in 10.3) or when mechanization is equalized ($m=0$):

$$-\frac{dX_1}{dX_2} = \frac{\lambda_2}{\lambda_1} = \frac{p_2}{p_1}, \qquad m=0 \tag{10.6a}$$

(For the other cases when the MRT is equal to the price ratio see (10.25) and (10.37).) Besides, (10.3a) is compatible with available stock of machines only if mechanization is uniform throughout the economy. That is easily seen. If output of machines is increased by one unit, output of baskets falls by λ_2/λ_1. Substitute into (10.4a):

$$\kappa_2(X_2+1) + \kappa_1\left(X_1 - \frac{\lambda_2}{\lambda_1}\right) = (\kappa_2 X_2 + \kappa_1 X_1) + \left(\kappa_2 - \frac{\kappa_1\lambda_2}{\lambda_1}\right) = \bar{K}.$$

The condition is satisfied only if $\kappa_2\lambda_1 - \kappa_1\lambda_2 = -m = 0$. For $m \neq 0$, any change in the proportion X_1/X_2 will leave either labour or machines unemployed.

The puzzle of (10.6) needs an explanation. Why does rm appear in the denominator? Because in a steady state equilibrium $r>0$ implies positive quantities of embodied labour and so total labour per unit of output depends on r. The direction of aggregate change depends on relative mechanization that may have any sign. dX_1/dX_2 is generally incompatible with full employment. Relative prices (p_2/p_1), on the other hand, reflect long-run full employment equilibrium when capital stock is fully adjusted to the rate of growth of labour.

All that is, of course, very different from standard neoclassical analysis. The relation between the two approaches can be established in the following way (Fig. 10.3).

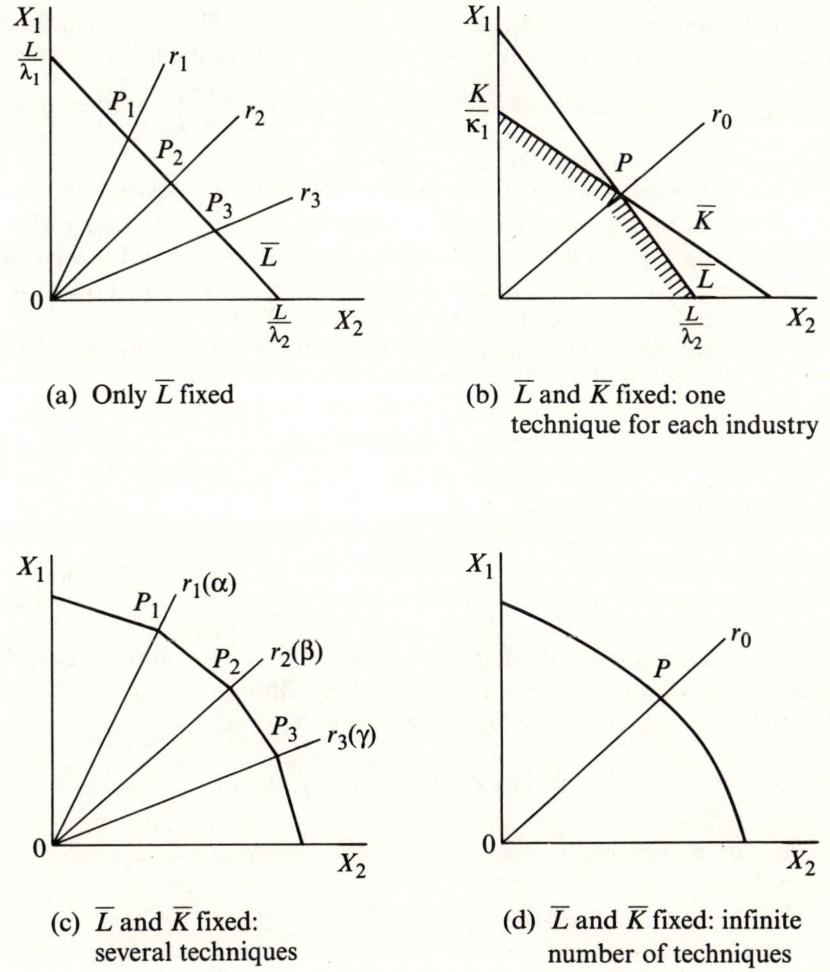

Figure 10.3 Transformation locus

Regardless of L, the ratio X_1/X_2 is determined by the rental rate and is represented by a ray from the origin. In Fig. 10.3a it is assumed that $r_1 < r_2 < r_3$: the slope of the output ray becomes flatter (less X_1 and more X_2) as r increases. Since only L is fixed, there is only one (labour) constraint. P_1, P_2, P_3 represent points of maximum output corresponding to rental rates r_1, r_2, r_3.

If also K is fixed, as it must be in the short run, we have two linear constraints denoted as $\bar{L}$ and $\bar{K}$ (Fig. 10.3b). Both resources are fully used only at the point P corresponding to the rental rate r_0. For $r_1 < r_0$, labour is not fully employed; for $r_1 > r_0$, capital is not fully used. The two constraints will coincide – and consequently, both resources will always be fully used as in Fig. 3a – only if the slopes in (10.3b) are equal $\left(\frac{\lambda_2}{\lambda_1} = \frac{\kappa_2}{\kappa_1}\right)$, i.e. when both industries are equally mechanized, $\kappa_1\lambda_2 - \kappa_2\lambda_1 = m = 0$.

When r_1 deviates from r_0, the economy may be able to choose another set of techniques that will employ resources more fully and produce higher output. In Fig. 10.3c, a different pair of techniques corresponds to each r. If the number of available techniques becomes infinite, the kinked transformation locus becomes a continuous curve (Fig. 10.3d).

If it is assumed that prices are fixed, the value of output may be maximized:

$$\max\ Y = \bar{p}_1 X_1(X_2) + \bar{p}_2 X_2$$

In the maximum we obtain:

$$-\frac{dX_1}{dX_2} = \frac{\bar{p}_2}{\bar{p}_1} \tag{10.7}$$

which is the neoclassical textbook result. The result holds in partial equilibrium with fixed prices. In a general equilibrium setting, prices are functions of r, i.e. of X_2. The maximization in b-prices:

$$\max\ \tilde{Y} = X_1(X_2) + \tilde{p}_2(X_2)X_2,\ \tilde{p}_2 = p_2/p_1$$

yields the following equilibrium condition

$$-\frac{dX_1}{dX_2} = (1 + \eta_{\tilde{p}_2 X_2})\frac{p_2}{p_1}, \qquad \tilde{p}_2 = \frac{p_2}{p_1} \tag{10.8}$$

The relation between MRT and price ratio depends on the elasticity of price ratio with respect to X_2. Only in the case $m = 0$, relative prices remain invariant to changes in output composition, $\eta\tilde{p}_2X_2=0$ and the neoclassical result (10.7) obtains.

In our model:

$$\eta\tilde{p}_2X_2=\frac{d\tilde{p}_2}{dX_2}\frac{X_2}{p_2}=-\frac{rm}{\lambda_1+rm}$$

and consequently:

$$-\frac{dX_1}{dX_2}=\frac{p_2}{p_1}\left(-\frac{rm}{\lambda_1+rm}+1\right)=\frac{p_2}{p_1}\frac{\lambda_1}{\lambda_1+rm} \qquad (10.8a)$$

For small *rm*, the marginal rate of transformation is approximately equal to the price ratio, $-dX_1/dX_2=p_2/p_1$, and at the limit ($rm=0$) it is exactly equal.

10.2 Dual (wage) curve

10.2.1 General considerations

An economy, in which fully employed labour force increases at the rate *g* and technology remains unchanged, is in a state of extended reproduction. If labour productivity increases, *g* will have to be replaced by $\pi=(1+g)(1+\gamma)-1$. Since in this case output per capita increases, which unnecessarily complicates the analysis, we shall assume constant technology. For the present purpose that is all we need. For $X_1/L=\tilde{w}=\frac{w}{p_1}$, which is the real wage, the first term in (10.1) becomes:

$$\tilde{w}=c=\frac{1-r\kappa_2}{r(\kappa_1\lambda_2-\kappa_2\lambda_1)+\lambda_1}, \quad \left(\frac{1}{v(g)}+g\right)=r(g) \qquad (10.9)$$

Output of basket industry per capita is, of course, the same as *consumption per worker*, $X_1/L=\tilde{w}=c$. On the other hand, *r* is the *rate of gross investment*, $r=(R+J)/\kappa=i$. Consequently the two functions – $\tilde{w}=f(r)$ and $c=f(i)$ – are identical since they reflect the dual aspect of the same structure of the economy. In order to refer to this duality I shall use interchangeably the terms dual or wage curve.[1]

If machine–worker ratios are equal in both industries, $\kappa_1\lambda_2=\kappa_2\lambda_1$, (10.9) becomes a straight line:

$$\tilde{w}=\frac{1}{\lambda_1}(1-r\kappa_2), \quad k_1=k_2$$

$$\tilde{w} = \tilde{W}\left(1 - \frac{r}{R}\right), \quad \tilde{w}(r=0) = \tilde{W}, \quad r(\tilde{w}=0) = R \qquad (10.10)$$

If machine–worker ratios in the two industries are different, $k_1 \neq k_2$, the wage curve (10.9) is a curve convex or concave towards the origin depending on the following conditions (bearing in mind that prices must be positive, $p_1/p_2 > 0$);

$$m = (\kappa_1\lambda_2 - \kappa_2\lambda_1) \gtreqless 0 \Rightarrow k_1 \gtreqless k_2 \Rightarrow \frac{d^2\tilde{w}}{dr^2} \gtreqless 0 \qquad (10.11)$$

$$m \begin{cases} >0 \text{ curve convex, basket industry more mechanized} \\ =0 \text{ straight line, equal degree of mechanization} \\ <0 \text{ curve concave, machine industry more mechanized} \end{cases}$$

If the machine industry is more mechanized, $k_1 < k_2$, the expression in brackets is negative, which renders the curve concave ($d^2w/dr^2 < 0$). This is the case portrayed in Fig. 10.4.

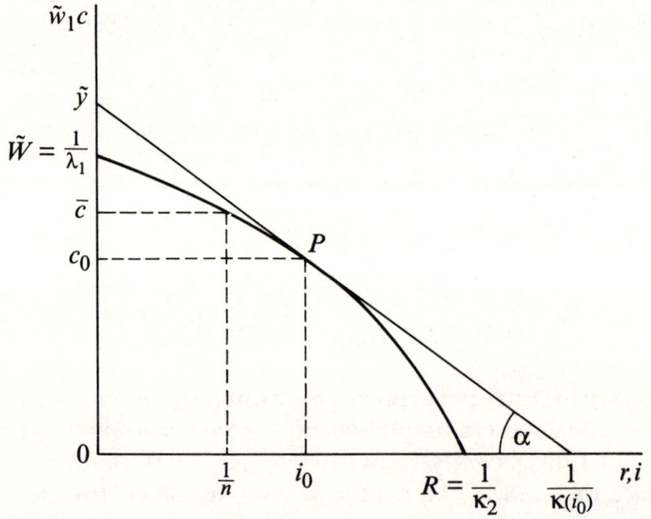

Figure 10.4 Dual (wage) curve with one technique in each industry and more mechanized machine industry (m<0)

The shape of the $\tilde{w} - r$ curve depends also on the standard of value used to express wages. If instead of being expressed in baskets, wages are expressed in machines, the curve is transformed into a straight line:

$$\tilde{w}_m = \frac{w}{p_2} = \frac{1}{\lambda_2}(1 - r\kappa_2),\ k_1 \neq k_2 \tag{10.12}$$

The result follows directly from the second of the price expressions (10.2), which means that in any multi-industry model with only one capital good, $\tilde{w}_m(r)$ will be a straight line.

Maximum rental is the same as before, $R = 1/\kappa_2$. Maximum wage must obviously change and is equal to $\tilde{w} = 1/\lambda_2$. The reduction to the straight line is in this case due to the fact that machines are produced by machine sector exclusively and so p_1 does not enter the determination of p_2. Note also that real wages expressed resp. in baskets (10.9) and machines (10.12) are simply equal to reciprocals of prices:

$$\tilde{w} = \frac{1}{p_1}, \qquad \tilde{w}_m = \frac{1}{p_2}, \qquad w = 1 \tag{10.13}$$

when prices are expressed in labour time.

Figure 10.4 invites some additional analysis.

Given g, the optimum point $P = (c_0, i_0)$ is established and the appropriate technology chosen. Any other point on the curve is, clearly, non-optimal. But whatever it is, we assume $X_1/L = \tilde{w} = c$, $I/K = r = i$. The distribution of income and output coincide. Gross investment rate i consists of replacement and new investment, $i = 1/v + g$. In a stationary economy $g = 0$ and so $i = 1/n$ to which the stationary consumption per capita $\bar{c}$ corresponds.

The dual curve may be decomposed into its two components: $\tilde{w}$–r and c–i curves. The $\tilde{w}$–r curve may be called *distribution curve*. Its dual, c–i curve, may be called *production curve*. In the former case i is fixed; in the latter case r is fixed.

10.2.2 The value of capital

A production system can produce either a maximum of X_1 or a maximum of X_2 or a combination of the two commodities. The value of combined output is equal to:

$$wL + rp_2K = Y \tag{10.14}$$

The value of capital (p_2K) may be determined in four different ways.

For $w = 1$, the value of final output is expressed in labour time. L is the value of consumer goods, $L = p_1X_1$, and the value of produced machines is given by the second term $rp_2K = p_2X_2$. The value of capital turns out to be the capitalized value of a production stream of machines:

$$p_2K=\frac{p_2X_2}{r} \tag{10.15}$$

If X_1 is not produced, $X_1=\tilde{w}=0, p_1=\infty$, total output consists of machines, $Rp_2K=p_2X_2=Y$ and value of capital stock is given as:

$$p_2K=\frac{Y}{R} \tag{10.15a}$$

However, neither are Y of (10.14) and Y of (10.15a) the same, nor has the same stock of machines of (10.15) and (10.15a) the same value because $p_2=f(r)$.

Since gross rental rate consists of replacement (depreciation) and net addition to capital stock, it is possible to write:

$$p_2X_2=\frac{1}{v}p_2K+gp_2K=D+gp_2K.$$

Consequently,

$$p_2K=\frac{p_2X_2-D}{g} \tag{10.16}$$

$$p_2K=\frac{Y-D}{G} \tag{10.16a}$$

which is the same value of capital as in (10.15) respectively (10.15a) but now expressed as net output capitalized at the rate of growth (G is maximal rate of growth when only machines are produced).

10.2.3 The geometry of the dual curve

Since outputs produced and distributed are the same, we may write on the per capita basis and using baskets as a *numéraire*:

$$\tilde{y}=c+i\tilde{p}_2\kappa=\tilde{w}+r\tilde{p}_2k,\ \tilde{w}=\frac{w}{p_1},\ \tilde{p}_2=\frac{p_2}{p_1},\ \tilde{y}=\frac{Y}{p_1L} \tag{10.17}$$

Derive the basket value of capital per capita:

$$\tilde{\kappa}=\frac{c=\tilde{w}}{r-i},\qquad \tilde{\kappa}=\tilde{p}_2\kappa$$

When r converges towards i also w converges towards c and at the limit:

$$\lim_{\Delta r \to 0} \bar{\kappa} = \lim_{\Delta r \to 0} -\frac{\Delta \tilde{w}}{\Delta r} = -\frac{d\tilde{w}}{dr} \tag{10.18}$$

The actual differentiation of the wage function gives:

$$-\frac{d\tilde{w}}{dr} = \frac{\lambda_2 \kappa_1}{(\lambda_1 + rm)^2} = \tilde{p}_2 k \tag{10.18a}$$

where $\lambda_2/(\lambda_1 + rm) = \tilde{p}_2$ by (10.1) and $\kappa_1/(\lambda_1 + rm) = K$ by (10.34). In Fig. 10.4 the slope of the tangent at point p is given as:

$$tg\alpha = \frac{\tilde{y} - \tilde{w}_0}{r_0} = \tilde{p}_2 k$$

Take capital–product ratio, which, as we know is the same evaluated either in b-prices or in l-prices

$$\tilde{\kappa} = \frac{\tilde{p}_2 K}{\tilde{Y}} = \frac{\tilde{k}}{\tilde{y}} = \frac{p_2 k}{y} \tag{10.19}$$

The tangent in Fig. 10.4 crosses r axis at:

$$\frac{\tilde{y}}{tg\alpha} = \frac{\tilde{y}}{\tilde{k}} = \frac{1}{\tilde{\kappa}} = \frac{1}{\kappa}$$

i.e. at the point that indicates product–capital ratio.

The elasticity of real wage rate with respect to the rental at the long-run equilibrium point $r = i$, $\tilde{w} = c$, is equal to the relative shares of rentals and wages:

$$-\eta_{\tilde{w}r} = -\frac{d\tilde{w}}{dr}\frac{r}{\tilde{w}} = \frac{r\tilde{k}}{\tilde{w}} = \frac{rp_2 k}{w} = \frac{rp_2 k/Y}{wL/Y} \tag{10.20}$$

In Fig. 10.4 the same elasticity will be:

$$-\eta_{ci} = -\frac{\tilde{y} - c}{i}\frac{i}{c} = \frac{\tilde{y} - c}{c} = \frac{i\tilde{p}_2 k}{c} = \frac{\tilde{I}/\tilde{Y}}{c/\tilde{y}} \tag{10.20a}$$

i.e. it measures the relative shares of investment ($i\tilde{p}_2K$=per capita investment in terms of baskets) and consumption.

10.3 Distribution (wage–rental) curve

10.3.1 Properties

Assume that resources L and K as well as output X_1 and X_2 are fixed at full capacity production. Consequently per capita consumption and the rate of investment are fixed and $c(i)$ curve collapses into one point $p=(c_0, i_0)$. On the other hand $w(r)$ curve is fully preserved. This is the *case investigated by Sraffa* (1960). He had to design his standard commodity with R as the standard ratio between final and intermediate deliveries of every commodity[2] in order to make sure that cost and price change in the same proportion. He then derived a linear relation between profits and wages:

$$r = R\left(1 - \frac{\tilde{w}}{\tilde{W}}\right) \tag{10.21}$$

which enabled him to show how profits can be increased only at the expense of wages. In the context of our analysis it is important to realize that the price–quantity duality generates a unique set of prices for every material configuration. In other words, to the point $p=(c_0, i_0)$ *only one ratio of relative prices* corresponds (cf. 10.1 and 10.2 where quantities and prices are derived from two pairs of linear equations having common parameters). If profits are increased, $r > i_0$ – and, therefore, wages are reduced, $\tilde{w} < c_0$ – the new prices will be inconsistent with the postulated production of baskets ($c_0\bar{L} = X_1$) and machines ($i_0\bar{K} = X_2$). Either profit rates or wage rates or both will fail to be equal in the two industries. The only way to make them equal is to postulate equal mechanization and exactly that was done in (10.10), which produced the same linear relation as (10.21).

The distribution curve has the following characteristics:

1. Technology $T(\lambda, \kappa, n)$ cannot be adapted to changes in $\tilde{w}$ and r;
2. whenever $(\tilde{w}, r) \neq (c, i)$ the allocation of resources is suboptimal;
3. whenever $\tilde{w} \neq c$ (and $r \neq i$) either exploitation emerges with part of gross profits channelled into the consumption of non-workers or a secondary distribution of income (by means of taxation) is used to adjust the disposable income to available supply of different commodities;
4. changes in $\tilde{w}$ and r, with given technology, must generate changes in prices p_1 and p_2, and they cannot be consistent.

10.3.2 Exploitation

The distribution curve makes sense only if for some reason economic agents do not maximize net output (consumption) of the society. Thus, in a privately owned economy entrepreneurs are supposed to maximize profits. Consequently the most profitable technology will be selected. Since capitalists are not expected to be altogether altruistic, profits must be sufficiently large to make possible both investment expenditures *and* a comfortable level of living. After all, neoclassical writers inform us that capitalists invest in order to consume. Consequently, $\pi > i$, where $\pi = r$ is gross profit. It is assumed that investment is sufficiently high (and capital stock adjusted) to ensure full employment. We, thus, have two points on the curve: p determined by i, as before and p' determined by π. Since the curve itself is determined by π, p' represents maximum profit while p is suboptimal because output of consumer good is not at its technologically possible maximum. The situation is portrayed in Fig. 10.5. (Cf. Lynn Mainwaring, 1984, p. 55, but the analysis is not rigorous.)

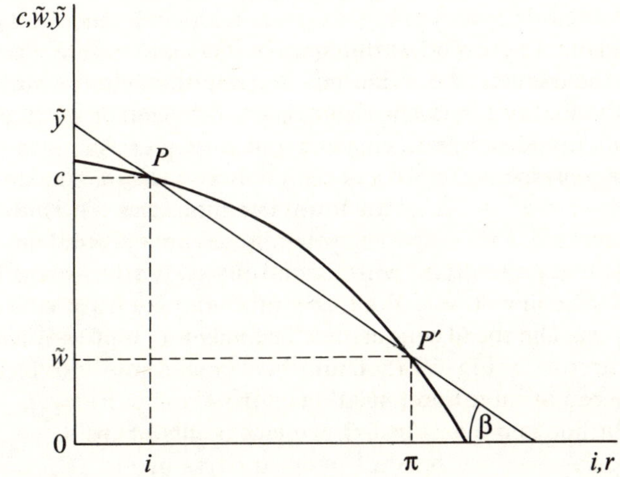

Figure 10.5 Capitalist exploitation

Draw a line through the points p and p'. At p consumption (c) and gross investment rate (i) are physical quantities implied by the given production and they do not change. At p' prices are formed at the profit rate π – and so is, naturally, $-\frac{d\tilde{w}}{dr} = \tilde{\kappa} = \tilde{p}_2\kappa$ – the slope of the wage curve is steeper at p' than at p. However, only prices involving π are used, while κ corresponds to i and therefore the slope of $\tilde{p}_{2K}$ is somewhere in between the slopes at p and p'. This is exactly the slope of the straight line through p and p' and it does not change. Per capita social product is given as the sum of consumption and gross investment:

$$\tilde{y} = c + i\tilde{p}_{2K} \qquad (10.22a)$$

social product is distributed among workers and capitalists by:

$$\tilde{y} = \tilde{w} + \pi\tilde{p}_{2K} \qquad (10.22b)$$

Social products are evaluated in the same prices and that produced is equal to the one distributed and therefore they represent the same line with the same slope. The value of $\tilde{y}$ is expressed in π-prices, but that does not affect the value of consumption since $\tilde{p}_1 = p_1/p_1 = 1 = \text{constant}$.

The economic interpretation of Figure 10.5 is now simple. Available per capita consumption is c, but workers receive only $\tilde{w}$. The difference $c - \tilde{w}$ is consumed by capitalists as measured per worker head. The necessary rental rate is $r = i$, but capitalists charge $r = \pi$, pocket the difference and finance their consumption $(c - \tilde{w})L$. The difference $(c - \tilde{w})$ measures exploitation. Besides, production may be inefficient because they choose the wrong technology. Prices – and the technology chosen – depend on π, which is the maximum profit, and not on i, which may maximize consumption. Thus, prices are different from the optimal ones and also they are inconsistent. Finally, since π-prices are oriented towards profits and not towards full employment requirement, there will generally be some unemployment.

If exploitation is eliminated, profits and investments are equal, $\pi = i$, points p and p' coincide and the value of $\tilde{y}$ may increase or decrease depending on m. The social product line is tangent to a differently chosen production curve at p (Fig. 10.4). Thus, the elimination of exploitation is the necessary condition for optimal allocation of resources.[3]

If a straight line is drawn through the end points of the wage curve – through $\tilde{W}$ and R – we get the Sraffian linear equation (10.21).

10.3.3 Changes in final product and capital intensities

The value of final output does not remain unchanged even if technology does and values are expressed in terms of baskets $(p_1 = 1)$.[4] The value of final output is smallest when $r = 0$ and consumption is maximal. In this case social product consists entirely of baskets and is equal to $\tilde{y} = 1/\lambda_1\ (r = 0)$. As r increases, the slopes of social product lines – either tangential to distribution curves ($tg\,\alpha$) if $r = i$, or intersecting with them ($tg\,\beta$) if $r(= \pi) > i$

– become steeper. It is the other way round if the distribution curve is convex toward the origin. In either case relative prices change although the marginal rate of transformation of baskets into machines remains constant. Full adaptation equilibrium k changes as well and in the same direction (10.35). However, the reasons for changes in the value of final output are different. If output is fixed and merely profit rate changes, changes in values are fictitious. If, however, investment rate changes in order to secure full employment, changes in values are real: higher i means that more labour must be allocated to supporting output and so real labour costs of net output increase.

Note the possibility of 'perverse' behaviour (discussed somewhat imprecisely by Nuti, 1977). If investment and profit rates (i and π in Fig. 10.5) change in such a way that the slope of $\tilde{y}$ line remains unchanged, $tg\beta = \tilde{\kappa} =$ constant, the social product line will shift in parallel to the line pp'. This implies that the same value of capital per worker (though evaluated at different prices) generates various outputs per worker at various profit rates. If, on the other hand, the $\tilde{y}$-line is rotated around p (or around $\tilde{y}$), the same consumption (or final output) per capita is possible at wildly different profit rates and capital per worker. The moral of the story is that there is no systematic relationship between per capita output or consumption and capital per worker and profit (interest) rates even if technology does not change.

Some simple relations between $\tilde{k}$, $\tilde{y}$ and $\tilde{\kappa}$ may be portrayed in the two diagrams (Fig. 10.6) which I borrow from Spaventa (1970, p. 134).

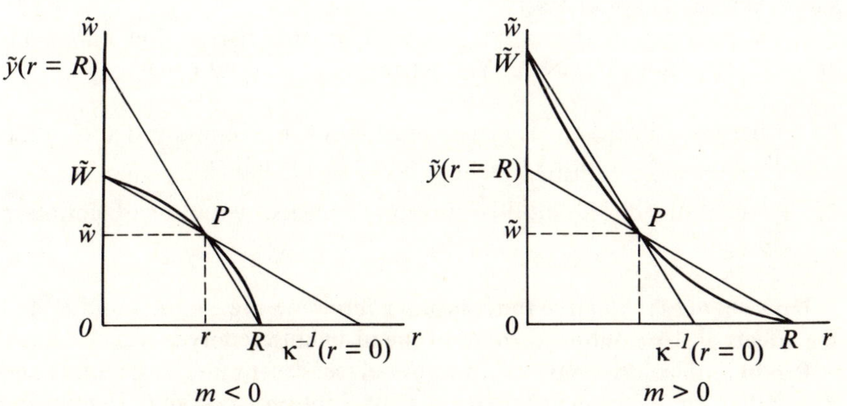

Figure 10.6 Final output per worker ($\tilde{y}$), capital per worker ($\tilde{k}$) and capital–output ratio (κ)

Recall (10.22b):

$$\tilde{y} = \tilde{w}(r) + r\tilde{p}_2(r)\kappa \tag{10.23}$$

For $r = 0$, final product reduces to $\tilde{y} = \tilde{W}$; for $\tilde{w} = 0$, it becomes $\tilde{y} = R\tilde{\kappa}(R)$, evaluated rep. at $\tilde{W}$- and R-prices. The slope of the line through the points $\tilde{y}(r = R)$ and p represents capital per worker, $\tilde{y}/R = \tilde{\kappa}(R)$. Output–capital ratio is equal to $\kappa^{-1} = \frac{\tilde{w} + r\tilde{\kappa}}{\tilde{\kappa}}$ which for $r = 0$ reduces to $\kappa^{-1} = \frac{\tilde{W}}{\tilde{\kappa}(0)}$, as shown on Fig. 10.6. In this way capital per worker varies as a function of r from a minimum $\tilde{k}(0) = \tilde{W}\kappa$ to a maximum $\tilde{k}(R) = \tilde{y}/R$ for $m < 0$ (machine industry more mechanized) and in a reverse fashion for $m > 0$ (machine industry less mechanized). Capital–output ratio varies between $\kappa(0)$ and $1/R$.

Quite generally, due to price effect, capital intensity may be a decreasing as well as increasing function of the rental rate if technology and quantity produced remain unchanged. If alternative technologies are available, an additional inquiry is necessary.

10.4 Production (consumption–investment) curve

10.4.1 Properties

Assume that $\tilde{w}$ and r, and consequently, p_1 and p_2 are fixed, and so is technology. Investment rate (i) and per capita consumption (c) change, which implies changes in the proportion of X_1 and X_2 produced and in the age structure of capital assets.

Corresponding to the point $P = (\tilde{w}, r)$ on the distribution curve, an optimal technology is chosen. Yet, whenever $c \neq \tilde{w}$ (and $i \neq r$):

1. either not all workers or not all machines will be employed and so the allocation of resources is again non-optimal; and
2. a secondary distribution of income is necessary and/or exploitation emerges.

Now changes in i lead to the rotation of chord in Fig. 10.5 around P' and the effects are analogous to those of the distribution curve.

Production curve may be interpreted as describing a set of island economies, each of them growing at a different rate, but all of them using the same technology and operating with the same profit rate. Such a situation is not analytically particularly interesting as all its essential elements have already been analysed elsewhere. However, if additional alternative restrictions are introduced, we encounter a new problem, described below.

10.4.2 The constant technology theorem

If there are two (or more) resources, it is generally not possible to vary the composition of output while retaining full employment of resources. In order to study the variations of output under full employment the number of resources must be reduced to one. That can be done in two ways: (a) by assuming labour abundant (procreation being governed by non-economic considerations) so that labour constraint is not binding and we are concerned with full use of capital only, or (b) by reproducing productive assets within one production period (replacing fixed capital by circulating capital) so that capital constraint is not binding. In both cases the following theorem (called erroneously 'non-substitution theorem'[5]) applies: *In an economy with single product industries there exists only one set of most efficient techniques; as a consequence, it also determines prices that remain unchanged even if the composition of demand changes.* In other words, prices are determined independently of demand. The latter depends on the rate of growth (g) and, in the case of many consumer goods, on consumer preferences. Once demand is given, individual industries produce as much as is required using individual minimum cost technologies.

1. If living labour is abundant, it is necessary to economize with embodied labour only, treating living labour as free. Thus, relative prices are fixed as given by price equations:

$$\frac{p_2}{p_1}=\frac{\kappa_2}{\kappa_1} \tag{10.24}$$

The composition of output changes according to (10.4a):

$$X_1=\frac{\bar{K}}{\kappa_1}-\frac{\kappa_2}{\kappa_1}X_2$$

The marginal rate of product transformation is constant and equal to relative prices:

$$-\frac{dX_1}{dX_2}=\frac{p_2}{p_1} \tag{10.25}$$

but full employment of labour obtains only by fluke.

2. More interesting is the case of circulating capital. Consider a two-industry economy with labour as the only primary resource:

$$\begin{aligned} (1-a_{11})\hat{X}_1 - a_{12}\hat{X}_2 &= X_1 \\ -a_{21}\hat{X}_1 + (1-a_{22})\hat{X}_2 &= X_2 \\ -\hat{\lambda}_1\hat{X}_1 - \hat{\lambda}_2\hat{X}_2 &= -L \end{aligned} \tag{10.26}$$

where X_1 is final and $\hat{X}_1$ is gross output. Columns of the coefficients represent net activity vector at unit of gross output level (*a* and *b* in Fig. 10.7). They determine final output frontier at the unit gross output level. If the same coefficients are divided by $\hat{\lambda}_1$ and multiplied by (since $\hat{\lambda}_1\hat{X}_1 = L$ for $\hat{X}_2 = 0$ and $\hat{\lambda}_2\hat{X}_2 = L$ for $\hat{X}_1 = 0$), the final output frontier will represent output possibilities determined by the availability of labour. The result is shown in Fig. 10.7, where, for example, coordinates of point *A* are $X_1 = (1-a_{11})L/\hat{\lambda}_1$, $X_2 = -a_{21}L/\hat{\lambda}_1$ (cf. Dorfman *et al.*, 1958, p. 224).

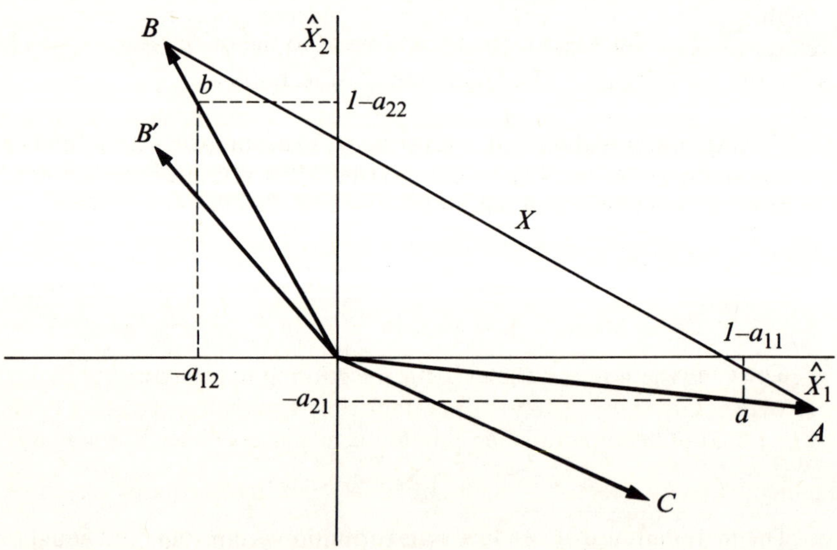

Figure 10.7 The final output frontier

Consider again the system (10.26) and the corresponding Fig. 10.7. The summation of the columns of (10.26) gives the price equations of a stationary economy (with zero rate of profit, $\pi = 0$):

$$(1-a_{11})p_1 - a_{21}p_2 - w\hat{\lambda}_1 = 0$$
$$-a_{12}p_1 + (1-a_{22})p_2 - w\hat{\lambda}_2 = 0 \qquad (10.27)$$

Solving for p_1 and p_2 we obtain:

$$\frac{w}{p_1} = \frac{(1-a_{11})(1-a_{22}) - a_{12}a_{21}}{\hat{\lambda}_1(1-a_{22}) + \hat{\lambda}_2 a_{21}}, \quad \frac{w}{p_2} = \frac{(1-a_{11})(1-a_{22}) - a_{12}a_{21}}{\hat{\lambda}_2(1-a_{11}) + \hat{\lambda}_1 a_{12}}$$
$$\frac{p_1}{p_2} = \frac{\hat{\lambda}_1(1-a_{22}) + \hat{\lambda}_2 a_{21}}{\hat{\lambda}_2(1-a_{11}) + \hat{\lambda}_1 a_{12}} \qquad (10.28)$$

For $L=1$, the straight line (the final output frontier) $X_2 = f(X_1)$ in Fig. 10.7 passes through the points $\left(-\frac{a_{12}}{\hat{\lambda}_2}, \frac{1-a_{22}}{\hat{\lambda}_2}\right)$ and $\left(\frac{1-a_{11}}{\hat{\lambda}_1}, -\frac{a_{21}}{\hat{\lambda}_1}\right)$ and its equation is:

$$X_2 = -\frac{\hat{\lambda}_1(1-a_{22}) + \hat{\lambda}_2 a_{21}}{\hat{\lambda}_2(1-a_{11}) + \hat{\lambda}_1 a_{12}} X_1 + \frac{(1-a_{11})(1-a_{22}) - a_{12}a_{21}}{\hat{\lambda}_2(1-a_{11}) + \hat{\lambda}_1 a_{12}} \qquad (10.29)$$

The rate of product transformation is equal to the price ratio:

$$-\frac{dX_2}{dX_1} = \frac{p_1}{p_2} \qquad (10.30)$$

and the intercept of the final output frontier with the X_2 axis measures real wage in terms of X_2, $\tilde{w}_2 = \frac{w}{p_2}$.

For $X_2 = 0$, we obtain the real wage in terms of X_1, $\tilde{w}_1 = \frac{w}{p_1}$, which is the intercept with the X_1 axis. The result correspond to neoclassical standards (Cf. Walsh, Gram, pp. 380–91). In a uniformly expanding economy (with $\pi = g$) (10.3) still holds (all non-labour technical coefficients are simply augmented by the factor $(1+g)$) and $\tilde{w}_i = \frac{w}{p_1}$ are intercepts of the wage frontier that is now equal to final output minus profits. But the effective wage frontier is reduced to only one point determined by g. The proportion X_2/X_1 can no longer vary without affecting prices. In an economy in which $\pi \neq g$, not only the wrong technology is chosen, but also $-dX_2/dX_1 \neq p_1/p_2$.

With one primary resource, changes in the rate of profit will lead to substitutions of techniques; with two primary resources – say labour and land – even changes in the composition of demand will generally lead to substitutions because the final output frontier is no longer a straight line. Prices and techniques may change even with one primary resource if there is joint production and/or the returns to scale. This case is ruled out in our model since all machines are identical and each industry produces one product. Finally, in the short run capital is also a scarce resource. Thus, a change in demand will cause a disequilibrium, most efficient techniques will no longer produce the necessary output mix, inputs will be substituted and prices temporarily changed. As soon as disequilibrium is eliminated – the stock of machines is adjusted – the economy will revert to old technology and the original prices will be reestablished. This observation should serve as a reminder that the labour theory of prices is an equilibrium theory.

10.5 Changes in capital intensity along the wage curve

Capital intensity may be defined with respect to labour and with respect to output and in either case it may be a quantity or a value relationship. The earlier list of capital intensities (section 6.3) is now completed by several additional concepts:

1. *Degree of mechanization* – Marx's technical composition of capital – is the number of machines per worker $\left(k=\frac{K}{L}\right)$.
2. *Value of capital per worker* is capital in terms of baskets per worker ($\tilde{k}=p_2/p_1k$), i.e. capital is evaluated in basket-prices.
3. *Organic composition of resources* is capital valued in labour time per unit of labour time, say per worker-year ($\omega=p_2k$).
4. *Technical capital–output ratio* (coefficient) is the number of machines per unit of output in each sector ($\kappa_1=K_1/X_1$).
5. *Technical capital–net output ratio* is the total number of machines per unit of consumer goods (K/X_1).
6. *Value of capital–net product ratio* is identical with organic composition ($p_2K/p_1X_1=p_2K/L=\omega$).
7. *Value capital–output ratio* is capital per unit of final output, both evaluated in either labour or basket prices ($\tilde{\kappa}=\kappa=p_2K/(p_1X_1+p_2X_2)$)

Organic composition belongs to both groups of measures – capital per worker and capital per unit of product – which indicates its special importance. For this reason organic composition was used for the classification of technological progress.

10.5.1 Capital–labour ratios

Consider the familiar quantity equations slightly modified:

$$\begin{aligned} \lambda_1 X_1 + \lambda_2 rK &= L \\ \kappa_1 X_1 + \kappa_2 rK &= K, \qquad rK = X_2 \end{aligned} \tag{10.31}$$

and express them in per capita terms:

$$\begin{aligned} \lambda_1 c + \lambda_2 rk &= 1 \qquad c = \frac{X_1}{L}, \qquad k = \frac{K}{L} \\ \kappa_1 c + \kappa_2 rk &= k, \end{aligned} \tag{10.32}$$

Two equations and three unknowns make possible that either c or k be expressed as a function of r. In the former case we get:

$$c = \frac{1 - r\kappa_2}{\lambda_1 + rm}, \qquad m = \kappa_1\lambda_2 - \kappa_2\lambda_1 \tag{10.33}$$

which is, of course, the same as (10.9). In the latter case we get:

$$k = \frac{\kappa_1}{\lambda_1 + rm} \tag{10.34}$$

There is a simple proportional relationship between k and the price ratio in (10.2):

$$\frac{p_2}{p_1} = \frac{\lambda_2}{\kappa_1} \frac{\kappa_1}{\lambda_1 + rm} = \frac{\lambda_2}{\kappa_1} k \tag{10.35}$$

and so the mechanization ratio behaves in the same way as the price ratio (see Fig. 10.2). If investment rate increases, overall mechanization intensity increases or decreases depending on whether machine industry ($m < 0$) or basket industry ($m > 0$) is more mechanized. As for efficient pricing $r = i$, the more mechanized machine industry will make the *overall mechanization intensity an increasing function of the rental rate*. This is a simple and rather obvious composition effect.

If baskets are used as a numéraire, the capital–worker ratio is equal to:

$$\tilde{k} = \frac{p_2}{p_1} k = \frac{\lambda_2 \kappa_1}{(\lambda_1 + rm)^2} \tag{10.36}$$

which is the same as (10.18a). This ratio is an increasing or decreasing function of $r = i$, depending on the relative mechanization of the two industries:

$$\frac{d\tilde{k}}{dr} = -\frac{2m}{\lambda_1 + rm}\tilde{k}\begin{cases} >0, m<0 \\ =0, m=0, \\ <0, m>0 \end{cases} \qquad (\lambda_1 + rm) > 0 \qquad (10.37)$$

Since the composition effect is now doubled (for k and p_2/p_1) it is perfectly possible that *capital intensity be an increasing function of the rental (profit) rate*.

If machines are valued in labour prices, capital per worker corresponds to Marx's organic composition of capital:

$$\omega = p_2 k = \frac{\lambda_2 \kappa_1}{(\lambda_1 + rm)(1 - r\kappa_2)} \qquad (10.38)$$

$$\frac{d\omega}{dr} = \frac{\kappa_1 \lambda_2 [\kappa_2(\lambda_1 + rm) - m(1 - r\kappa_2)]}{[(\lambda_1 + rm)(1 - r\kappa_2)]^2} \gtreqless 0, \; m \lesseqgtr \frac{\kappa_2 \lambda_1}{1 - 2r\kappa_2}, \qquad (10.39)$$

$$\lambda_1 + rm > 0$$

$$1 - r\kappa_2 > 0$$

The result is quite interesting. We know that $(\lambda_1 + rm) > 0$ because prices must be positive $(p_2/p_1 = \lambda_2/(\lambda_1 + rm))$, and similarly $(1 - r\kappa_2) > 0$ because outputs must be positive $(X_1/X_2 = (1 - r\kappa_2)/r\kappa_1)$. Consequently, whenever machine industry is more mechanized, $m < 0$, capital intensity increases with the increase in the rental rate. But it may increase even when machine industry is equally $(m = 0)$ or less mechanized if $m < \lambda_1\kappa_2/(1 - 2r\kappa_2)$ and $2r\kappa_2 < 1$. The latter condition says that the rates of growth must not be exorbitantly high, $r < 1/2\kappa_2$. The lowest bound for m generating increasing capital intensity is $m < \kappa_2\lambda_1$, for $r = 0$. Since m is not likely to deviate greatly from zero, it may be taken as generally true that organic composition *increases* with r, $d\omega/dr > 0$. This interpretation turns the well-known Marx's contention that organic composition of capital increases with investment – into a correct conjecture.

The synchrony principle provides the explanation why for $m = 0$, ω does not and k does remain unchanged. If investment rate increases, labour cost per unit of output increases, $\delta p_1/\delta i > 0$, $\delta p_2/\delta i > 0$. Thus, labour price of machine will increase whatever relative mechanization. However, if machine price is expressed in terms of baskets (p_2/p_1), it will not change because for $m = 0$ both prices are equally affected.

Three important conclusions follow: (1) Capital intensity (capital per worker) varies with the rental rate depending on what prices are used in evaluating capital. (2) Relative mechanization plays an important role in determining increasing or decreasing variations. (3) If either prices are used and the machine industry is more mechanized ($m<0$), higher rental rate increases capital intensity; if the machine industry is less mechanized, and labour prices are used (organic composition) higher rental rates may increase, leave unchanged or decrease capital intensity depending on $m \lesseqgtr \kappa_2\lambda_1/(1-2r\kappa_2)$. As long as $r>1/(2\kappa_2)$, even $m>0$ will generate increasing ω.

10.5.2 Capital–output ratios

Technical capital–net output ratio obviously increases whenever the rate of investment increases:

$$\frac{K}{X_1}=\frac{K_1}{X_1}+\frac{K_2}{X_1}=\kappa_1+\kappa_2\frac{X_2}{X_1}=\kappa_1+\kappa_2\frac{i\kappa_1}{1-i\kappa_2} \tag{10.40}$$

When i increases, relatively more machines must be produced and so X_2/X_1 increases.

More complicated are changes of value capital coefficients. If such a coefficient is defined with respect to net output, and labour prices are used, it is nothing else but an organic composition of resources, $p_2K/p_1X_1 = p_2K/L=\omega$. We have already discussed that case and so let us consider capital coefficients defined with respect to final output (recall $p_2=\lambda_2/(1-r\kappa_2)$, $X_2=r\kappa_1 L/(\lambda_1+rm)$):

$$\tilde{\kappa}=\kappa=\frac{p_2K}{p_1X_1+p_2X_2}=\frac{p_2X_2}{r(L+p_2X_2)}=\frac{\kappa_1\lambda_2}{\lambda_1+rm(2-r\kappa_2)} \tag{10.41}$$

$$\frac{d\kappa}{dr}=-\frac{2\kappa_1\lambda_2(1-r\kappa_2)m}{[\lambda_1+rm(2-r\kappa_2)]^2}\begin{cases}>0, & m<0\\ =0, & m=0\\ <0, & m>0\end{cases}\quad 1-r\kappa_2>0 \tag{10.42}$$

The composition effect is present in the usual way.

We may now also show why ω behaves differently from all other measures of capital intensity.

$$\frac{1}{\kappa}=\frac{L}{p_2K}+\frac{p_2X_2}{p_2X_2}r=\frac{1}{p_2k}+r=\frac{1}{\omega}+r \tag{10.43}$$

$$\omega=\frac{\kappa}{1-r\kappa} \tag{10.43a}$$

The organic composition of resources increases with r faster than the capital–product ratio.

The following relation holds as well:

$$\tilde{w}=\frac{X_1}{L}=\frac{1}{p_1}=\left(\frac{p_2}{p_1}k\right)\left(\frac{1}{p_2 k}\right)=\frac{\tilde{k}}{\omega}, \quad w=1 \tag{10.44}$$

Since $\tilde{w}$ is a decreasing function of r, ω increases faster than $\tilde{k}$.

10.5.3 Variations of final product and capital intensities

The value of final product ($\tilde{y}$) does not remain constant. It is a function of the rental (investment) rate. Recall the following eight expressions:

$$\tilde{y}=\tilde{w}+r\tilde{k} \tag{10.21b}$$

$$\tilde{k}=-\frac{d\tilde{w}}{dr}=\frac{\kappa_1\lambda_2}{(\lambda_1+rm)^2} \tag{10.18d}$$

$$\tilde{y}=\frac{\tilde{k}}{\kappa} \tag{10.19}$$

$$\tilde{w}=\frac{1-r\kappa_2}{\lambda_1+rm} \tag{10.9}$$

$$k=\frac{\kappa_1}{\lambda_1+rm} \tag{10.34}$$

$$p_2=\frac{\lambda_2}{1-r\kappa_2}, \quad \frac{p_2}{p_1}=\frac{\lambda_2}{\lambda_1+rm} \tag{10.2}$$

$$\omega=\frac{\kappa}{1-r\kappa} \tag{10.43a}$$

For concave wage curves ($k_2>k_1$), the slope becomes steeper as r increases and, consequently, $\tilde{y}$ and capital intensities increase. For convex wage curves ($k_1>k_2$) it is the other way round, i.e., capital intensities *decrease* as r increases. Variations are shown in Fig. 10.8, which corresponds to Fig. 10.6. Inserting $r=0$ and $r=R$ into these formulae and observing $\lambda_1>\lambda_2$, $\kappa_1<\kappa_2$, i.e. the machine industry is assumed more mechanized, we obtain the following intervals of variations:

$$\tilde{k}(0)=\tilde{p}_2 k=\frac{\lambda_2}{\lambda_1}\frac{\kappa_1}{\lambda_1} \le \tilde{k} \le \tilde{k}(R)=\frac{\kappa_2}{\kappa_1}\frac{\kappa_2}{\lambda_2}$$

$$\tilde{y}(0)=\tilde{W}=\frac{1}{\lambda_1} \le \tilde{y} \le \tilde{y}(R)=\frac{\kappa_2}{\kappa_1\lambda_2}$$

$$\kappa(0)=\tilde{p}_2\kappa_1=\frac{\lambda_2}{\lambda_1}\kappa_1 \leq \kappa \leq \kappa(R)=\kappa_2$$

$$k(0)=\frac{\kappa_1}{\lambda_1} \leq k \leq k(R)=\frac{\kappa_2}{\lambda_1}$$

$$\omega(0)=p_2k=\kappa(0) \leq \omega \leq \omega(R)=\frac{\kappa_2}{1-\frac{1}{\kappa_2}\kappa_2}=\infty$$

When basket industry is more mechanized (convex wage curve), the intervals remain the same but the inequalities are reversed. Because of the homogeneity of labour and baskets, λ_1, κ_2 and the product $\kappa_1\lambda_2$ are comparable across techniques. Except for k, the bounds of the intervals consist only of those coefficients. Thus, they are also comparable across techniques (for a given r).

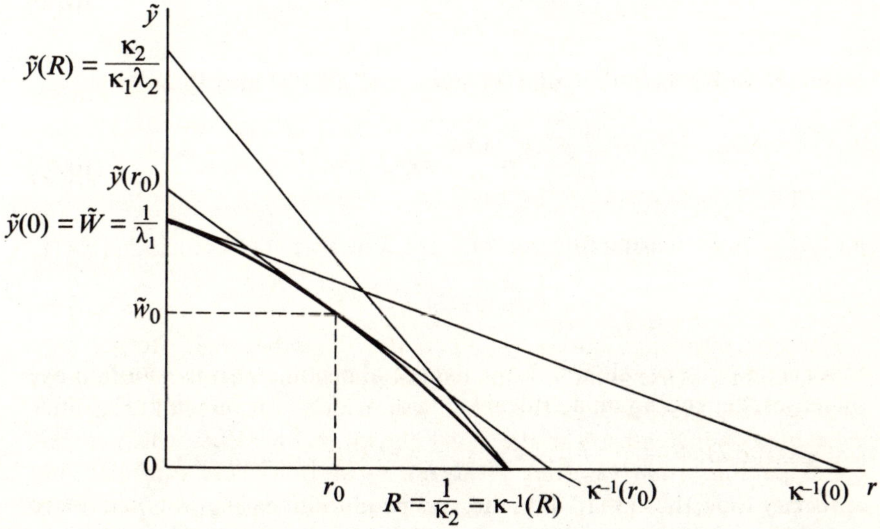

Figure 10.8 *Variations of final product* ($\tilde{y}$), *capital–worker* ($\tilde{k}=\tilde{p}_2k$) *and capital–output* $\left(\kappa=\frac{p_2\kappa}{p_1X_1+p_2X_2}\right)$ *ratios as functions of rental rate. Values in terms of baskets and* $m<0$

10.6 Relations between output and capital

Output is either net (baskets) or final (baskets and machines) and output, as well as capital, can be evaluated either in labour time (p_j) or in terms of baskets ($p_j = p_j/p_1$), i.e. in labour of the constant production. In the later case, values are denoted with a tilde. It turns out that a change of the numéraire is not at all an innocent affair.

10.6.1 Labour time values

Net output per capita evaluated in labour time:

$$p_1\tilde{w} = \frac{p_1 X_1}{L} = 1 \tag{10.45}$$

is invariant to changes in r: the value added by living labour is always equal to the value of net output. This is, in fact, the definition of net output.

Final output per capita in terms of labour:

$$y = \frac{p_1 X_1 + p_2 X_2}{L} = 1 + \frac{p_2 X_2}{L} \tag{10.46}$$

increases with r as both p_2 and X_2 increase (Fig. 10.1 and 10.2). Now:

$$\frac{p_2 X_2}{L} = \frac{p_2 r K}{L} = r p_2 k = r\omega \tag{10.47}$$

and $r\omega$ is an increasing function of r. It follows from (10.46) and (10.47):

$$y = 1 + r\omega(r) \tag{10.48}$$

Since ω may rise or fall, it follows that social product also rises or falls as r increases, depending on a critical value of m. Also, as shown in Fig. 10.9: $\omega = tg\alpha$ and $\overline{ar}_0 = \frac{y}{tg\alpha} = \frac{y_0}{\omega_0} = \frac{1}{\omega} + r_0 = \frac{1}{\kappa(r_0)}$ by (10.43), and $\overline{ao} = \frac{1}{\omega_0}$.

It may look that in (10.48) marginal product of capital is equal to the rental rate. However, this is not so because in a general equilibrium framework r is a function of ω (given technology). Thus, using (10.38) and (10.39):

$$\frac{\delta y}{\delta \omega} = r + \frac{\delta r}{\delta \omega}\omega = r + \frac{(\lambda_1 + rm)(1 - r\kappa_2)}{\kappa_2(\lambda_1 + rm) - m(1 - r\kappa_2)} \tag{10.49}$$

and in general $\delta y/\delta\omega \neq r$. Equality holds in one case: for $r=\dfrac{1}{\kappa_2}=R$ (no consumption).

10.6.2 Values in terms of baskets

Let per capita final output be expressed in baskets. That implies dividing (10.46) through p_1:

$$\tilde{y}=\frac{X_1}{L}+\frac{p_2}{p_1}\frac{X_2}{L}=\tilde{w}+\frac{p_2}{p_1}rk=\tilde{w}(r)+r\tilde{k}(r) \qquad (10.50)$$

Note that r is a function of $\tilde{k}$ and also that $-\dfrac{\delta\tilde{w}}{\delta r}=\tilde{k}$ from (10.18). Consequently:

$$\frac{\delta\tilde{y}}{\delta\tilde{k}}=\frac{\delta\tilde{w}}{\delta r}\frac{\delta r}{\delta\tilde{k}}+\frac{\delta r}{\delta\tilde{k}}\tilde{k}+r=r \qquad (10.51)$$

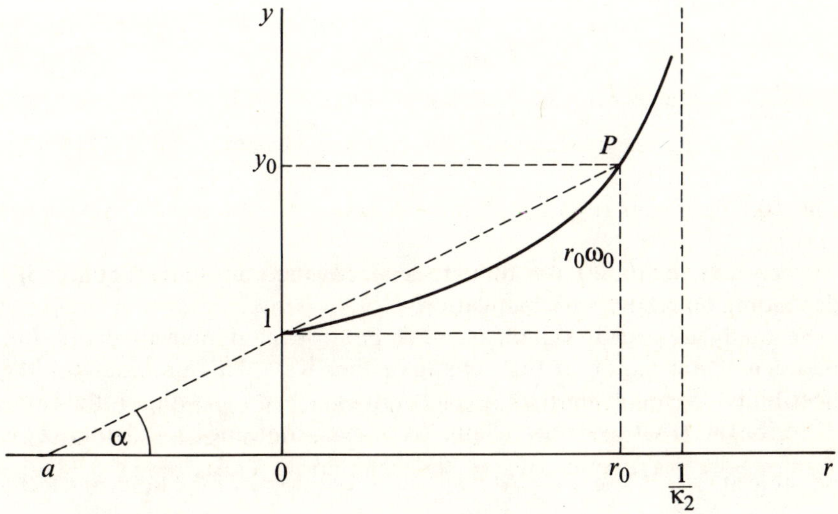

Figure 10.9 Labour value of final output ($m \gtreqless 0$)

Finally a neat result: when baskets are used as a *numéraire* to evaluate final product, marginal product of capital is equal to the rental rate.

The relation between final output and rental rate is not so neat. From (10.50) and (10.37):

$$\frac{\delta \tilde{y}}{\delta r}=\frac{\delta \tilde{w}}{\delta r}+\tilde{k}+r\frac{\delta \tilde{k}}{\delta r}=r\frac{\delta \tilde{k}}{\delta r}\gtreqless 0 \text{ for } m\lesseqgtr 0 \tag{10.52}$$

For $r>0$, $\tilde{y}$ moves in the same way as does $\tilde{k}$.

Assume again that machine industry is more mechanized ($m<0$). The characteristic points of the curve are:

$$\text{for } r=0, \qquad \tilde{y}(0)=\tilde{w}(0)=\frac{1}{\lambda_1}$$

$$\text{for } r=R=\frac{1}{\kappa_2} \qquad \tilde{y}(R)=\frac{\tilde{k}}{\kappa_2}=\frac{1}{\lambda_2}$$

At the point $r=R$, all capital is used for machine production, $K=K_2$. Consequently, $R=\frac{X_2}{K_2}=\frac{1}{\kappa_2}=\frac{1}{\kappa}$.

From (10.52) and (10.37):

$$\frac{\delta \tilde{y}}{\delta r}=r\frac{\delta \tilde{k}}{\delta r}\begin{cases}=0, & r=0\\ =-\dfrac{\kappa_2}{\lambda_2}\,\dfrac{2m}{\lambda_1\kappa_2+m}, & R=\dfrac{1}{\kappa_2}\end{cases}$$

Fig. 10.10 portrays the rising final product curve in terms of baskets for $m<0$.

According to (10.52), $\tilde{y}$ is an increasing, constant or falling function of r depending on relative mechanization.

Secondly, as already stated, at switch points capital intensity drops, but between switch points it may change either way. This provides for the possibility of capital reversal (capital intensity and r moving in the same direction) even without reswitching. Moreover, the same capital intensity is possible at two different r's. At $r=\frac{1}{n}$ and r_3 the slopes of the tangents at the wage curves are the same, and so they are at r_2 and r_5, which means that capital per worker ($\tilde{k}$), which discontinuously diminished at r_1, reaches the same value at r_3 as it had at $r=\frac{1}{n}$, and similarly at r_2 and r_5 separated by the

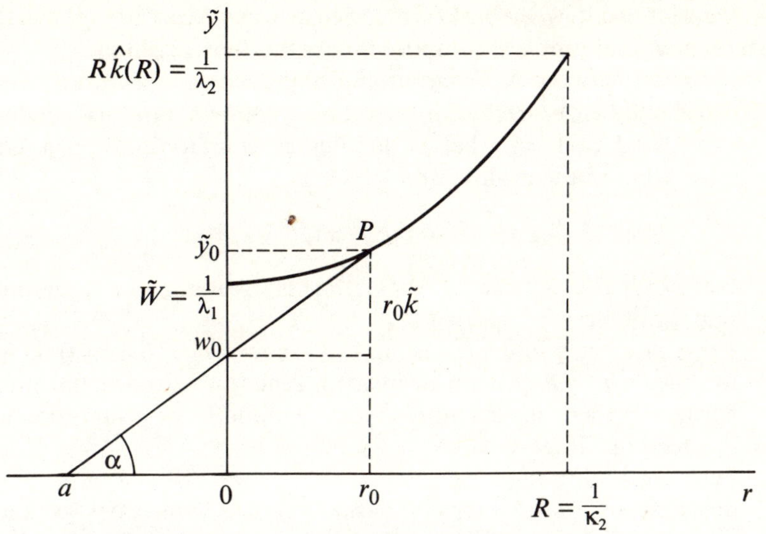

Figure 10.10 Final product in terms of baskets ($m<0$)

switch point r_4. A continuous monotonic technological frontier eliminates capital reversal. Similar reasoning applies to distribution curve (recall Fig. 10.6).

We are now ready to describe properties of the technological frontier in a systematic fashion.

Capital–labour ratio is given by $tg\ \alpha = \frac{r_0\tilde{k}}{r_0} = \tilde{k}$. It follows that $\overline{ar_0}$ represents product–capital ratio, $\frac{1}{\kappa(r_0)} = \frac{\tilde{y}}{\tilde{k}} = \frac{\tilde{w}}{\tilde{k}} + r_0$. At the point $r=R$, product–capital ratio amounts to $\frac{\tilde{y}(R)}{\tilde{k}(R)} = \frac{R\tilde{k}(R)}{\tilde{k}(R)} = R = \frac{1}{\kappa(R)}$, which was already indicated. Also, $\overline{ao} = \frac{\tilde{w}_0}{\tilde{k}}$.

The value of final product as a function of rental rate behaves very differently when expressed in terms of baskets as compared with values in labour time. The labour time values always increase, the basket values may also decrease or remain constant, depending on the relative mechanization of industries. That should be obvious. An increase in r means increase in embodied labour and, consequently, of total labour time since the current labour time remains unaffected. The same increase in r means more machines and less baskets and so the size of the *numéraire* changes.

10.6.3 Relations systematized

We may now summarize the findings of the preceding sections:

1. The results are crucially dependent on whether net or final product is considered and on whether labour or commodities are used as *numéraires* in the evaluation.

Net product, p_1X_1

2. Net product evaluated in labour time is invariant to changes in the rental rate because $p_1X_1 = L$.
3. Per capita net product (consumption) in terms of baskets (real wage rate $\tilde{w} = w/p_1 = X_1/L$) is a decreasing function of the rental rate (r) because higher r means more investment and less consumption for a given labour force.
4. Per capita output of baskets may be expressed as a ratio of two measures of capital intensity: basket value of capital per worker ($\tilde{k}$) and organic composition (ω), both functions of $r(\tilde{w} = \tilde{k}/\omega)$. When machine industry is more mechanized ($m < 0$), both indexes increase but ω increases faster than $\tilde{k}$ as r increases and technology is given. When basket industry is sufficiently more mechanized ($m > \kappa_2\lambda_1/(1 - 2r\kappa_2)$), both indexes decrease but $\tilde{k}$ decreases faster. For $m = 0$, $\tilde{k}$ is constant while ω increases.

Final product, $Y = p_1X_1 + p_2X_2$,

A. Technology fixed, labour as a numéraire *(*$w = 1$*)*

5. Final product per capita evaluated in labour time (y) is an increasing or decreasing function of the rental rate (r) depending on a critical value of m.
6. Capital per worker (organic composition, ω) may increase or decrease depending on whether the relative mechanization is smaller or greater than a critical value, $m \lesseqgtr \kappa_2\lambda_1/(1 - 2r\kappa_2)$. Consequently y may be either increasing or decreasing function of capital intensity.
7. Notional marginal product of capital, resulting from the comparison of two steady state equilibria, is generally different from the rental rate, $\delta y/\delta\omega \neq r$.

B. Technology fixed, baskets as a numéraire *(*$p_1 = 1$*)*.

8. Final product per capita in terms of baskets ($\tilde{y}$) changes in the same direction as capital per worker ($\tilde{k}$) when r increases. Thus, as r increases, $\tilde{y}$ may increase, remain unchanged or decrease, depending on which industry is more mechanized.

9. It follows from (8) that $\tilde{y}$ is an increasing function of capital intensity $\tilde{k}$.
10. Notional marginal product of capital is equal to the rental rate, $\delta\tilde{y}/\delta\tilde{k}=r$.

In conclusion, we may note that standard neoclassical assumptions are inconsistent with labour values (conclusions 1, 2, 6, 7) and are partly (8) or fully (3, 9, 10) consistent with values in terms of consumer commodity when technology is fixed. It turns out that labour theory, being more general, provides a basis for a rigorous analysis of neoclassical assumptions.

10.7 Wicksell effects

Since C.G. Uhr (1951) introduced the therm, the change of the value of capital stock, as a function of the interest rate, from one steady state to another, has been called the *Wicksell effect*.

The value of capital changes because the quantity changes and/or the price changes. Thus, the Wicksell effect represents the sum of real Wicksell effect (RWE) and price Wicksell effect (PWE). Evaluate capital per worker in *l*-prices ($p_2k=\omega$) and *b*-prices ($\tilde{p}_2k=\tilde{k}$) and consider changes caused by an increase in the rental rate, i.e. changes in the value of capital from one steady state to another:

$$\begin{aligned}\frac{d\omega}{dr}&=p_2\frac{dk}{dr}+k\frac{dp_2}{dr}, \qquad w=1\\ \frac{d\tilde{k}}{dr}&=\tilde{p}_2\frac{dk}{dr}+k\frac{d\tilde{p}_2}{dr}, \qquad p_1=1\end{aligned} \tag{10.53}$$

Both – quantity and price – effects may be algebraically either positive or negative. Using (10.34) we may relate RWE to relative mechanization:

$$\frac{dk}{dr}\gtreqless 0 \text{ when } m\lesseqgtr 0 \tag{10.54}$$

PWE is always positive for *l*-price, and may have either sign for *b*-prices (10.2). Thus, PWE depends on the choice of *numéraire*, while RWE is in this respect invariant. For *b*-prices PWE and RWE have the same sign since p_2/p_1 and k move together.

In the case of *b*-prices, price effect may also be neutral,

$$k\frac{d\tilde{p}_2}{dr}=0$$

That will happen when the ratio of prices ($\tilde{p}_2 = p_2/p_1$) does not change, which implies linear wage curve (equal mechanization in both sectors).

Let us now split the wage curve into its two components, distribution and production curve. Consider first the distribution curve ($i = i_0$). Since quantity of capital does not change, total effect reduces to price effect. It follows the PWE is positive for *l*-prices and may be either positive or negative for *b*-prices.

In the case of production curve ($r = r_0$), prices do not change and RWE reduces to composition effect (10.54).

Note that whenever $r \neq i$, prices become arbitrary (in the sense that they are no longer optimal, labour prices).

If there are more efficient techniques, commodity and factor prices remain unchanged at switch points. Consequently, RWE can be studied at switch points and we shall see (section 11.3) that it is always negative since at switch points both ω and $\tilde{k}$ are decreasing functions of r. Between the switch points ω and $\tilde{k}$ may move in any direction.

Changes in the value of output may also be studied in terms of Wicksell effects. Consider per capita product in labour values:

$$y = rp_2k + w, \qquad w = 1$$

Total differentiation gives:

$$dy = rp_2dk + p_2kdr + rkdp_2 \tag{10.55}$$

The change of the value of social product consists of two components: a real one (change of the number of machines evaluated at constant prices, rp_2dk) and a price change (the remaining two terms). Both effects may be positive, negative or zero. In the last case the price effect is called neutral, which implies:

$$p_2dr + rdp_2 = 0 \tag{10.56}$$

The relation (10.56) is apparently satisfied in two cases: (a) when rental rate and machine price do not change and (b) for:

$$\frac{p_2}{r} = -\frac{dp_2}{dr}$$

But (b) is impossible because $dp_2/dr > 0$ and p_2 and r are, of course, positive. Thus, only the case (a) applies. If the price effect is neutral, (10.55) gives:

$$\frac{dy}{dk}=rp_2 \tag{10.57}$$

which is a neoclassical result.

If per capita product is evaluated in terms of baskets:

$$\tilde{y}=r\tilde{p}_2k+\tilde{w},\ \tilde{y}=y/p_1,\ \tilde{p}_2=p_2/p_1,\ \tilde{w}=1/p_1$$

the relation (10.55) is turned into:

$$d\tilde{y}=r\tilde{p}_2dk+\tilde{p}_2kdr+rkd\tilde{p}_2+d\tilde{w} \tag{10.58}$$

and (10.56) into:

$$\tilde{p}_2kdr+rdk\tilde{p}_2+d\tilde{w}=rkd\tilde{p}_2=0 \tag{10.60}$$

because $\tilde{p}_2kdr=-d\tilde{w}$ by (10.18). The price effect is neutral when the *relative* commodity prices do not change ($\tilde{w}$ and r do change) which implies a linear wage curve.

Split again the dual curve into its two components, distribution and production curves. Consider first distribution curve with $i=i_0$, $c=c_0$. Since $dk=0$, the entire effect is price effect:

$$dy=p_2kdr+rkdp_2$$
$$d\tilde{y}=\tilde{p}_2kdr+rkd\tilde{p}_2+d\tilde{w}=rkd\tilde{p}_2$$

Whenever r increases, dp_2 also increases and price effect is always positive in l-prices, $dy>0$. The b-price of machines may change in either direction, depending on relative mechanization. Consequently $d\tilde{y}\gtreqless 0$ for $m\lesseqgtr 0$.

As for production curve ($r=r_0$, $w=w_0$), only the quantity of capital (the number of machines) changes and the effect is purely real.

11 Technological frontier

The analysis of substitution in neoclassical exchange economics is replaced by analysis of alternative production techniques in the neo-Marxian production economics. Instead of substituting labour by capital one substitutes labour intensive by capital intensive techniques. In terms of mathematics, neoclassical economics is oriented towards calculus, neo-Marxian economics towards linear algebra. The former uses smooth curves, the latter analyses discrete changes – which, by the way, is obviously closer to what happens in real economies. Consequently, the former focuses on marginal adjustments, which are often of no practical interest; the latter deals with discrete changes and can sharply distinguish between partial and total adjustments.

In the general equilibrium framework, we are interested in the full impact that a technological change exerts on an economy. Thus, changes in individual techniques will be considered in the context of technologies. It is often erroneously claimed that the stronger results linear economics can achieve as compared with the traditional neoclassical approach are due to the unrealistic assumption of fixed coefficients. In fact, assuming that there are many alternative techniques means assuming that there are many technical coefficients, i.e. that they are variable. Any smooth curve may be approximated by linear segments as well as one likes. A reverse procedure is generally not possible, at least not in a simple way.

After the foregoing brief introduction, let me define the terms that will be used:

1. A *process* or a *technique* or an *activity* is a method of production used. There are as many processes (techniques, activities) in use as there are industries.
2. A *technology* is a set of techniques (processes, activities), one technique for each industry.
3. A *book of blueprints* or a *spectrum of techniques* is the complete set of all known techniques, not all of which are efficient. As such it contains all possible technologies. If there are n industries and for each of them k techniques are available, the book of blueprints will contain $n \times k$ techniques and k^n technologies.
4. An *efficient technology* is the one which is not dominated by another technology over the entire range of admissible rental rates. It may be

dominated for some of the rental rates. Efficient technologies generate the *technological* frontier.

11.1 The impossibility of reswitching

Before we proceed, a careful analysis of several issues is called for.

Technological frontier has a number of properties that are not immediately obvious. Since wage curves, $\tilde{w}(r)$, represent second degree functions, alternative efficient technologies are usually represented by curves intersecting twice. At the first intersection the economy switches from technology α to technology β, at the second intersection the economy switches back to technology α. Generally, that is an error: in an economy with one (composite) capital good always, and with more capital goods in some cases, there can be no reswitch. The parameters of our function cannot vary freely. They are subject to two limitations: (a) for a technique to be efficient, a higher labour coefficient implies lower capital coefficient and vice versa, (b) generally at a switch point only one industry can change its technique, as will be proved below.

The implication of (a) is that for each pair of *efficient* techniques one technique can have either maximum wage $\left(\tilde{W}=\frac{1}{\lambda_1}\right)$ greater or maximum growth rate $\left(R=\frac{1}{\kappa_2}\right)$ greater, but not both. Since the curves cannot cross twice, linear wage functions cannot cross at all. An efficient technology is dominating over the entire admissible range. If one likes, one may call the two conclusions Nonreswitching ($m \neq 0$) and Nonswitching ($m=0$) Theorems.

As a consequence of the limitations imposed on coefficients, two curves representing alternative efficient technologies may intersect in six different ways of which four are shown in Fig. 11.1. (In the remaining two cases both curves are convex.) Recall that $m>0$ ($m<0$) reflects higher degree of mechanization in the basket (machine) industry, and generates convex (concave) curves. Also recall that λ_1 and κ_2 are comparable across techniques. Figure 11.1 shows that wage curves intersect twice in such a way as to either originate from or terminate at the same point. That leaves only one possibility for intersection in the interval $0<r^*<R$ (as already noted by Morishima, 1966, p. 524). Note that if the vertical axis is shifted from $r=0$ to $r=1/n$, when economy becomes stationary, in the cases (a) and (b) wage curves start from as well as end in different points.

Take the case (c) for further analysis (Fig. 11.2). At $r<r^*$, technology α produces higher net output; at $r>r^*$, β is more productive. Since the machine industry keeps the old technique, $\lambda_2^{\alpha}=\lambda_2^{\beta}$ and $\kappa_2^{\alpha}=\kappa_2^{\beta}$. The basket

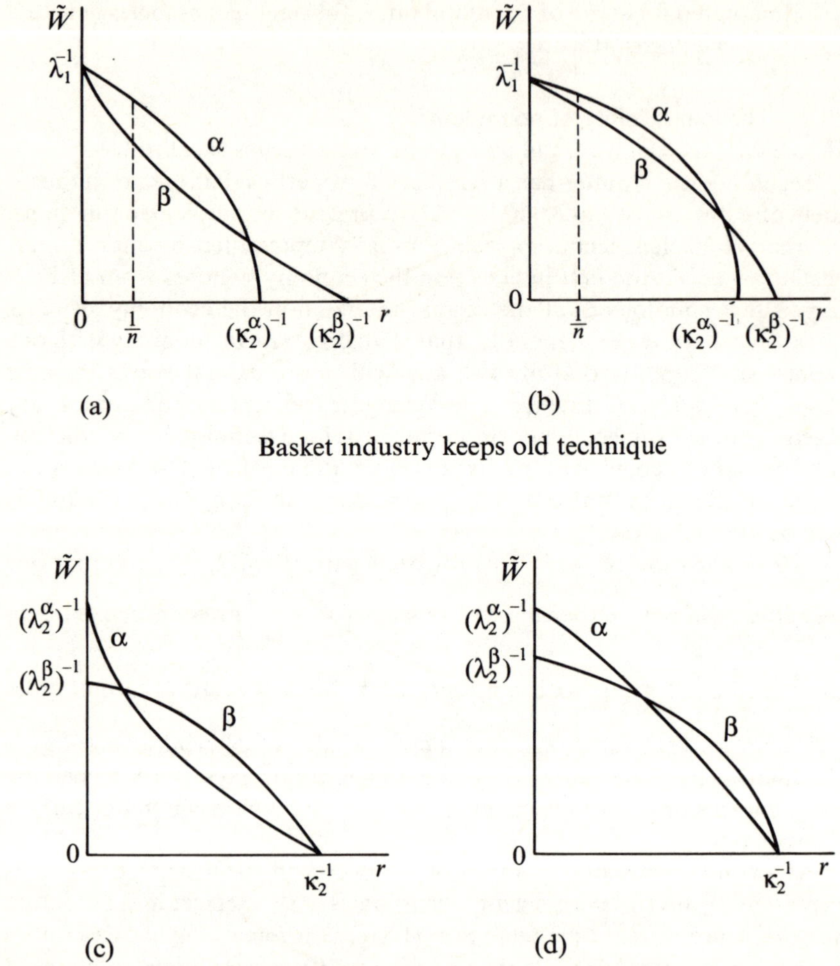

Figure 11.1 Four possible pairs of efficient technologies

industry replaces the technique α, which has lower labour coefficient, by technique β, which has higher labour coefficient, and so $\lambda_1^\alpha < \lambda_1^\beta$, $\kappa_1^\beta > \kappa_1^\alpha$. Technology α implies higher mechanization of the basket industry ($m > 0$), technology β reverses relative mechanization ($m < 0$). Consequently, relative price falls for α and increases for β (cf. Fig. 11.2).

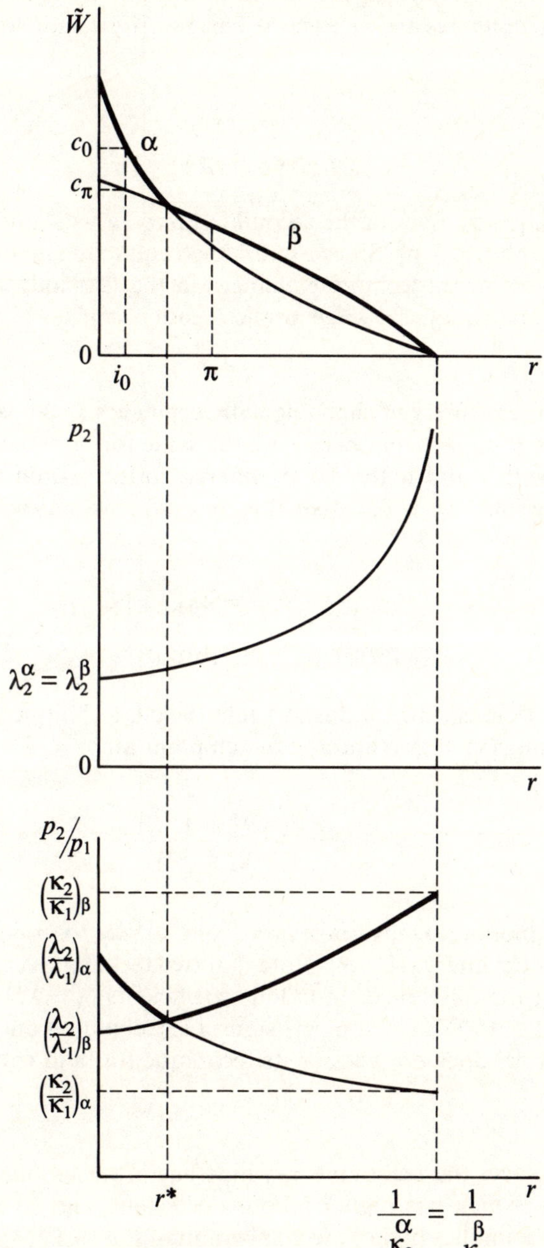

Figure 11.2 Switch point and prices

Note that equal real wages and rental rates imply equal prices for two alternative techniques and vice versa. This is easily demonstrated. Consider the price equations:

$$p_1 = w\lambda_1 + rp_2\kappa_1$$
$$p_2 = w\lambda_2 + rp_2\kappa_2$$

If the technique changes in the second industry, $\kappa_1^\alpha = \kappa_1^\beta$ and $\lambda_1^\alpha = \lambda_1^\beta$. Equal real wage implies $p_1^\alpha = p_1^\beta$. Since r is assumed equal, the first equation holds only if $p_2^\alpha = p_2^\beta$. If the technique changes in the first industry, p_2 remains unchanged and equal real wage implies again $p_1^\alpha = p_1^\beta$.

11.2 The impossibility of changing both techniques at the same time

A switch point implies that prices are the same for both technologies. For otherwise, with r and w the same, different prices would mean that one technology is inefficient. To satisfy this condition, we may write two pairs of equations:

$$p_2 r\kappa_1^\alpha + \lambda_1^\alpha = p_1 = p_2 r\kappa_1^\beta + \lambda_1^\beta \qquad (11.1)$$

$$p_2 r\kappa_2^\alpha + \lambda_2^\alpha = p_2 = p_2 r\kappa_2^\beta + \lambda_2^\beta \qquad (11.2)$$

Suppose that the machine industry keeps the old technique, as in Fig. 11.2. Then, by using (11.1), we find the switch point at:

$$r^* = \frac{\lambda_1^\beta - \lambda_1^\alpha}{\kappa_1^\alpha - \kappa_1^\beta} \frac{1}{p_2(r^*)} \qquad (11.3)$$

Since $p_2(r)$ monotonically increases from $p_2 = \lambda_2$ to $p_2 = \infty$, r^* can be anywhere in the interval $[O, R]$. Note that two techniques can be equiprofitable only if the differences in labour coefficients $(\lambda_1^\beta - \lambda_1^\alpha)$ and in capital coefficients $(\kappa_1^\beta - \kappa_1^\alpha)$ have opposite signs, i.e. techniques are efficient. If the basket industry does not change its technique ((a) and (b) in Fig. 11.1)), (11.2) gives:

$$r^* = \frac{\lambda_2^\beta - \lambda_2^\alpha}{\lambda_2^\beta \kappa_2^\alpha - \lambda_2^\alpha \kappa_2^\beta} \qquad (11.4)$$

Thus, *providing that techniques are efficient*, there is always a positive rental rate at which switch can occur.

Suppose, now, that we change both techniques simultaneously. It follows from (11.2) that:

$$p_2 = \frac{\lambda_2^\beta - \lambda_2^\alpha}{r^*(\kappa_2^\alpha - \kappa_2^\beta)} \tag{11.5}$$

Substitute p_2 from (11.5) into (11.1) to obtain the condition for a simultaneous change of techniques:

$$\frac{\lambda_1^\beta - \lambda_1^\alpha}{\lambda_2^\beta - \lambda_2^\alpha} = \frac{\kappa_1^\alpha - \kappa_1^\beta}{\kappa_2^\alpha - \kappa_2^\beta} \tag{11.6}$$

The condition requires linear dependence of techniques, (such as $\lambda_j^\beta = \lambda_j^\alpha + s$, $\kappa_j^\alpha = \kappa_j^\beta + t$) or proportionality of coefficients (such as $\kappa_j^\alpha = t\lambda_j^\alpha$, $\kappa_j^\beta = t\lambda_j^\beta$) which are very special cases. Proportional coefficients represent equal organic composition of resources; in this case both industries cease to be profitable for the same r and, consequently, both techniques must be changed.

Alternatively we may postulate that at switch points relative prices (basket-prices) must be the same:

$$\tilde{p}_2^\alpha = \tilde{p}_2^\beta = \Rightarrow \frac{\lambda_2^\alpha}{\lambda_1^\alpha + rm^\alpha} = \frac{\lambda_2^\beta}{\lambda_1^\beta + rm^\beta}$$

$$r^* = \frac{\lambda_2^\beta \lambda_1^\alpha - \lambda_2^\alpha \lambda_1^\beta}{\lambda_2^\alpha m^\beta - \lambda_2^\beta m^\alpha} \tag{11.7}$$

With unchanged basket production technique, (11.7) reduces to (11.4). With unchanged machine production technique, (11.7) reduces to (11.3) which may be written as:

$$r^* = \frac{\lambda_1^\beta - \lambda_1^\alpha}{m^\alpha - m^\beta} \tag{11.3a}$$

With equal mechanization, $m^\alpha = m^\beta = 0$, price ratio curves collapse into a single horizontal straight line because price ratios are no longer a function of r. Any r will do and all that matters is the proportionality of labour coefficients.

Note that this analysis is conducted in terms of full resource coefficients. Direct coefficients behave differently. The relation between direct and full coefficients is given by:

$$\hat{\lambda} = \lambda(I - A), \; \hat{\kappa} = \kappa(I - A) \qquad (2.8)$$

Thus, although full coefficients will change only in one industry, direct coefficients will change in both. Moreover, depending on how A changes, full and direct coefficients may even not move in the same direction. This problem is considered in section 16.2.

11.3 Changes in capital intensities

Let us now search for additional techniques in the book of blueprints. Altogether there will be four technologies consisting of five techniques, three in the basket industry and two in the machine industry (Fig. 11.3). It is immediately clear that δ is an inefficient technology, better than α and β for some values of r but fully dominated by γ.

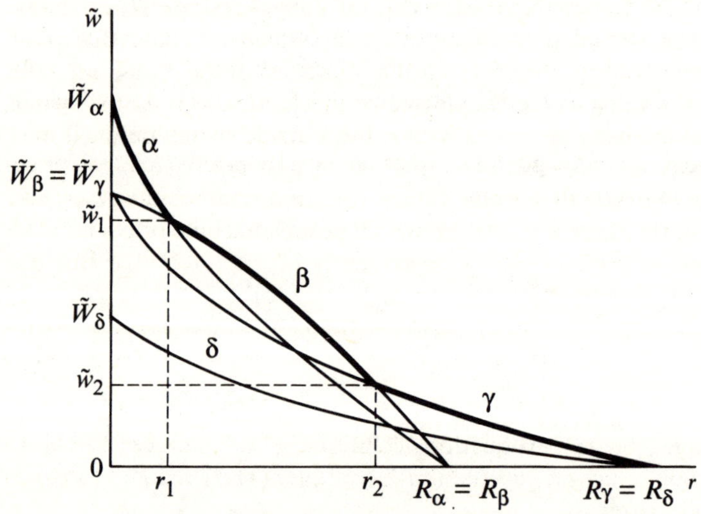

Figure 11.3 Technological frontier

Thus, it will never be used. Next, we see that at r_2 a second switch point appears (machine industry changes its technique). In β and γ we recognize the case (a), in α and β the case (c) from Fig. 11.1. In technology β the relative mechanization is reversed as compared with α and γ, $k_1 < k_2$, and therefore wage curve is concave to the origin. At the rental rate r_1 the system switches from α to β, at r_2 from β to γ because they yield higher $\tilde{w}$ than the alternatives.

Consider now what happens to capital intensities at switch points. The relation (10.34) gives the number of machines per worker, $k = \kappa_1/(\lambda_1 + rm)$.

For $r=0$, from (10.9) $\tilde{W}=1/\lambda_1$. Next, $\tilde{W}_\alpha > \tilde{W}_\beta$ implies $\lambda_1^\alpha < \lambda_1^\beta$. Since no technique in a pair of efficient techniques can be dominant over the whole range, $\lambda_1^\alpha < \lambda_1^\beta$ implies $\kappa_1^\alpha > \kappa_1^\beta$ (for the same n). The technique in the machine industry does not change, $\kappa_2^\alpha = \kappa_2^\beta$. For the same rental rate r_1 and the same wage rate, $\tilde{w}_1 = (1-r_1\kappa_2^\alpha)/(r_1 m^\alpha + \lambda_1^\alpha) = (1-r_1\kappa_2^\beta)/(r_1 m^\beta + \lambda_1^\beta)$. It follows that $r_1 m^\alpha + \lambda_1^\alpha = r_1 m^\beta + \lambda_1^\beta$. Since in (10.34) for the technique α the numerator is greater and the denominator is the same at $r=r_1$, this technology is more mechanized, $k^\alpha > k^\beta$. At the switch point of r_2, technical coefficients of the first industry remain unchanged, $(\lambda_1^\beta = \lambda_1^\gamma,\ \kappa_1^\beta = \kappa_1^\gamma)$ while $m^\beta < 0$ and $m^\gamma > 0$ (concave and convex wage curve). Consequently $k^\beta > k^\gamma$. Note that k's are not fixed but are increasing or decreasing functions of r depending on $m \gtrless 0$.

Next, we compare capital intensity in terms of capital–labour ratio (with baskets serving as a *numéraire*). By (10.18) capital–labour ratio is equal to the slope of the tangent to the w–r curve, $\tilde{k} = -dw/dr$. If we look at points r_1 and r_2 on Fig. 11.3, β appears to be less capital intensive (slope flatter) than α at r_1 and more capital intensive than γ at r_2 (slope steeper). That is due to the fact that the technology frontier is a falling function of the rental rate. The relations are the same as for the degree of mechanization. At the switch points, capital intensity decreases with r, but outside switch points it may move either way.

Capital per worker in labour values (organic composition, $\omega = p_2 k$) behaves also in the same way. At the switch points machine prices must be the same while $k^\alpha > k^\beta$, $k^\beta > k^\gamma$. Consequently $\omega^\alpha > \omega^\beta$, $\omega^\beta > \omega^\gamma$. But not necessarily $\omega^\alpha(r_1) > \omega^\gamma(r_2)$.

Finally, value capital coefficient displays the same characteristics. Write:

$$\kappa = \frac{p_2 K}{p_1 X_1 + p_2 X_2} = \frac{p_2 K}{L + p_2 r K} = \frac{p_2}{\dfrac{1}{k} + p_2 r}, \qquad X_2 = rK,\ p_1 X_1 = L \qquad (11.8)$$

Since p_2 must be the same for both technologies, κ follows k and so $\kappa^\alpha > \kappa^\beta$, $\kappa^\beta > \kappa^\gamma$. Outside switch points changes in ω and κ are given by (10.39) and (10.42).

The general conclusion is simple enough. All four measures of capital intensity display the neat neoclassical property of capital intensity being a decreasing function of the rental rate *at the switch points*. That is the result of the structure of the model – of which more below – and of the assumption that n is the same for alternative technologies. *Between the switch points* capital intensity may move either way depending on the relative mechanization of the two industries (m). Neither hold neoclassical conclusions for *successive switch points*. At the switch points the change is discontinuous, between them it is continuous.

If we assume a continuous technology frontier, the number of switch points and efficient wage curves will be infinite and the frontier becomes an envelope of efficient wage curves. Now neoclassical postulates may be violated because:

$$\frac{d\tilde{k}}{dr}=\frac{d}{dr}\left(-\frac{d\tilde{w}}{dr}\right)=-\frac{d^2\tilde{w}}{dr}$$

and changes in $\tilde{k}$ depend on the shape of the frontier (and similarly for other measures of capital intensities). At convex portions of the frontier $\tilde{k}$ will behave neoclassically (even if the constituent wage curves are concave), at concave portions antineoclassically (the constituent wage curves can be only concave) and at the inflection points it will not change.

Two final points may be made:

1. Figure 11.2 also helps to elucidate different behaviour of economic agents depending on social institutions. Rational economic agents will attempt to minimize cost of production and that will drive them towards the technology frontier. However, even with perfect competition, they will not reach the frontier unless social institutions are right as well. Since in capitalism $\pi > i$, the technology chosen will generally be wrong. In Fig. 11.2 the rate of profit π will induce capitalists to choose technology β as the most profitable one. Yet the actual investment rate i_0 makes technology α more productive. The loss of per capita consumption, due to the wrong choice of technology, is equal to $c_0 - c_\pi$. Maximizing the rate of profit does not imply maximizing consumption and output.
2. The second point concerns the time preference explanation of interest. It is said that higher interest rate reflects the request for higher consumption in the future. Consider stationary economy with $r = 1/n$ and zero interest rate (Fig. 11.4). An *increase* of the rate of interest (that moves r beyond r_1) causes technique α to be replaced by the *less* productive β and that *lowers* per capita consumption.

Finally, as already stated, at switch points capital intensity drops, but between switch points it may change either way. This provides for the possibility of capital reversal (capital intensity and r moving in the same direction) even without reswitching. Moreover, the same capital intensity is possible at two different r's. At $r=\frac{1}{n}$ and r_3 the slopes of the tangents at the wage curves are the same, and so are those at r_2 and r_5, which means that capital per worker ($\tilde{k}$), which discontinuously diminished at r_1, reaches the

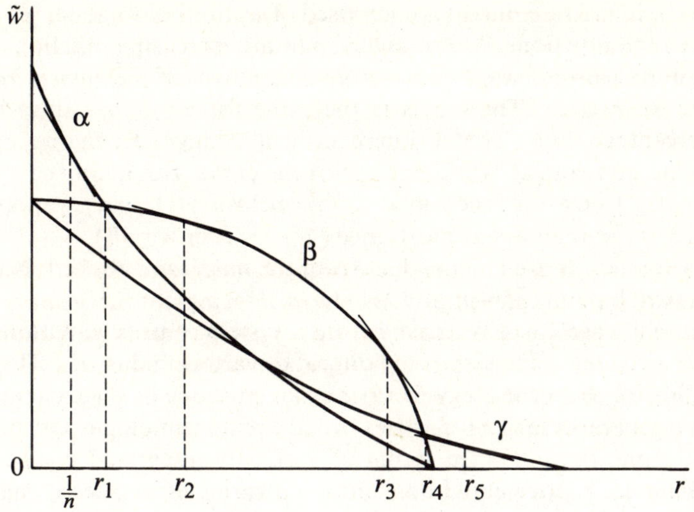

Figure 11.4 Capital reversal at r_3 *and* r_5

same value at r_3 as it had at $r=\frac{1}{n}$, and similarly at r_2 and r_5 separated by the switch point r_4. A continuous monotonic technological frontier eliminates capital reversal. Similar reasoning applies to distribution curve (recall Fig. 10.6).

We are now ready to describe properties of the technological frontier in a systematic fashion.

11.4 The properties of technological frontier systematized

1. At switch points prices of the same commodities produced by alternative techniques must be the same. If any price were different, $p_i^\alpha \neq p_i^\beta$, industry i would stay with a more profitable technique, which is contrary to the definition of the switch point. Since $\tilde{w}=1/p_1$, equal real wages imply equal basket prices and so the only additional condition is the equality of machine prices, $p_2^\alpha = p_2^\beta$, provided that machines do not change.
2. As a consequence of characteristic (1), outside switch points one system is always more productive than the other and so must have higher real wages and lower machine and/or basket prices.
3. Technological frontier $\left(\tilde{w}=\frac{w}{p_1}=\tilde{w}(r)\right)$ is a strictly decreasing function

of the rental rate since it is composed of sections of wage curves which are such functions. Alternatively, p_j/w are increasing functions of r.

4. Comparisons of wage curves are independent of the *numéraire* used for the system. The r axis is the same for all curves since it is a percentage rate. The $\tilde{w}$ intercept will change depending on the numéraire, and so will the shape of the curve. But in any case $\tilde{w}$ is a strictly decreasing function of r and conclusions (1) and (2) apply. The curves can intersect at most once (for $r < R$ or $\tilde{w} < \tilde{W}$).
5. Switch points are independent from the *numéraire* applied. Namely, at switch points $p_i^\alpha = p_i^\beta$ and also $(p_i/p_j)^\alpha = (p_i/p_j)^\beta$.
6. Since a wage curve is derived from a system of price equations, it is independent of the size of the output of various industries. The same holds for the technology frontier as an envelope of wage curves.
7. In a general case of n industries the adjacent technologies can differ in only one technique (in terms of vertically integrated coefficients). There are n price equations and $n+2$ variables: n prices, wage and rental rate. Let $w=1$, which leaves us with one degree of freedom. It will be used by adding one equation for an alternative technique. In other words, $n-1$ industries use identical techniques and so we are effectively left with one industry that can use two different techniques. We have two equations with two unknowns, p_i and r, and the system is determined.[1] Thus, the same prices satisfy two technologies differing in one technique. If some pairs of alternative techniques are dependent in particular ways the two technologies may differ in more than one technique. If by chance three wage curves happen to intersect at the same point, one of them is irrelevant because it will be dominated by one of the other two.
8. In an n-industry economy with one capital good there can be no reswitching.[2] Namely, the price equation belonging to the capital good industry uniquely determines the best technique for any given r. Hence, that technique cannot recur.
9. It will be shown later (section 15.2) that reswitching may occur in a two-sector circulating capital model when both commodities are used as inputs and in a three-sector full-coefficients fixed capital model with two capital goods. Generally, at least two capital goods are necessary for reswitching to become possible.
10. With continuous spectrum of technologies, technological frontier is generally unattainable under private ownership regime. The same is true for discrete technologies (kinked frontier) and substantial differencies between profit and investment rates.
11. With discontinuous technologies, capital per worker is a strictly decreasing function of the rental rate *at the switch points* for all three

measures of capital (number of machines, machines evaluated in terms of baskets, and machines evaluated in labour time), and so is capital per unit of output, provided that the durability of machines is the same for alternative techniques. Thus, there can be no capital reversal (value of capital and r moving in the same direction). Between the switch points, and successively from one to the other switch point capital intensity may vary in either direction depending on relative mechanization and so capital reversal occurs whenever the new technology includes more mechanized machine industry ($m<0$) except for ω-intensity.

12. Continuous monotonic technological frontier consists of switch points only. Capital intensities may behave perversely depending on the shape of the frontier-envelope. Reswitching is possible (for different curvatures of the envelope and the wage curves containing two or more capital goods), but capital reversal is impossible (for a monotonic frontier).

The technology frontier is represented by an envelope of the wage curves. The efficient curves (technologies) are tangent to the envelope; others will be scrapped as inferior. Thus, technology frontier consists of efficient techniques available at certain points of time. Each point on the technology frontier indicates maximum consumption possible for a given investment rate. If the number of techniques is sufficiently large, the envelope will be almost continuous.

In order to locate a production point on the technology frontier, one has to apply labour-time prices. That, of course, is not a surprise because labour-time prices were derived from the price–quantity duality and so they must be production efficient. In the programming context this duality is directly interpretable as the solutions of primal and dual problems: technology frontier is the result of maximization of output c and at the same time a result of minimization of cost $\tilde{w}$. The optimum allocation of resources is achieved when the two points on the frontier coincide.

11.5 Quasi-production function

For a given $i=r$, technology frontier implies the choice of technology that will generate the highest consumption per capita (real wage $\tilde{w}$). That technology implies a certain capital–labour ratio $\tilde{k}=\tilde{p}_2k$. If the technology frontier is smooth with monotonously changing slope, $\tilde{k}(r)$ is uniquely determined so that inverse function $r(\tilde{k})$ also exist. We may, thus, search for the best technology in the following way: for a given $r=r_0$, find capital intensity $\tilde{k}$ that will maximize real wage. For that purpose (10.50) may be written as:

$$\tilde{y} = \tilde{w}(r) + r\tilde{k}(r) = f(\tilde{k}),\ r = r_0 \tag{11.9}$$

The function (11.9) looks like a production function. For an unknown technology (depending on $\tilde{k}$) and $r = r_0$, the real wage $\tilde{w}(r_0)$ is determined. How do we find the optimal capital intensity $\tilde{k}^*$? Under what conditions is the most profitable technique, associated with $\tilde{k}^*$, also the most efficient? For this purpose use Fig. 11.5 adapted from Joan Robinson (1956, p. 412) and J.D. Harris (1973). Robinson described the resulting curve as 'productivity curve'; Harris renamed it 'profitability curve'.

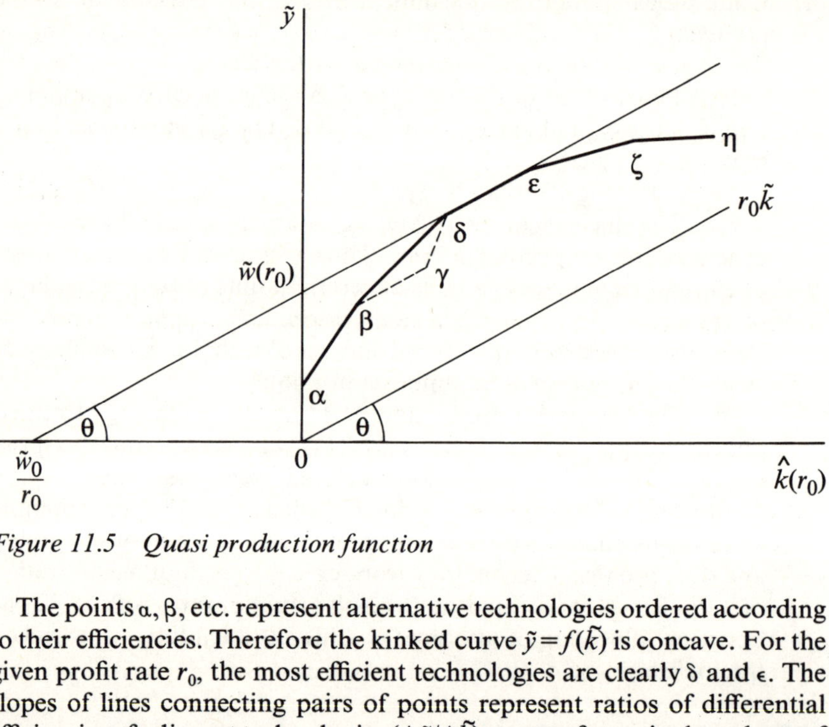

Figure 11.5 Quasi production function

The points α, β, etc. represent alternative technologies ordered according to their efficiencies. Therefore the kinked curve $\tilde{y} = f(\tilde{k})$ is concave. For the given profit rate r_0, the most efficient technologies are clearly δ and ϵ. The slopes of lines connecting pairs of points represent ratios of differential efficiencies of adjacent technologies ($\Delta\tilde{y}/\Delta\tilde{k}$), a sort of marginal products of capital. As long as the successive slopes are steeper than the slope of $r_0\tilde{k}$, it pays to continue the search for the most efficient technology. The prescribed profit is always covered but the real wage (consumption) is maximized only when the wage lines touches quasi production curve, i.e. for $\tilde{k}_\delta \leq \tilde{k}^* \leq \tilde{k}_\epsilon$.

The curve is a *quasi* production function because it depicts rational choice among possible combination of techniques and not technological relationship between output and input, given the technology. A technology such as γ, which is better than β, will never be considered because it is always possible to increase profitability by a linear combination of efficient technologies β and δ. For that reason increasing returns (slope $\overline{\gamma\delta}$) will never occur. Technologies δ and ϵ are equally profitable and correspond to a switch point on the wage curve. The point where the wage line $\epsilon\delta\tilde{w}(r_0)$ cuts the horizontal axis represents the ratio of 'factor incomes' $\tilde{w}_0/r_0$ (because $tg\,\theta = r_0$). *A different* r_0 *will generate different ordering of technologies and a different* $\tilde{y} = f(\tilde{k})$ *curve*. But the curve will always be concave.

The above exercise provides a link with the standard neoclassical analysis by means of rigorously defined concepts. Assume continuity so that $\tilde{y}(\tilde{k})$ becomes a well-behaved quasi-production function, $\tilde{y}'(k) > 0$, $\tilde{y}''(k) < 0$. From (10.51):

$$\tilde{y}'(\tilde{k}) = r \tag{11.10}$$

which looks like marginal product of capital as required by the neoclassicals. Continuous technological frontier is represented by:

$$\tilde{w} = \tilde{w}(r)$$

We know from (10.18a) that $d\tilde{w}/dr = -\tilde{k}$ for the point where the wage curve touches the frontier. That can also be derived neoclassically:

$$\begin{aligned} &\tilde{w} = \tilde{y}(\tilde{k}) - r\tilde{k} = \tilde{y}(\tilde{k}) - y'(\tilde{k})\tilde{k} \\ &\frac{d\tilde{w}}{d\tilde{k}} = -\tilde{y}''(\tilde{k})\tilde{k} > 0,\ \tilde{y}''(\tilde{k}) = \frac{dr}{d\tilde{k}} < 0 \qquad (11.11) \\ &\frac{d\tilde{w}}{dr} = \frac{d\tilde{w}}{d\tilde{k}}\frac{d\tilde{k}}{dr} = -\tilde{k} \end{aligned}$$

However, the result is not valid for *l*-prices; it holds only for *b*-prices.

Neoclassical postulates may be graphically represented as in Fig. 11.6 (Harris, 1978, p. 218). They seem to be satisfied by the quasi-production function.

All we need is to derive the consequences:

$$\tilde{w}''(r) = -\frac{d\tilde{k}}{dr} = -\frac{1}{\tilde{y}''(\tilde{k})} > 0 \tag{11.12}$$

the technology frontier must be convex, in order to generate the desirable neoclassical effects.

This neat result obtains necessarily only for one-product economies that generate convex technological frontiers due to diminishing returns. If there are two or more products, the quasi-production function in Fig. 11.5 will generally be different for each r, as already noted, and so will the optimal technology. Successive optimal technologies may move $\tilde{k}$ in any direction. Although the 'marginal product of capital' ($\tilde{y}'$) is a monotonously decreasing function of capital intensity ($\tilde{k}$) for any single quasi-production function, $\tilde{y}'$ and $\tilde{k}$ are not necessarily related in that way for optimal $\tilde{k}$'s belonging to a set of feasible different quasi-production functions. Consequently, the technology frontier is not necessarily convex, as we have already established before.

The simple production function of neoclassical textbooks is a construct devoid of meaning. The quasi-production function is logically consistent, but it requires a number of qualifications. That, of course, restricts its usefulness.

11.6 The determination of the technology frontier

11.6.1 The problem

For a given growth rate, we want to choose such a combination of techniques that will maximize net output. That will bring the economy to the technology frontier.

In a standard linear programme, output prices and resources are known. The task consists of finding the technology that will maximize the value of output and minimize cost subject to constraints. Since labour and capital are in fixed supply, we must use constraint inequalities and it is always possible that one of the resources will not be fully used.

Our problem is different. First output prices are not known. Second, in the long run any number of machines may be produced making possible the full employment of available labour. Thus, labour is the only scarce resource and we use constraint equalities.

The value of net product is:

$$p_1 X_1 = L, \qquad w = 1$$

and so maximizing X_1 implies minimizing p_1. That determines primal and dual of the programme:

$$\begin{array}{ll} \max X_1 & \min p_1 \\ s.\text{ to } \lambda_1 X_1 + \lambda_2 X_2 = \bar{L} & s.\text{ to } r p_2 \kappa_1 + \lambda_1 = p_1 \\ \qquad \kappa_1 X_1 + \kappa_2 X_2 = \bar{K} & \qquad r p_2 \kappa_2 + \lambda_2 = p_2 \\ \qquad X_1, X_2 > 0 & \qquad p_1, p_2 > 0 \end{array} \tag{11.13}$$

The problem may be further simplified by eliminating the second constraint equations.

They may be written as:

$$X_2 = \frac{r\kappa_1}{1 - r\kappa_2} X_1, \qquad p_2 = \frac{\lambda_2}{1 - r\kappa_2}$$

The substitution into first constraint equations defines the optimization problem:

$$\max X_1 = \left(\lambda_1 + \lambda_2 \frac{r\kappa_1}{1 - r\kappa_2}\right)^{-1} \bar{L}, \quad \min p_1 = \lambda_1 + \lambda_2 \frac{r\kappa_1}{1 - r\kappa_2} \qquad (11.14)$$

The book of blueprints may contain *m* techniques (λ_1, κ_1) for the first industry and *n* techniques (λ_2, κ_2) for the second industry (the durability of machines is assumed invariable) and so the task is to find one (or two, in a switch point) combination(s) of techniques that will generate the optimum result. It is obvious from (11.14) that maximization and minimization will produce the same result.

11.6.2 The solution

Redefine the primal in the following way:

$$\max X_1$$
$$\text{subject to } \lambda_1 X_1 + \lambda_2 X_2 = \bar{L}$$
$$r\kappa_1 X_1 - (1 - r\kappa_2) X_2 = 0$$

The programme says: search for technology $T(\lambda_1, r\kappa_1)$, which will maximize X_1 given the two constraint equations. Fig. 11.7 depicts the constraint equations, which we may slightly rewrite:

$$\text{Labour constraint:} \quad X_2 = \frac{\bar{L}}{\lambda_2} - \frac{\lambda_1}{\lambda_2} X_1 \qquad (11.15)$$

$$\text{Capital constraint:} \quad \frac{X_2}{X_1} = \frac{r\kappa_1}{1 - r\kappa_2}$$

We may assume that the economy has been growing at the equilibrium rate *g* with its structure (X_2^0/X_1^0) fully adjusted to the technology used. At some point a re-examination of the book of blueprints is undertaken (technological change would have the same effect) with an intention of

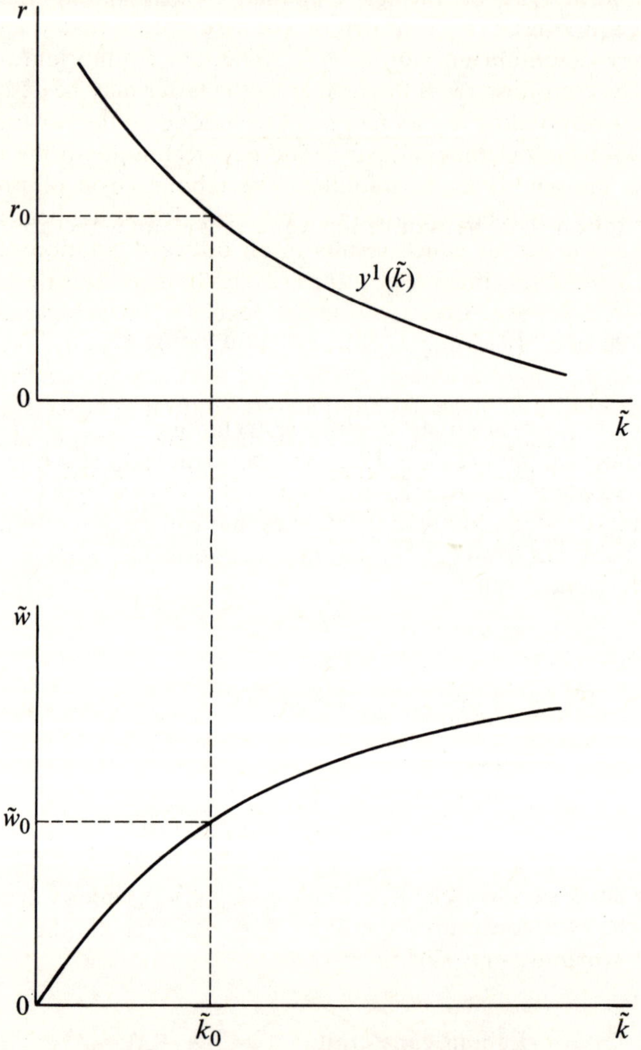

Figure 11.6 ***Neoclassical relations between consumption per capita ($\tilde{w}$), capital intensity ($\tilde{k}$) and the interest rate (r)***

finding an alternative technology that will increase the equilibrium output of X_1. It is assumed that all obviously inferior techniques (both labour and capital coefficients higher) have already been eliminated and so we have to examine only those techniques for which lower λ_1 implies higher κ_1 (or vice versa). Since each of the two industries can find an alternative technique with either λ_1 or κ_1 lower, the new technology may be composed in four different ways. Figure 11.7 is drawn on the assumption that λ_2 and κ_1 are lower. The old equilibrium output is X_1^0. The new equilibrium output is $X_1^* > X_1^0$. The transition from the former to the latter may be described in two steps corresponding to the changes of techniques in the two industries. We start with the machine industry. The new technique in the machine industry is chosen so as to minimize the labour costs of producing machines. Why – will be explained in a moment. It just happens that this technique has lower λ_2, which results in an outward rotation of labour constraint around $\bar{L}/\lambda_1$ into the position $(\bar{L}/\lambda_1) - A$, increasing the output of machines to $X_2(0) = A$. Lower λ_2 implies higher κ_2, which results in an inward rotation of the capital constraint, $X_2'/X_1' > X_2^0/X_1^0$. Given r, relative outputs depend only on capital coefficients, and any increase in any κ_1 expands the output of machines relative to the output of baskets. Given $\bar{L}$, higher output of machines ($X_2' > X_2^0$) may mean lower output of baskets. But if the labour price of machines is sufficiently reduced, even higher output of machines will release some labour, which will be used to increase the output of baskets ($X_1' > X_1^0$).

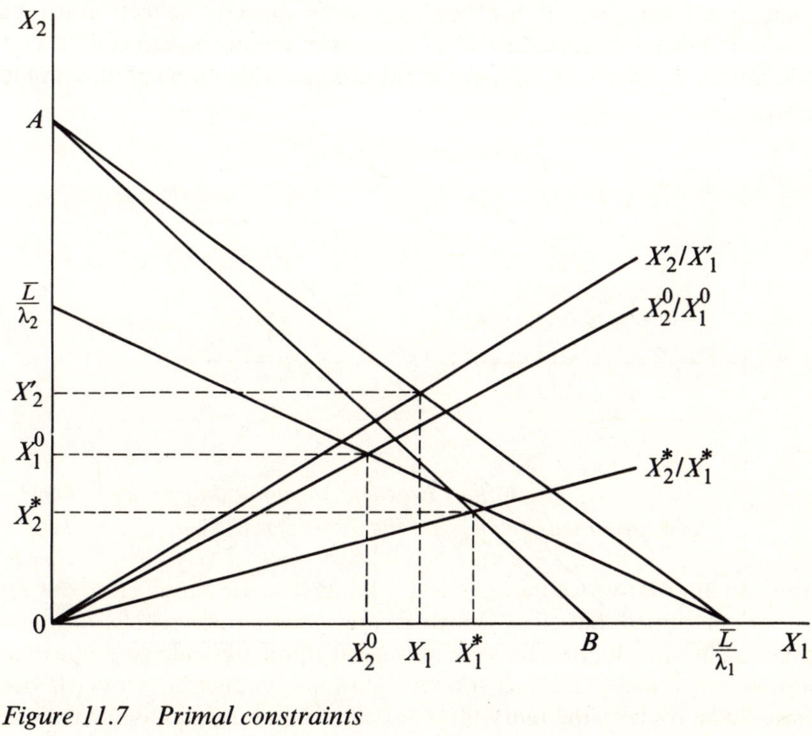

Figure 11.7 Primal constraints

Next we examine the basket production techniques. Suppose that the best one lowers κ_1 and so the output of machines decreases to X_2^*. At the same time the concomitant increase in λ_1 rotates labour constraint into the position AB. The resulting X_1^* is the highest possible.

The new optimum is a long-run equilibrium, after the necessary structural adjustments will have been carried out. In the short run it may not be an equilibrium at all. In our case the new absolute output of machines – and, consequently, the new relative output of machines – is lower than in the old equilibrium. This is due to the fact that the capital–labour ratio has been reduced. Since $X_2 = rK$ and we examine technological change for $\bar{L}$ and r fixed, $X_2^* < X_2^0$ implies $k^* < k^0$. Now, lower k for given $\bar{L}$ means that part of inherited capital stock is redundant. The redundant machines will, of course, not be thrown away but will be used instead of some of the new machines. Thus, X_2 will be reduced and X_1 expanded until capital stock is adjusted to labour. If it were the case that $X_2^* > X_2^0$, the output of the machines would have to be increased at the expense of baskets. In either case full employment is preserved. The adjustment is not a one-period affair because replacement is a function of the age structure of capital. Thus, complete adjustment will be achieved only after n years, n being the life span of machines. But for all practical purposes the later effects must be considered negligible, particularly if the investment rate is high and the new X_2/X_1 does not differ very much from the old one which is what one should expect.

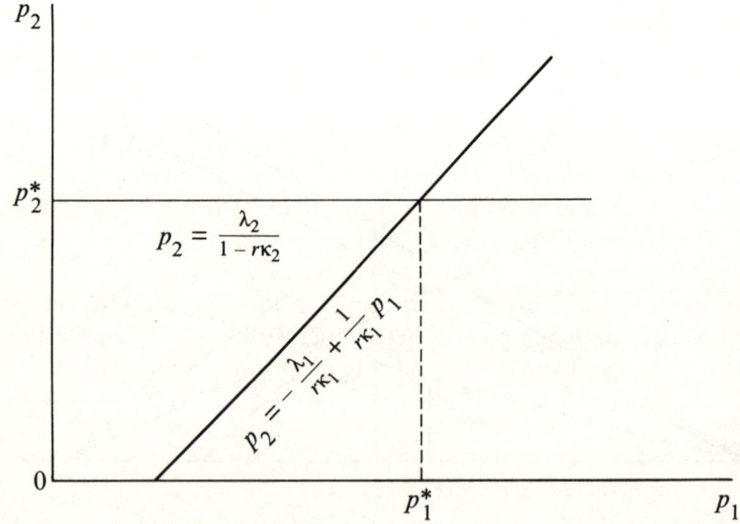

Figure 11.8 Dual constraints

The dual problem now looks as follows:

$$\begin{aligned} &\min \quad p_1 \\ &s.\text{ to} \quad p_2 r\kappa_1 + \lambda_1 = p_1 \\ &\qquad\quad p_2 r\kappa_2 + \lambda_2 = p_2 \end{aligned}$$

Since p_1 does not appear in the second constraint, the solution becomes utterly simple. First, choose a technique for the machine industry that will minimize p_2. That is also intuitively obvious: since machines are produced only by machines (and labour), we have to minimize their labour costs of production thus making more labour available for the basket sector. Second, substitute the minimal p_2 into the first constraint equation and find the cost minimizing technique for the basket sector (Fig. 11.8). A smaller κ_1 rotates the constraint line into a steeper position and reduces p_1. The resulting greater λ_1 translates the line towards right and increases p_1. The optimal combination (λ_1, κ_1) generates the maximal net result of the two movements.

The foregoing procedure may also be restated as follows (note that the format is not the standard one):

$$\begin{aligned} &\text{Primal: max} \quad X_1 &&\text{Dual: min} \quad p_1 \\ &\quad s.\text{ to} \quad TX = Q &&\quad s.\text{ to} \quad WT = p \\ &\qquad\qquad X > 0 &&\qquad\qquad p > 0 \end{aligned} \tag{11.16}$$

where the symbols used are:

$$T = \begin{bmatrix} \lambda_1 & \lambda_2 \\ r\kappa_1 & r\kappa_2 - 1 \end{bmatrix} \quad X = \begin{bmatrix} X_1 \\ X_2 \end{bmatrix}, \quad Q = \begin{bmatrix} \bar{L} \\ 0 \end{bmatrix}, \quad W = [1 \quad p_2], \quad p = [p_1 \quad 0]$$

The technology matrix T represents the book of blueprints and has m columns $(\lambda_1; \kappa_1)$ and n columns $(\lambda_2; \kappa_2)$ from which two optimal columns have to be chosen. Consequently X and p will have $m+n$ elements.

It was shown that the dual solution is easier, because it consists of two independent steps. This property may be used to simplify the primal solution. The minimization of p_2 determines the machine sector technology $(\lambda_2^*, \kappa_2^*)$. That being known and $\bar{L}$ being given, we may use (10.1):

$$X_1 = \frac{1 - r\kappa_2^*}{\lambda_1(1 - r\kappa_2^*) + \lambda_2^* r\kappa_1} \bar{L} \tag{11.17}$$

and find the technique $(\lambda_1^*, r\kappa_1^*)$ which maximizes X_1. If K proves insufficient, the output of X_2 is increased at the expense of X_1 until the proper proportion is reached. If there is surplus output capacity, X_1 is increased at the expense of X_2. In the transition period a different technology may be required. Once proportions are right, $T(\lambda_j^*, r\kappa_j^*)$ maximizes X_1. The economic meaning of the procedure ought to be obvious: minimizing p_2 means minimizing the expenditure of labour time on the production of machines necessary for the replacement of scrapped machines and for the employment of increasing labour force. The less labour is expended on the production of machines, the more is left for the production of baskets. In this sense the minimum p_2 is a condition for the maximum X_1. The decomposable input matrix makes it possible to solve the programme in stages.

The procedure suggested applies when technological change is unembodied or when optimal techniques in the two industries are independent $[(\lambda_1, \kappa_1, n)$ does not depend on the choice of $(\lambda_2, \kappa_2, n)]$. Otherwise minimizing p_2 may mean choosing the smallest or inadequate and not the most productive machine.

Essentially the same approach may be used in a multi-industry economy. First study the machine sector in isolation and minimize the labour value of produced machines. The assortment of the produced machines is irrelevant, because changes in demand do not change prices. In the second step use optimal machine prices to find the basket-sector technology that will minimize prices of consumer goods.

Somewhat differently and more formally we may proceed as follows. In order to define the symbols to be used, consider an economy in which two industries produce consumer goods X_1 and X_2 and the other two industries produce machines X_3 and X_4. When installed, these machines produce two kinds of capital goods, K_1 and K_2, which are the same as X_3 and X_4 and are used to produce any of the four commodities. There are, thus, eight capital coefficients, $\kappa_{ij} = \frac{K_1}{X_j}$, $i = 1,2$, $j = 1,2,3,4$.

The book of blueprints has, of course, more than four techniques. The system of balances is given by:

$$r \begin{bmatrix} 0 & 0 & 0 & 0 \\ 0 & 0 & 0 & 0 \\ \kappa_{11} & \kappa_{12} & \kappa_{13} & \kappa_{14} \\ \kappa_{21} & \kappa_{22} & \kappa_{23} & \kappa_{24} \end{bmatrix} \begin{bmatrix} X_1 \\ X_2 \\ X_3 \\ X_4 \end{bmatrix} + \begin{bmatrix} X_1 \\ X_2 \\ 0 \\ 0 \end{bmatrix} = \begin{bmatrix} X_1 \\ X_2 \\ X_3 \\ X_4 \end{bmatrix}$$

$$rAX + hC = X \tag{11.18}$$

where C is the consumption vector of constant structure and scalar h indicates the level of consumption. Technology matrix:

$$\begin{bmatrix} A \\ \cdots \\ \lambda \end{bmatrix}$$

has several alternative processes (columns) for the production of every commodity. The usual summation of columns evaluated at appropriate prices leads to price equations:

$$rpA + w\lambda = p$$

The programme follows straightforwardly (for a similar approach, see Abraham-Frois and Berrebi, 1988):

$$\begin{array}{llll} \max & 0 \cdot X + \bar{L} \cdot h = h\,\bar{L} & \min & p \cdot 0 + w \cdot \bar{L} = w\bar{L} \\ s.\text{ to} & -(I - rA)X + \bar{C}h \leq 0 & s.\text{ to} & -p(I - rA) + w\lambda \geq 0 \\ & \lambda X = \bar{L} & & p\bar{C} = \bar{L} \\ & X \geq 0 & & p \geq 0 \\ & h > 0 & & w > 0 \end{array} \qquad (11.19)$$

Now the programme has the standard form. Since $\bar{L}$ is fixed, the programme says: maximize the level of consumption and minimize labour costs. For surplus product, prices are zero; for non-profitable activities, production is zero. Evidently, $h > 0$ and that implies equality in the $p\bar{C} = \bar{L}$ constraint.

Similarly, full employment $\lambda X = \bar{L}$ implies positive wages, $w > 0$. Initially, $w > h$. In the optimum $h^* = w^* = 1$ for prices in labour units.

As already stated, $\bar{C}$ has constant structure in the primal. The dual is more flexible in this respect, because prices do not depend on the structure of demand.

It is possible to achieve some simplification if the programme is slightly reformulated. Let the net output column vector be given:

$$\bar{C} = \{\bar{X}_1\ \bar{X}_2\ 0\ 0\}$$

Then simply maximize the *value* of net output (consumption) and minimize its labour input:

$$\begin{array}{ll} \max p\bar{C} & \min \lambda X \\ s.\text{ to } p(I - rA) \leq \lambda & s.\text{ to } (I - rA)X \geq \bar{C} \\ \quad p \geq 0 & \quad X \geq 0 \end{array} \qquad (11.20)$$

The minimization of labour input will generally result in labour different from that available, say less, $\lambda X^* = L^* < \bar{L}$. But we know that L is linearly homogeneous function of C and so if $hL^* = \bar{L}$, all we have to do is expand C by the same factor. Thus, $C^* = h\bar{C}$ is maximum net output that can be produced with available labour L using optimum technology:

$$\begin{bmatrix} A^* \\ \cdots \\ \lambda^* \end{bmatrix}$$

given the rate of gross investment r. Clearly, the value of the programme is $p^*(h\bar{C}) = \lambda(hX^*) = \bar{L}$. The partial derivative of the value of the programme must be equal to the i-th dual variable:

$$\frac{\delta L(C)}{\delta C_i} = p_i$$

In other words, prices are marginal labour costs in producing consumer goods. We also know that these prices are unique since $L(C)$ is differentiable (Bliss, 1973, pp. 365–6).

PART V

EXTENSIONS

12 Joint production

12.1 Stationary economy

Let us now assume that both industries produce both commodities – baskets and machines – as joint products. At the same time the two industries continue to specialize in their original products. Thus each industry produces one main and one subsidiary product. In industry I baskets are the main and machines the subsidiary product and in industry II it is the other way round.

12.1.1 Price equations

It will be convenient to start our analysis by writing down new value balances:

$$\begin{aligned} p_2R_1 + wL_1 &= p_1X_1^1 + p_2X_2^1 \\ p_2R_2 + wL_2 &= p_1X_1^2 + p_2X_2^2 \end{aligned} \tag{12.1}$$

where X_i^j represents product i produced by industry j. X_1^1 and X_2^2 are the main products, X_2^1 and X_1^2 are the subsidiary ones. R_i is replacement investment. Let us define technical coefficients in relation to the main products and add coefficients defining the relations between main and subsidiary products:

$$\begin{aligned} \rho_1^* &= \frac{R_1}{X_1^1}, & \rho_2^* &= \frac{R_2}{X_2^2} < 1 \\ \lambda_1^* &= \frac{L_1}{X_1^1}, & \lambda_2^* &= \frac{L_2}{X_2^2} \\ a &= \frac{X_2^1}{X_1^1}, & b &= \frac{X_1^2}{X_2^2} \end{aligned} \tag{12.2}$$

Since industry II specializes in producing machines, it produces more machines than necessary for its own reproduction, $X_2^2 > R_2$ and consequently $\rho_2^* < 1$. Taking labour as a *numéraire* ($w = 1$) and dividing the first equation by X_1^1 and the second one by X_2^2, we get the following price equations:

$$p_2\rho_1^* + w\lambda_1^* = p_1 + p_2\frac{X_2^1}{X_1^1} = p_1 + p_2 a$$

$$w=1 \qquad (12.3)$$

$$p_2\rho_2^* + w\lambda_2^* = p_1\frac{X_1^2}{X_2^2} + p_2 = p_1 b + p_2$$

Note that λ_1^* and ρ_1^* are no longer labour and replacement coefficients comparable with those of the single product industries since they include also labour and replacement attributable to subsidiary products.

The technology of the system may now be represented as follows:

		Activities at unit levels	
Outputs	X_1	1	b
	X_2	a	1
Inputs	L	$-\lambda_1^*$	$-\lambda_2^*$
	R	$-\rho_1^*$	$-\rho_2^*$

(12.4)

There is also a subtle change in the dimensional characteristics of X_1 and X_2. So far X_1 meant the number of *baskets* and X_2 the number of *machines*. In defining a and b, they become indices of the levels of activities, i.e. *pure* numbers. Activity I will run at the level X_1 and will, of course, produce X_1 baskets (and also aX_1 machines), and activity II will be operated at the level X_2 and produce X_2 machines (and also bX_2 baskets).

A standard activity analysis does not distinguish primary factors from produced factors. For our purpose this distination is vital and so the input matrix will be composed of technical coefficients of produced factors only. The input (A) and output (B) matrices look as follows

$$A = \begin{bmatrix} 0 & 0 \\ \rho_1^* & \rho_2^* \end{bmatrix} \quad B = \begin{bmatrix} 1 & b \\ a & 1 \end{bmatrix}$$

The price system (12.3) may now be written in a compact notation:

$$pA + \lambda^* = pB, \qquad w=1 \qquad (12.3a)$$

The solution of this matrix equation is a row vector of prices:

$$p = \lambda^*(B-A)^{-1} \qquad (12.3b)$$

Since $B \neq \mu I$, ($\mu >$ dominant root), matrix $(B-A)^{-1}$ is not necessarily semipositive and there is no guarantee that all prices will be positive. Alternatively we may write:

$$(B-A)=(I-A^*), \qquad A^*=\begin{bmatrix} 0 & -b \\ \rho_1^*-a & \rho_2^* \end{bmatrix}.$$

As A^* is not semipositive, $A^* \ngeq 0$, there is no guarantee that the solution vector will be positive. This is the standard conclusion concerning joint production. Let us investigate the problem in some more detail.

The two price equations (12.3) determine the two labour prices and their ratio:

$$\begin{aligned} p_1 &= \frac{\lambda_2^*(\rho_1^*-a)+\lambda_1^*(1-\rho_2^*)}{b(\rho_1^*-a)+(1-\rho_2^*)}w \\ p_2 &= \frac{\lambda_2^*-\lambda_1^*b}{b(\rho_1^*-a)+(1-\rho_2^*)}w \\ \frac{p_1}{p_2} &= \frac{\lambda_2^*(\rho_1^*-a)+\lambda_1^*(1-\rho_2^*)}{\lambda_2^*-\lambda_1^*b} \end{aligned} \tag{12.5}$$

Since X_2^1 is a subsidiary product, $X_2^1 < R_1$, and consequently $\rho_1^*-a>0$. If it were the case that $X_2^1 \geq R_1$, the second industry would not be necessary, and the economy would be reduced to one industry. From (12.2), $\rho_2^*<1$ and consequently $(1-\rho_2^*)>0$. Thus the labour price of baskets must be positive, $p_1>0$. As it stands, the price of machines may become negative. For it to be positive in (12.5) it is necessary that $\lambda_2^*>\lambda_1^*b$, i.e.:

$$p_2>0 \text{ if } \frac{L_2}{L_1}>\frac{X_1^2}{X_1^1} \text{ or } \frac{X_1^1}{L_1}>\frac{X_1^2}{L_2} \tag{12.6}$$

the ratio of the number of workers employed in the two industries must be higher than the ratio of outputs of baskets in the two industries. Or, main output per worker in the first industry must be higher than subsidiary output per worker in the second industry. Suppose it was not. Then the machine industry would produce more baskets per worker than the basket industry, while at the same time producing more than necessary for the replacement of old machines, $X_2^2>R_2$. Consequently, net output (production of baskets) would be maximized if all labour were allocated to the second industry. This means that the inferior technology of the first industry would not be used and the entire economy would consist of the second industry only, which would produce a surplus of machines. Barring that degenerate case, both industries will be operating and both prices will be positive. In general, if an economy operates both industries, prices will be positive. Negative prices could appear only if one or the other industry is not operating because that industry uses an inferior technique. This is not likely to occur in practice because specialized industries are more productive and relation coefficients a and b are not rigidly fixed but can vary within certain intervals. The availability of alternative techniques eliminates inferior techniques and makes possible specialization. If condition (12.6) is satisfied in a stationary economy it will always be satisfied in a growing economy because growth implies relative expansion of industry II and, therefore, an increase in the ratio L_2/L_1.

If we are interested in a possible generalization to a multisectoral economy, the conditions for positive prices must be presented in the matrix form.

From (12.3b):

$$(B-A)^{-1}=\frac{1}{(1-\rho_2^*)+(\rho_1^*-a)b}\begin{bmatrix}1-\rho_2^* & -b\\ \rho_1^*-a & 1\end{bmatrix}$$

The multiplicative term is clearly positive, but the adjoint of the matrix (B–A) is not semipositive because of the presence of the term $-b$ (the same as in A'). For that reason also labour coefficients must be examined. The multiplication $\lambda^*=[\lambda_1^*\lambda_2^*]$ and adjoint gives:

$$\lambda_1^*(1-\rho_2^*)+\lambda_2^*\,(\rho_1^*-a)>0 \Rightarrow L_1(1-\rho_2^*)+\lambda_2^*(R_1-X_2^1)>0$$

$$-\lambda_1^*b+\lambda_2^*>0 \qquad\qquad \Rightarrow \frac{L_2}{L_1}>\frac{X_1^2}{X_1^1}$$

The first condition is clearly satisfied which means that the price of the consumer good is always positive. The second condition is equal to (12.6).

Joint production technology is depicted in Fig. 12.1. Two industries are now two processes using technologies α and β to produce the same pair of goods in the quantities A and B given labour resources $\bar{L}$. Rays α and β define a convex polyhedral cone that determines producible combinations of outputs. Given labour $\bar{L}$, any combination of outputs can be produced within the triangle OAB. Technologies α and β are efficient, i.e. no process can produce more of both products, and so the labour constraint line HG is downward sloping.

Suppose the required combination of goods is C, then technology γ represents the linear combination of technologies α and β, $\mu\alpha+(1-\mu)\beta=\gamma$, $0<\mu<1$. Prices and quantities must be positive. The line HG represents also linear combinations of the same vectors, except that μ is not restricted to values below unity. Suppose very little replacement is required, so that even process α produces too many machines. The required proportion is δ, but such a technology does not exist. Formally, D can be reached by

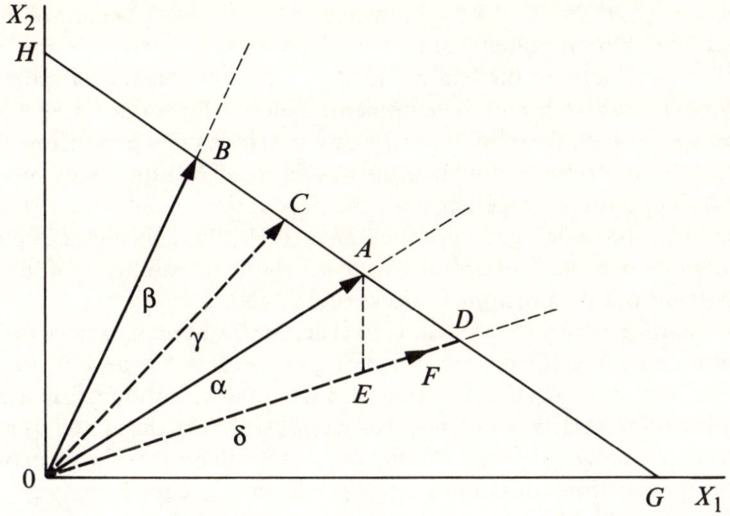

Figure 12.1 Joint production

expanding labour in α ($\mu > 0$) and allocating negative labour to β. This is equivalent to saying that equations (12.1) must be solved by using *both* processes. Since using both processes produces too many machines, the solution will show negative p_2. Negative quantities of labour and negative prices are meaningless. Thus, instead of using equalities we must work with inequalities and use the programming format.

It is immediately obvious that only α (i.e. the process specializing in baskets) will be used, that quantities *E* can be produced and that *EA* machines are superflous. If the unnecessary machines can be freely disposed of, $p_2 = 0$. If the handling of waste incurs costs, an additional process must be added that produces negative machines. That makes sense.

In the case of single product industries, at any time one best combination of processes was operated regardless of demand changes. This constant technology theorem holds no longer in joint-production economy where changes in demand require the use of different technologies. Suppose technology δ existed. It is clearly inferior to α when *C* is demanded but it is superior to α when *F* is demanded. The reason why we do not encounter this problem in an economy with one-product industries lies in the fact that output vectors are represented by coordinate axes and so the cone represents the entire positive quadrant.

With *n* commodities there will be an *n*-dimensional convex polyhedral cone within which output proportions will generate positive prices,

$C=\{b\epsilon B, b\epsilon R^h, BX^*=X, \lambda^*X^*\leq L\}$ where X^* represents vector of main products and the components of each vector b consist of one main and $n-1$ subsidiary products. In the real world any change in demand proportions will stimulate research and development, which will produce a new cone with positive prices. Also, in the real world of n industries producing $m\geq n$ single and joint products, not all industries produce the same assortment of joint products, which, together with the production of substitutes (sheep produce meat and wool, cows produce meat and leather, plastics may partly substitute leather, etc.), enormously increases the possibility of adjusting aggregate output proportions to those of demand.

Note that for $n>m$, the system is overdetermined and competition will eliminate $n-m$ inferior processes making $m=n$. If $m>n$ and $m-n$ products are not wanted (because they are harmful or produced in excess quantities) additional $m-n$ disposal processes will close the model. If $m-n$ products are wanted, $m-n$ additional processes will be introduced in order to adopt proportions of commodities produced to requirements of consumption. In case of a corner solution, the most profitable process may produce commodities in exactly that proportion market demands. Then the number of processes is smaller than the number of commodities but that, of course, is a fluke. Thus, in general, the number of processes and commodities will be equal, $n=m$ (Steedman, 1976; Schefold, 1978).

If subsidiary products are eliminated, the system (12.5) is reduced to (3.6) with $\rho_j=\kappa_j/n$

$$p_1=\lambda_1+\frac{\rho_1\lambda_2}{1-\rho_2}, \qquad a=b=0$$

$$p_2=\frac{\lambda_2}{1-\rho_2}, \qquad b=0 \qquad (12.5a)$$

$$\frac{p_1}{p_2}=\frac{\lambda_1}{\lambda_2}+\frac{\lambda_2\rho_1-\lambda_1\rho_2}{\lambda_2}, \qquad a=b=0$$

It is of some interest to note that the original p_2 of the single product industry system does not change even if the industry I applies a joint-products technology. This asymmetry results from X_2 being a means of production and X_1 net output. Since X_2 is used in industry I while X_1 is not used in industry II the dependence is unilateral and the conditions of production in I do not influence prices in II.

One additional characteristic of the price system (12.3) is also of some interest. It follows immediately from the first and the second equation:

$$\begin{aligned} p_1&=\lambda_1^*+p_2(\rho_1^*-a)>\lambda_1^* \\ p_2&=\lambda_2^*+p_2\rho_2^*=p_1b\gtreqless\lambda_2^* \end{aligned} \qquad (12.7)$$

The price of the basket is always greater than the corresponding labour coefficient. The same cannot be said for the price of the machine, which depends on the difference $(p_2\rho_2^* - p_1 b)$. For $p_2 > \lambda_2^*$, this difference implies:

$$p_2 R_2 > p_1 X_1^2 \text{ and } p_2 X_2^2 > wL_2$$

i.e. value of replacement investment is greater than value of subsidiary output in machine industry, which implies that the value of the main product is greater than the wage bill in the same industry. The condition is satisfied for single-commodity industries because $X_1^2 = 0$. In the case of joint production it depends on the technology used. One should also bear in mind that λ_1^* and λ_2^* do *not* represent direct labour per unit of commodity 1 and 2.

12.1.2 Quantity equations

We shall next consider balances of labour and capital resources:

$$L_1 + L_2 = L$$
$$K_1 + K_2 = K$$

Since machines last n years, we may replace capital stock engaged by capital used, i.e.:

$$R_1 + R_2 = R$$

and total replacement in a stationary state is equal to total output of machines, $R = X_2$. Applying technical coefficients defined in (13.2) we obtain quantity equations:

$$\lambda_1^* X_1^1 + \lambda_2^* X_2^2 = L \qquad (12.8)$$

$$\rho_1^* X_1^1 + \rho_2^* X_2^2 = L \qquad (12.9)$$

to which we must add two technologically determined relations:

$$X_1^1 + bX_2^2 = X_1$$
$$aX_1^1 + X_2^2 = X_2$$

Now we have four equations from which we can determine four unknowns, X_1^1, X_2^2, X_1 and X_2,

$$X_1^1 = \frac{(1-\rho_2^*)L}{\lambda_1^*(1-\rho_2^*)+\lambda_2^*(\rho_1^*-a)}, \qquad X_2^2 = \frac{(\rho_1^*-a)L}{\lambda_1^*(1-\rho_2^*)+\lambda_2^*(\rho_1^*-a)}$$

$$X_1 = \frac{b(\rho_1^*-a)+(1-\rho_2^*)}{\lambda_1^*(1-\rho_2^*)+\lambda_2^*(\rho_1^*-a)}L, \qquad X_2 = \frac{a(1-\rho_2^*)+(\rho_1^*-a)}{\lambda_1^*(1-\rho_2^*)+\lambda_2^*(\rho_1^*-a)}L \qquad (12.10)$$

$$\frac{X_1^1}{X_2^2} = \frac{1-\rho_2^*}{\rho_1^*-a}, \qquad \frac{X_1}{X_2} = \frac{b(\rho_1^*-a)+(1-\rho_2^*)}{\rho_1^*-a\rho_2^*}$$

All quantities are clearly positive when both industries are operating. We also see that:

$$\frac{L}{X_1} = \frac{p_1}{w} = p_1, \qquad w=1 \qquad (12.11)$$

as it should be: p_1 is labour time spent on the production of one unit of net output as in (12.5).

If subsidiary products are not produced, $a=b=0$, (12.10) reduces to (3.4) with $\rho_j = \kappa_j/n$:

$$X_1 = \frac{1-\rho_2}{\lambda_2\rho_1+\lambda_1(1-\rho_2)}L, \qquad a=b=0$$

$$X_2 = \frac{\rho_1}{\lambda_2\rho_1+\lambda_1(1-\rho_2)}L, \qquad a=0 \qquad (12.10a)$$

$$\frac{X_1}{X_2} = \frac{1-\rho_2}{\rho_1}, \qquad a=b=0$$

Again as with prices, commodity X_2 is an exception. But this time the joint output of b is allowed without disturbing the total output of X_2. In other words, subsidiary machines ($a>0$) influence the total output of machines (X_2) but not their price; subsidiary baskets ($b>0$) influence the price of machines (p_2) but not their output. Output and prices of baskets always change when a subsidiary output appears anywhere in the system.

12.1.3 Other effects

At the level of an economy $p_1X_1 = L$ represents living labour and p_2X_2 represents embodied labour. Such a distinction cannot be made in a determinate way at the level of separate industries.

It has already been mentioned that λ_1^* and λ_2^* do not represent direct labour coefficients. Consequently, it is impossible to disaggregate labour values into living and embodied (direct and indirect) labour in a determined way. This is due to the fact that we have only two equations:

$$\begin{aligned}\lambda_1 X_1 + \lambda_2 X_2 &= L \\ \rho_1 X_1 + \rho_2 X_2 &= X_2\end{aligned} \tag{12.13}$$

for the determination of four unknowns, of the coefficients λ_1, λ_2, ρ_1 and ρ_2. It is, of course, always possible to use the available two degrees of freedom in various ways. The most natural procedure is to impose global proportion to individual industries, i.e. to assume that the ratio of indirect and direct labour be equal throughout the economy:

$$\sigma = \frac{p_2 X_2}{p_1 X_1} = \frac{p_2 R}{L} = \frac{p_2 \rho_i X_i}{\lambda_i X_i} = \frac{p_2 \rho_i}{\lambda_i} \tag{12.14}$$

This adds the one missing equation. The two other equations are simply the price equations:

$$\begin{aligned}p_1 &= \lambda_1 + p_2 \rho_1 = \lambda_1 (1 + \sigma) \\ p_2 &= \lambda_2 + p_2 \rho_2 = \lambda_2 (1 + \sigma) \\ p_2 &= \frac{\lambda_2}{1 - \rho_2}\end{aligned} \tag{12.15}$$

and the argument is exactly the same as before, $\frac{1}{1-\rho_2}$ being the sum of an infinite series:

$$\sum_{k=0}^{\infty} \rho_2^{\kappa}$$

Also, price ratios are equal to labour coefficient ratios, $p_1/p_2 = \lambda_1/\lambda_2$.

The ratio $\sigma = \frac{p_2 R}{L}$ is a sort of organic composition of capital, the difference being that $\omega = \frac{p_2 K}{L}$ is the ratio of capital in labour value per unit of labour, while σ is replacement in labour value per unit of labour. Obviously $\omega = n\sigma$. An interesting conclusion follows: while equal organic composition of capital is a serious restriction for single product industries, it is no restriction at all for joint product economies. However, in the latter case it does not apply to industries (which produce joint products) but to products (regardless of the industry in which they are produced).

It is, of course, always possible to have a mixed case: joint products in one industry and one product in the other. In such a case we have two equations with three unknowns. The available degree of freedom may be used to apply the organic composition of the single product industry to the system as a whole and the above conclusion remains valid.

12.2 Expanding economy

It is now a very simple job to describe a uniformly growing economy without technological progress. Since the labour force is growing at the rate g, so is the output of machines. The quantity equations are similar to (5.3):

$$\begin{aligned} \lambda_1^* X_1^1 + \lambda_2^* X_2^2 &= L \\ \kappa_1^* X_1^1 + \kappa_2^* X_2^2 &= K \end{aligned} \qquad (12.16)$$

Since capital is being replaced at the rate $\frac{1}{v}$ and expands at the rate g, the machine industry must deliver $\left(\frac{1}{v}+g\right) K = X_2$ machines. Thus the second equation will have to be multiplied by: $r = \frac{1}{v} + g$:

$$r\kappa_1^* X_1^1 + r\kappa_2^* X_2^2 = X_2 \qquad (12.17)$$

A comparison between (12.16), (12.17) and (12.8) shows that the two systems are formally the same. All we have to do is to replace ρ_i^* by $r\kappa_i^*$ and the solution of the systems follows straightforwardly from (12.10):

$$\begin{aligned} X_1 &= \frac{b(r\kappa_1^* - a) + (1 - r\kappa_2^*)}{\lambda_1^*(1 - r\kappa_2^*) + \lambda_2^*(r\kappa_1^* - a)} L \\ X_2 &= \frac{a(1 - r\kappa_2^*) + (r\kappa_1^* - a)}{\lambda_1^*(1 - r\kappa_2^*) + \lambda_2^*(r\kappa_1^* - a)} L \\ \frac{X_1}{X_2} &= \frac{r(b\kappa_1^* - \kappa_2^*) + (1 - ab)}{r(\kappa_1^* - a\kappa_2^*)} \end{aligned} \qquad (12.18)$$

Price equations represent no difficulty either since the same substitution will do the trick:

$$\begin{aligned} rp_2\kappa_1 + w\lambda_1^* &= p_1 + ap_2 \\ rp_2\kappa_2^* + w\lambda_2^* &= bp_1 + p_2 \end{aligned} \qquad (12.19)$$

$$p_1 = \frac{\lambda_2^*(r\kappa_1^* - a) + \lambda_1^*(1 - r\kappa_2^*)}{b(r\kappa_1^* - a) + (1 - r\kappa_2^*)} w$$

$$p_2 = \frac{\lambda_2^* - \lambda_1^* b}{b(r\kappa_1^* - a) + (1 - r\kappa_2^*)} w \tag{12.20}$$

$$\frac{p_1}{p_2} = \frac{\lambda_2^*(r\kappa_1^* - a) + \lambda_1^*(1 - r\kappa_2^*)}{\lambda_2^* - \lambda_1^* b} = \frac{rm^* + (\lambda_1^* - a\lambda_2^*)}{\lambda_2^* - b\lambda_1^*}, \qquad m^k = \kappa_1^*\lambda_2^* - \kappa_2^*\lambda_1^*$$

Equal pseudo mechanization ($m^* = 0$) does not render price ratio equal to the ratio of labour coefficients ($p_1/p_2 \neq \lambda_1^*/\lambda_2^*$), although it is equal to the ratio of derived labour coefficients of (12.15).

We have also to show that prices and quantities are positive. For that we have to examine the two expressions in brackets. $(r\kappa_1^* - a) > 0$ implies $rK_1 > X_2^1$, which is certainly true because X_2^1 is a subsidiary product and therefore not sufficient to cover the investment needs in its industry. Next, $(1 - r\kappa_2^*) > 0$ implies:

$$r\frac{K_2}{X_2^2} < 1$$

Which is true because $rK_2 < X_2^2$. The third condition, $\lambda_2^* - \lambda_1^* b > 0$, is the same as before.

For $g = 0$, r reduces to $\frac{1}{n}$ and prices and quantities reflect stationary systems (12.5) and (12.10). If subsidiary products are not produced, $a = b = 0$, prices and quantities are those of single product industries in (5.4) and (5.9). In either case for $w = 1$ prices are exact labour time prices and $p_1X_1 = L$.

If (12.19) is transformed into value balances by multiplying the first equation by X_1 and the second one by X_2:

$$\begin{aligned} rp_2K_1 + wL_1 &= p_1X_1^1 + p_2X_2^1 \\ rp_2K_2 + wL_2 &= p_1X_1^2 + p_2X_2^2 \end{aligned} \tag{12.21}$$

it becomes obvious that the exchange between the two industries remains indeterminate. All we know is that wages must buy consumption goods, $w(L_1 + L_2) = p_1(X_1^1 + X_1^2)$, and that rentals must buy machines, $rp_2(K_1 + K_2) = p_2(X_2^1 + X_2^2)$. But that may be done in many different ways. One possibility to close the system is to assume that each industry first covers its own needs and exchanges only the surpluses. In that case industry I will exchange its surplus in baskets for the surplus in machines of industry II:

$$p_1X_1^1 - wL_1 = p_2X_2^2 - rp_2K_2 \tag{12.22a}$$

That, of course, implies the equality of deficits as well:

$$rp_2K_1 - p_2X_2^1 = wL_2 - p_1X_1^2 \tag{12.22b}$$

12.3 The wage curve

The wage curve for joint production has essentially the same characteristics as for single-product industries. The main difference is that, for obvious reasons, it touches the two axes at different points.

From (12.18) we have:

$$\frac{X_1}{L} = \tilde{w} = \frac{r(b\kappa_1^* - \kappa_2^*) + (1 - ab)}{rm^* + (\lambda_1^* - a\lambda_2^*)}, \qquad m^* = \kappa_1^*\lambda_2^* - \kappa_2^*\lambda_1^* \tag{12.23}$$

We cannot find maximum $\tilde{W}$ and R by simply putting $r=0$ and $\tilde{w}-0$ because that would have no economic meaning; even when only one industry is operating it produces both products and so neither $\tilde{w}$ nor r can be zero.

If only machine industry is operating, the quantity equation for labour reduces to:

$$\lambda_2^* X_2^2 = L, \qquad X_1^1 = X_2^1 = 0 \tag{12.24}$$

At the same time per capita output of baskets will be:

$$\tilde{w} = \frac{X_1^2}{L} = \frac{bX_2^2}{L} \tag{12.25}$$

Substituting X_2^2/L from (12.24) we get:

$$\tilde{w} = \frac{b}{\lambda_2^*} \tag{12.26}$$

which is the new abscissa axis.

Similarly when only basket industry is operating, the quantity equation for capital reduces to:

$$\kappa_1^* X_1^1 = K, \; X_2^2 = X_1^2 = 0 \tag{12.27}$$

The rental (investment) rate is:

$$r = \frac{X_2^1}{K} = \frac{aX_1^1}{K} \tag{12.28}$$

Substitution gives:

$$r = \frac{a}{\kappa_1^*} \tag{12.29}$$

which is the new ordinate axis. The curve is shown in Fig. 12.2.

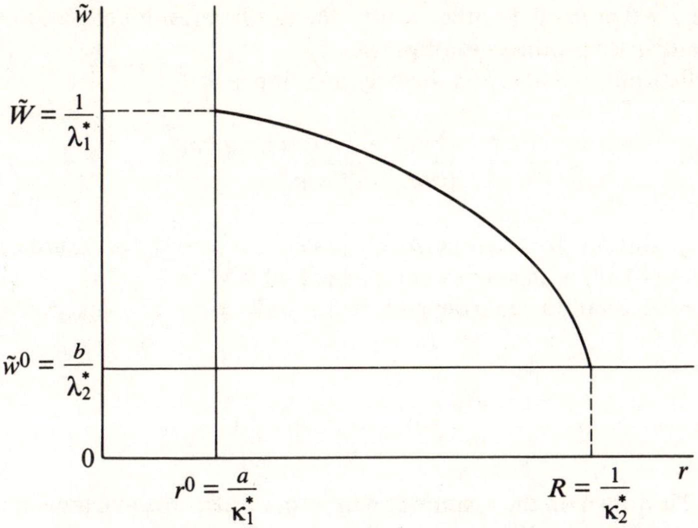

Figure 12.2 The wage curve for joint production in both industries

If $r = \frac{a}{\kappa_1^*}$ is substituted into (12.23), the maximum wage turns out to be $\tilde{W} = \frac{1}{\lambda_1^*}$ and if $\tilde{w} = \frac{b}{\lambda_2^*}$ is substituted, the maximum rental is found to be $R = \frac{1}{\kappa_2^*}$. Both are formally the same as in single product industries but λ_1^* and κ_1^* are no longer single direct technical coefficients since they are calculated with respect to main and not with respect to total products.

Per analogiam with the single-product industries, $m^* = \kappa_1^*\lambda_2^* - \kappa_2^*\lambda_1^*$ may be taken as describing relative mechanization in the two industries. Note that $m^* \neq m$, but $m^* = 0$ when $m = 0$. If the degree of mechanization in both industries is the same, $m^* = 0$, the wage function (12.23) becomes linear, but not so simple as the Sraffa function:

$$r = r^0 R\left(\frac{1-ab}{r^0 - abR} - \frac{\tilde{w}}{\tilde{w}^0 \tilde{W}}\frac{\tilde{w}^0 - ab\tilde{W}}{r^0 - abR}\right) \tag{12.30}$$

$$m^* = \lambda_2^*\kappa_1^* - \lambda_1^*\kappa_2^* = 0,\ \tilde{W} = \frac{1}{\lambda_1^*},\ R = \frac{1}{\kappa_2^*},\ \tilde{w}^0 = \frac{b}{\lambda_2^*},\ r^0 = \frac{a}{\kappa_1^*}$$

If subsidiary products are eliminated, $ab = 0$, the function (12.30) reduces to Sraffian function $r = R\ (1 - \tilde{w}/\tilde{W})$. Note that either a or b may remain positive, $a > 0$ or $b > 0$. In other words, the Sraffian result holds even if one of the industries produces joint products.

The distribution curve has the negative slope:

$$\frac{d\tilde{w}}{dr} = \frac{(b\kappa_1^* - \kappa_2^*)(\lambda_1^* - a\lambda_2^*) - (1-ab)m^*}{[rm^* + (\lambda_1^* - a\lambda_2^*)]^2} < 0$$

if the conditions for non-negative price (12.6) and for non-negative quantities (12.18) of machines are satisfied ($\lambda_2^* > \lambda_1^* b, \kappa_1^* > \kappa_2^* a$). The sign of the second derivation again depends on the index of relative mechanization m^*:

$$\frac{d^2w}{dr^2} \gtreqless 0 \quad \text{if} \quad m^* \lesseqgtr 0$$

Fig. 12.2 is drawn on the assumption $m^* < 0$, i.e. that the machine industry is more mechanized. Clearly, for $m^* = 0$ the distribution curve becomes a straight line.

We easily find that both prices increase if the rental (investment) rate increases and that the price ratio p_2/p_1 increases, decreases or remains constant depending on whether the machine industry is more, less or equally mechanized. The output ratio X_1/X_2 always decreases as the investment rate increases. Thus, all findings for the single product industries, given in Table 6.1, remain in force. If the technical constraint (12.6) is satisfied, joint production economy behaves in the same way as single-product industries.

13 Rent

13.1 Differential and absolute rents

Labour is now no longer the only primary factor; 'land' emerges as another one. The term 'land' may be used to denote all non-reproducible factors. Thus, we have to play with three balls at the same time: with two primary factors and one produced factor.

13.1.1 Extensive and intensive margins of cultivation

If plots of land are of different 'quality' (fertility, location), the same technology applied to different plots will produce different outputs (differential fertility), or will generate different costs (different locations) or both. More generally: different technologies, each of them minimizing costs, will produce different net outputs on different plots of the same size. If not all land is used, the worst plot will generate no rent. Compared with the worst plot, others will produce more output and these productive differentials will be measured by rent. If demand increases (and technology does not change), even less productive plots will be brought to cultivation and intramarginal plots will generate increased rents. The worst plot represents the extensive margin of cultivation. Marx called the corresponding rent Differential Rent I.

In the other analytical case, conditions are reversed: land remains the same but technique changes. Successive doses of capital and labour applied to the same plot of land will generate decreasing returns. Increased demand will push prices upwards and will be met by introducing a hitherto inferior technique capable of increasing *yields per acre* at *higher unit costs*. This higher cost technique marks the intensive margin of cultivation and the rent generated by the original technique is Marx's Differential Rent II.

13.1.2 Orders of rentability

The ranking of land in terms of 'quality' is not uniquely determined by natural conditions. It may change if economic conditions change. The price of land is equal to rent capitalized at the ruling interest rate.

$$p_2 = \frac{V}{\pi}$$

If demand increases, rents (v_i) will increase unequally and if interest rate (π) changes, different techniques will be chosen again changing rents. The former case is depicted in Fig. 13.1 adapted from Ziercke (1988).

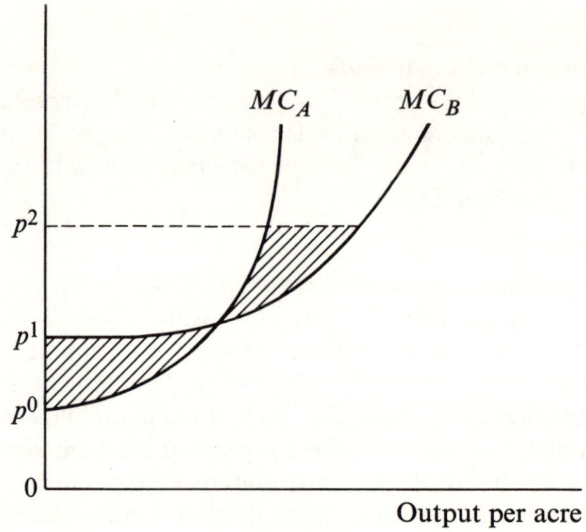

Figure 13.1 Changing order of rents

A and *B* are two plots of land and *A* is more fertile. For a while the returns are constant, but eventually become diminishing (e.g. marginal costs are rising). If the price rises above p^0, *A* will begin to generate rent, which is represented by the area between marginal cost curve and the price line. At $p = p^1$, inferior plot *B* is brought under cultivation. At first it generates no rent. If marginal cost curves of the two plots cross, as they do in Fig. 14.1, *B* will generate greater rent than *A* for all prices greater then p^2, and so the order of rentability is reversed.

Similarly the order of profitability may be reversed depending on the interest rate. Consider a number of different plots of land cultivated by means of the same technique. Profit net of interest will be different on each plot and so plots may be arranged in order of profitability. A change in interest rate will change the profits differently and so the order of profitability will be changed as well. The situation is similar to *w–r* relationship with different plots playing the role of different technologies while at the 'switch points' (which may be multiple) one plot is replaced by another as the most profitable. Instead of being related to capital of equal size, which produces the order of profitability, net profits may be related to land of equal size thus ordering plots in terms of rentability. Again, changes in the interest rate will change that order. Finally, different interest rates may induce the application of different minimum cost techniques and the order of profitability/rentability will change again.

In conclusion, there is no single, 'natural', way of ordering different plots of land.

13.1.3 Private and social regimes of land ownership

Consider the successive introduction of more productive more costly techniques, *a*, *b*, *c*, etc. into cultivation of *homogeneous* land. The book of blueprints does not change (no technological progress). Under these circumstances two resource allocations are possible, one inefficient and the other efficient. If land is privately owned, landowners will insist on preserving their rent and no amount of competition will make possible the introduction of technique *b* before it generates the same rent as technique *a*. Yet, it is clearly socially desirable that a more costly technique *b* be introduced as soon as the price covers its costs with no surplus left for rent. The difference is the rent that is exclusively due to the private ownership of land and so conceptually (but not otherwise) corresponds to Marx's Absolute Rent.[1]

The process is depicted in Fig. 13.2 which, with necessary adaptation, I borrow from H. Kurz (1978). For simplicity, I now assume that the techniques have fixed coefficients.

$\mathscr{R}_a$, $\mathscr{R}_b$, etc. are rent lines representing total amounts of rent generated by techniques *a*, *b*, etc. over the entire area as demand and, consequently, price increase. A more costly technique produces higher output per acre – otherwise it would not be introduced – and so its rent line must be steeper than the one of a cheaper technique that starts at lower prices. When the price reaches the level $p=a$, technique *a* is introduced. Under *social* ownership technique *b* is introduced at $p=b$. At that price, technique *a* generates differential rent $\mathscr{R}=b'$. As demand increases, technique *b* gradually replaces technique *a* over the entire land area, product price remains unchanged and total rent decreases. When *a* is completely displaced, differential rent disappears and from this point onwards further increase in demand generates price increase and the emergence and gradual increase of new rent. At $p=c$, the new rent reaches its peak, which happens to be lower than the former peak, $\mathscr{R}(c)<\mathscr{R}(b)$. At this point it becomes profitable to introduce technique *c*, which starts a new round. At $p=d$, rent reaches a new peak, which happens to be the same as the first one, $\mathscr{R}(d)=\mathscr{R}(b)$.

Under *private* ownership, production is inefficiently organized. Technique *b* cannot be introduced at $p=b$ because at that point it cannot cover

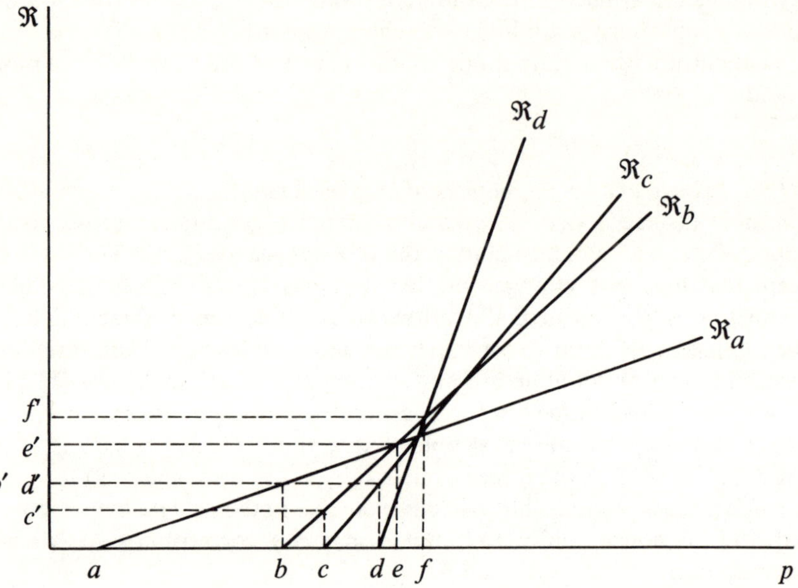

Figure 13.2 Differential rent II as dependent on techniques and product prices under social and private ownership regimes

the already established $\mathscr{R}=b'$. That will be possible only at a higher price $p=e$, and as a consequence rent will have risen in the meantime to $\mathscr{R}=e'$. When *b* has spread over the entire area, differential rent will disappear, but absolute rent will remain and will increase with each new round. Technique *c*, although *less costly* than technique *d*, will *never* be introduced because it is not sufficiently rent efficient. Technique *d* will not be introduced at $p=d$ but at $p=f$ and that will further inflate rent to $\mathscr{R}=f'$. In short, while under social ownership rent oscillates between zero and some point b' and new more intensive techniques are introduced as soon as they become profitable, under private ownership of land the introduction of new techniques is delayed until both profit and already established rent are covered. As a result, rent increases all the time and prices are always higher. That is shown in Fig. 13.3 where rent is portrayed as a function of demand.

At a'' demand generates sufficiently high prices to make the cultivation profitable. Technique *a* is introduced. At that level of demand not all area is

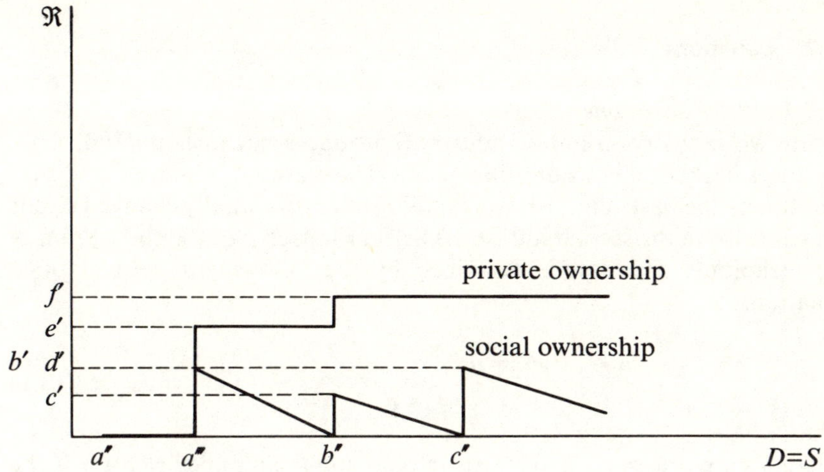

Figure 13.3 Differential rent II as a function of demand = supply equilibria under social and private ownership regimes

cultivated and so for a while supply can follow demand at unchanged price and zero rent. At $D=a'''$ all land is cultivated, supply can no longer increase and unsatisfied demand generates increases in price. Under *social* ownership at the rent level $\mathcal{R}=b'$, more productive (and more costly) technique *b* is introduced. As it gradually replaces technique *a*, supply increases at unchanged prices and falling total rent. At $D=b''$ all land is cultivated by technique *b*, rent is reduced to zero, supply cannot be increased until increased price makes possible the introduction of technique *c*. And so on. Under *private* ownership rent must increase to $\mathcal{R}=e'$ before technique *b* can be introduced. Since at that level of demand both *a* and *b* generate the same rent, the replacement of *a* by *b* does not change prices. At $S=c$ supply possibilities are exhausted and the more productive technique *d* can be introduced only at the rent level $\mathcal{R}=f'$.

As already noted, 'social' rent oscillates between zero and some point $\mathcal{R}=b'$ and new more productive techniques are introduced as soon as they become profitable. Under private ownership the introduction of new techniques is delayed until both profit and already established rent are covered. As a result, supply is always smaller, prices are higher and rent increases all the time. The difference between 'social' and 'private' rent is Absolute Rent, which may be taken as a measure of inefficiency of the regime of private land ownership.

13.2 Equations

13.2.1 Price equations

In our two-industry economy Industry II produces machines and Industry I produces baskets of consumption goods. There are k qualities of land that are used by the basket industry only. (Nothing is essentially changed if rent appears also in the second industry.) Select for each plot the cost minimizing technique. The case is described by the following system of price equations:[2]

$$\begin{aligned} &p_2 r\kappa_2 + w\lambda_2 = p_2 \\ &p_2 r\kappa_1^{(i)} + w\lambda_1^{(i)} + \mathrm{v}_i\zeta_i = p_1, \qquad i=1,\dots k \end{aligned} \tag{13.1}$$

where p's are prices, κ's and λ's are capital and labour coefficients, r is the capital rental rate, v's are unit rents and ζ's are land input coefficients (acreage per basket). Observe that $\mathrm{v}_i = gp_3^{(i)}$ is rent per acre of land of type i, p_3 is the price of that land and g is the rate of growth of economy with no technological progress; g plays the role of interest rate. $T_i = T_i(\kappa_1^{(i)}\lambda_1^{(i)})$ is the cost minimizing technique applied to the ith plot of land. Since we are here examining the *extensive* margin of cultivation, the worst plot bears no rent. Suppose that this is the plot number one and so:

$$\mathrm{v}_1 = 0, \qquad \mathrm{v}_i > 0, \qquad i=2,\dots k \tag{13.1a}$$

The system is now closed: the first two equations determine prices of the two products and the last $k-1$ equations determine that many rents (i.e. that many prices of land). Prices of products are labour prices determined at the extensive margin of cultivation. Rents (and, consequently, prices of land) depend on the quality of land *and* the price of product as well as on the interest rate g. If p and g change, the ranking of rent generating lands may change.

Consider now the *intensive* margin of cultivation. The quality of land is uniform but the demand for baskets surpasses the supply and part of land must be more intensively cultivated. At any time there can be only two different techniques applied (unless two techniques just happen to produce the same output at the same cost): the original technique a, which produces less at lower unit cost, and the new technique b, which produces more at higher unit cost. As the demand increases, technique b will gradually replace technique a until eventually only b will be used and Differential Rent II will be wiped out. Further increase in demand will initiate a new cycle with the introduction of a still more intensive technique c.

The intensive margin of cultivation may also be described by system (13.1) taking into account that land is homogeneous and that two different techniques, say *a* and *b*, are necessary to determine the rent in the production of one product.

Under *private* ownership the group of rent equations reduces to

$$\begin{aligned} p_2 r\kappa_1^a + w\lambda_1^a + v\zeta_1^a &= p_1 \\ p_2 r\kappa_1^b + w\lambda_1^b + v\zeta_1^b &= p_1 \end{aligned} \qquad (13.1b)$$

Price of equipment (p_2) is determined by the first equation of (13.1). Price of consumer good (p_1) is determined by demand in (13.1.b), supply being fixed by application of technique *a*. The only remaining unknown is rent v. Further increase in demand in an economy with *private* land ownership increases price up to the level where it covers the established rent and the greater costs (per unit of output) of the more productive technique *b*. At that moment *b* will be introduced and further increase in demand will be covered by gradual replacement of *a* by *b* on the entire land area at unchanged price.

Under *social* ownership the rent equations are:

$$\begin{aligned} p_2 r\kappa_1^a + w\lambda_1^a + v\zeta^a &= p_1 \\ p_2 r\kappa_1^b + w\lambda_1^b &= p_1 \end{aligned} \qquad (13.1c)$$

Quantities supplied are determined by technology *a* and are fixed. Increased demand generates increases in price and rent. Technique *b* is introduced as soon as the price covers costs and at that price *b* gradually replaces *a* until the rent is wiped out. At any time only one technique generates rent except when supply just matches demand and there is no rent. Note that market forces by themselves will not achieve this result since the same homogeneous land must at the same time generate positive and zero rent and the land must be cultivated by two techniques in proportions that will enable full employment of labour.

If there is more than one land-using industry, land will have to be distributed among them in such a way as to *minimize* total rent (production costs being kept at minimum by the competition among firms). If rent were higher than minimum, that would mean that demand for a certain consumer good could have been satisfied but was not. There will be as many equations as there are industries plus possibly an additional equation for an alternative technique for the industry that happened to determine rent. As excess demand develops in various markets, more intensive high-cost high-yield techniques will gradually spread over the area until rent is wiped out.

After that, a rise in prices in one of the markets may temporarily generate new rent and so initiate a new round of intensification of production.

The introduction of joint products would not change the foregoing analysis except that prices would be determined in a more complicated fashion. More than two joint products would require additional equations for all prices to be determined. Also, the specific condition for the non-negativity of prices would have to be observed. Since in neither case is the determination of rents affected, we may stay with the simpler case of one-product industries. In that case cultivation at the extensive margin implied production of the same commodity at several plots of different qualities. Cultivation at the intensive margin implied production of the same commodity on homogeneous land by pairs of specifically different techniques (higher production associated with higher unit costs).

13.2.2 Quantity equations

It is, as always, helpful to consider the dual aspect of the problem. Price equations (13.1) are then complemented by quantity equations:

$$\begin{aligned} \lambda_1 X_1 + \lambda_2 X_2 &= L \\ r\kappa_1 X_1 + r\kappa_2 X_2 &= rK = X_2 \\ \zeta_1 X_1 + \zeta_2 X_2 &= Z \end{aligned} \tag{13.2}$$

In (13.1) land was used only in the first industry and so $\zeta_2 = 0$. The system is clearly overdetermined. If *only one* technology were available, either some land or some labour would be left unemployed in a general case. Thus, we use a third process using an alternative technique in one of the industries.

The alternative technique may be applied either in the industry using land or in the other industry. The first procedure was suggested by P. Sraffa and was discussed above. It implies shifting the intensive margin with transitory (social ownership) or permanent (private ownership) rent. The second procedure was suggested by J.E. Woods (1987) as an alternative to Sraffa's approach. Yet, his algebra apparently prevented him seeing the economic implications. The case is sufficiently interesting to merit brief discussion.

Sraffa's case So far we have been concerned with the full use of land. What happened to the employment of labour was not considered, and the analysis was of the partial equilibrium type. Now we consider what happens in general equilibrium when X_1 represents net product to be maximized.

In order to avoid overdetermination of the system, we introduce an additional variable by adding an alternative process:

$$\lambda_1^a X_1^a + \lambda_1^b X_1^b + \lambda_2 X_2 = L$$
$$r\kappa_1^a X_1^a + r\kappa_1^b X_1^b + r\kappa_2 X_2 = X_2 \qquad (13.3)$$
$$\zeta_1^a X_1^a + \zeta_1^b X_1^b = Z$$

As long as land is not scarce, the land equation is not necessary and the more cost efficient technique *a* is used. When all land is brought under cultivation and the number of workers continues to increase, additional workers will be employed by the use of more costly and more productive technique *b*. Thus, at any time all land will be used (after it has become scarce for the first time) and all labour will be employed. The system of equations (13.3) determines the output of two composite goods and the distribution of land between the two regimes of cultivation for any given number of workers (L). Analogous results are obtained if in (13.3) land and alternative techniques are used in the machine industry. Only in the case no alternative technique *b* existed, additional workers would remain unemployed, but such a possibility does not look realistic in the modern economy.

Woods's case Take the simplest possible case when land is used either (a) in the second or (b) in the first industry. By assumption two alternative techniques are available, (a) in the first or (b) in the second industry. Whenever two techniques are available, resources must somehow be distributed between two processes producing the same commodity. The following two sets of balance equations emerge:

$$\lambda_1^a X_1^a + \lambda_1^b X_1^b + \lambda_2 X_2 = L$$
$$r\kappa_1^a X_1^a + r\kappa_1^b X_1^b + r\kappa_2 X_2 = X_2 \qquad (13.3a)$$
$$\zeta_2 X_2 = Z$$

$$\lambda_1 X_1 + \lambda_2^a X_2^a + \lambda_2^b X_2^b = L$$
$$r\kappa_1 X_1 + r\kappa_2^a X_2^a + r\kappa_2^b X_2^b = X_2^a + X_2^b \qquad (13.3b)$$
$$\zeta_1 X_1 = Z$$

There are three equations and three variables, where *a* and *b* stand for the two techniques used in the same industry. The techniques are efficient, i.e. none is dominating in the sense that none of them produces more of both commodities because otherwise the less efficient technique would never be used. In order for all outputs to be positive, the solution vector must lie in the cone generated by the output vectors (depending on L but neglecting Z) of the two technologies, α (consisting of technique *a* and the other industry technique) and β (technique *b* and the other industry).

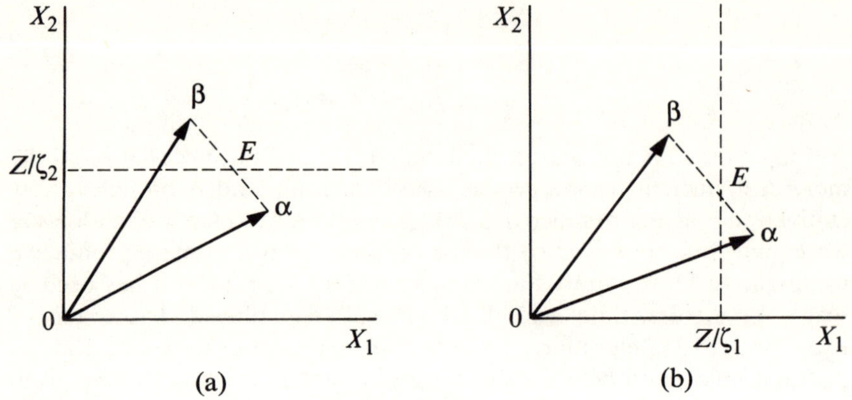

Figure 13.4 Production with limited labour and land

In Fig. 13.4a technology α leaves land not fully used, while technology β hits the land limit before labour is fully employed, which causes unemployment. In Fig. 13.4b the situation is reversed. At *E*, which is a convex combination of outputs generated by technologies α and β, both land and labour are fully used.

The model has some odd features such as real wage (in terms of machines) being an *increasing* function of the rental rate, $d\tilde{w}/dr > 0$. At *E* there is no rent. The appearance of a positive or a negative rent indicates that either labour or land is not fully used. But the main point is that *E* does not represent equilibrium. In both cases technology α produces higher net output X_1 although either land (in (a)) or labour (in (b)) is not fully employed. Technology β will never be used. Thus, Woods' solution, when all three resources are fully used, implies *disguised unemployment* of one of the resources at the cost of a smaller net output. While in Sraffa's case (alternative techniques in the land using industry) both primary resources are fully used, in the two Woods's cases (alternative technique in the non-land using industry) either land or labour must be left partly unemployed.

13.3 Distribution surface

Since rent is a demand (distribution) and not a supply (cost) phenomenon, a three-dimensional wage surface with dual properties does not make sense. While $\tilde{w} = c$, and $r = i$, there is no production counterpart for real rent $\tilde{v}$. But a distribution surface, with fixed quantities of commodities produced, may be a useful analytical construct.

Consider the case in which two different techniques are used to produce two different commodities on rent-bearing lands of equal quality.[3] Equal quality is an economic description of the fact that rent per acre is the same. In this case both basket and machine industry use land and pay rent:

$$\begin{aligned} p_2 r\kappa_1 + w\lambda_1 + v\zeta_1 &= p_1 \\ p_2 r\kappa_2 + w\lambda_2 + v\zeta_2 &= p_2 \end{aligned} \tag{13.4}$$

where $\zeta_i = Z_i/X_i$ and Z_i represents the land area occupied by industry i. Solving the equations, we obtain prices and their ratios:

$$\begin{aligned} p_1 &= w\left(\lambda_1 + \frac{r\kappa_1}{1-r\kappa_2}\lambda_2\right) + v\left(\zeta_1 + \frac{r\kappa_1}{1-r\kappa_2}\zeta_2\right) \\ p_2 &= \frac{w\lambda_2}{1-r\kappa_2} + \frac{v\zeta_2}{1-r\kappa_2} \end{aligned} \tag{13.5}$$

$$\frac{p_1}{p_2} = \frac{w[\lambda_1 + r(\kappa_1\lambda_2 - \kappa_2\lambda_1)] + v[\zeta_1 + r(\kappa_1\zeta_2 - \kappa_2\zeta_1)]}{w\lambda_2 + v\zeta_2} \tag{13.6}$$

As machines continue to be inputs in both industries, while baskets are not inputs, p_2 is determined by the second equation only, while p_1 depends on both equations. The introduction of rent adds fully symmetrical terms to both price equations, which reflects the fact that land appears as a primary factor symmetrical to labour. Also, an increase in land intensity of a commodity as measured by output (ζ_i) increases the relative price of that commodity:

$$\frac{\delta(p_i/p_j)}{\delta\zeta_i} > 0$$

For $v=0$, the two expressions are reduced to (10.2) determining labour prices.

Equal mechanization of the two industries, $\kappa_1\lambda_2 = \kappa_2\lambda_1$, is no longer sufficient to make the price ratio equal to the ratio of direct labour coefficients. Even the addition of an analogous equal mechanization with respect to land, $\kappa_1\zeta_2 = \kappa_2\zeta_1$, will not do. However, if we impose these two conditions on the expression for p_1, we obtain a linear relation between real wage, rental rate and real rent:

$$r\kappa_2 + \tilde{w}\lambda_1 + \tilde{v}\zeta_1 = 1, \quad p_1 = 1 \tag{13.7}$$

Moreover, if the extreme values for the variables in (13.5)

$$\begin{aligned} \tilde{W} &= \frac{1}{\lambda_1}, & r = \tilde{v} = 0 \\ R &= \frac{1}{\kappa_2}, & \tilde{w} = \tilde{v} = 0 \\ \tilde{V} &= \frac{1}{\zeta_1}, & \tilde{w} = r = 0 \end{aligned} \tag{13.8}$$

are substituted into (13.7), the three-factor version of Sraffa's equation emerges:

$$r = R\left(1 - \frac{\tilde{w}}{\tilde{W}} - \frac{\tilde{v}}{\tilde{V}}\right) \tag{13.9}$$

Divide (13.3) through p_1 so as to obtain real wage (w) and real rent (v) in terms of baskets, and rearrange:

$$\tilde{w} = \frac{1 - r\kappa_2}{\lambda_1 + rm} - \frac{\zeta_1 + rm^k}{\lambda_1 + rm}\tilde{v}, \quad m = \kappa_1\lambda_2 - \kappa_2\lambda_1, \quad m^* = \kappa_1\zeta_2 - \kappa_2\zeta_1 \tag{13.10}$$

For $\tilde{v} = 0$, (13.10) reduces to the wage curve (10.11). For $m = m^* = 0$, $\tilde{w}(r, \tilde{v})$ becomes a plane. The distribution surface $\tilde{w}\ (r, \tilde{v})$ is clearly a declining function of $\tilde{v}$ because both the numerator and the denominator of the fraction associated with $\tilde{v}$ must be positive due to $r < \frac{1}{\kappa_2}$.

Putting always the third variable equal to zero in (13.10), three partial relationships – three planes of a box, $\tilde{w}(r)$, $\tilde{w}(\mathrm{v})$ and $\tilde{v}(\mathrm{r})$ – may be analysed. The three functions are shown in Fig. 13.5, which is adapted from Metcalfe and Steedman (1972).

It is assumed that the machine industry does not change the technique and therefrom the common R. The values of extreme points are given in (13.8). The projection in the first quadrant ($\tilde{v} = 0$) is the familiar wage curve. It is assumed that basket industry is more mechanized than the other industry when technology α is in use and less mechanized in the case of β technology. The price equations (13.4) indicate that rent plays mathematically the same role as wage and so the projection in the fourth quadrant ($\tilde{w} = 0$) may be similarly interpreted with the ratio K/Z replacing K/L. The third partial relationship ($r = 0$), projected in the second quadrant, is linear

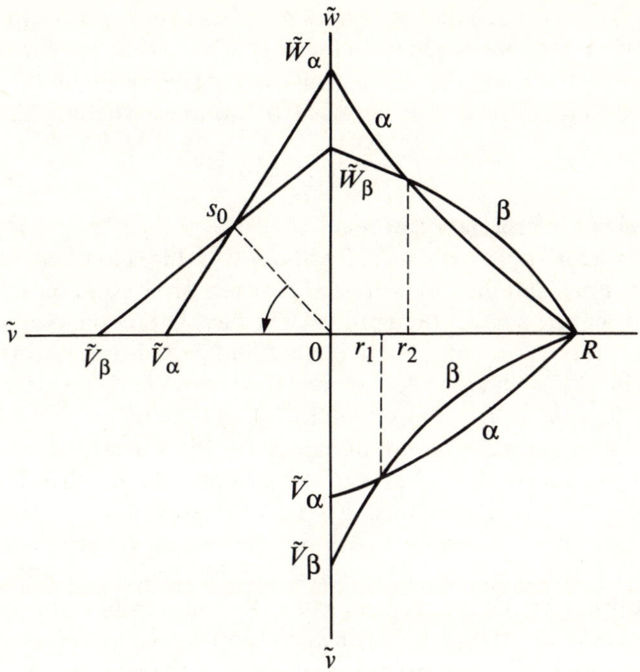

Figure 13.5 Projections of the distribution surface

as it follows from (13.10). From (13.8), $\tilde{V}=1/\zeta_1$, $\tilde{W}=1/\lambda_1$, and so the slopes of the lines are given by $\tilde{V}/\tilde{W}=\lambda_1/\zeta_1=L_1/Z_1=1/z_1$. Since machine industry technique does not change, it is obvious that technology α is more land intensive than β, $z^\alpha > z^\beta$.

For a small r, technology α generates higher real wage (for $\tilde{v}=0$), but higher real rent is produced by technology β (for $\tilde{w}=0$). Denote the rent–wage ratio as $s=\tilde{v}/\tilde{w}$. Then the former case implies $s=0$, the latter $s=\infty$, and somewhere in between there will be a switch point where both technologies generate equal $\tilde{w}$, $\tilde{v}$ and r. For $r=0$, the switch point occurs for the rent–wage ratio $s=s_0$: as the rent–wage ratio increases from $s<s^0$ to $s>s^0$, economy switches from the more land-intensive technology α to less land-intensive technology β. The same switches occur in the entire interval $0\leq r<r_1$ as a function of s. In the next interval $r_1<r<r_2$ only α is used as s changes from $s=0$ ($\tilde{v}=0$) to $s=\infty$ ($\tilde{w}=0$). In the last interval $r_2<r<R$, there is a 'wrong' switch from β to α.

As we saw earlier (section 11.3), our model with one capital good (in the absence of rent) generates a neoclassical switch at r_2 from more capital-intensive technology α to a less capital-intensive β as the rate of interest increases. By contrast, it also generates switches in either direction of land intensity when the rent–wage ratio increases. Note that the perverse land intensity switch caused by increasing rent–wage ratio in the interval $r_2<r<R$ occurs without the presence of double switching in the $\tilde{w}$–r quadrant.

13.4 A labour interpretation of rent

In a modern economy wages make for about two thirds to three quarters of national income, and the rest is divided between profits and rent, the latter being several times smaller than profits. The fact that rent makes for only a small part – about 2% – of GNP in industrialized countries justifies the use of models in which land is neglected and labour represents the only primary factor. At least as a first approximation. Land complicates the analysis; nevertheless, as shown above, rent caused by the scarcity of land can be consistently included in the theory of price formation. As already Ricardo knew, prices will be determined by the processes at the extensive and intensive margin of cultivation. With no rent included, such prices will be labour prices. It remains to derive some implications.

The fact that prices are determined at the margin has one important consequence. Without rent, by setting $w=1$, prices become *absolute* labour time prices and the value of net output is equal to the labour time currently expended, $p_1X_1=L$. That is generally no longer true; one does not imply the other. Prices, being determined by marginal processes with no rent, are still *relative* labour prices, but $p_1X_1=L$ must be imposed as a matter of definition of net output in order to derive the appropriate value of w. Consider value balances corresponding to price equations (13.1):

$$\begin{aligned} &p_2rK_2+wL_2=p_2X_2 \\ &p_2rK_1+wL_1+\Sigma v_iZ_i=p_1X_1, \quad v_1=0, \quad v_i\geq 0, \quad i\geq 2 \end{aligned} \tag{13.11}$$

where $K_1=\Sigma K_1^{(i)}$ and $L_1=\Sigma L_1^{(i)}$ represent capital and labour applied to all k qualities of land. The price of baskets, being determined by the worst land cultivated, contains more labour than necessary on the average, $p_1X_1>L$.

Since $rp_2(K_1+K_2)=p_2X_2$, the exchange condition for the two sectors is:

$$rp_2K_1=wL_2$$

and the first value balance reads:

$$rp_2K_1+wL_1+\Sigma v_iZ_i=w(L_1+L_2)+\Sigma v_iZ_i=p_1X_1 \tag{13.12}$$

For $w=1$, $\Sigma v_i Z_i = p_1 X_1 - L$. Rent represents the difference between the value of net output (evaluated at labour prices generated by the cultivation of the worst land and the most intensive technology) and labour time available and used.

If the value of net output is to be made equal to L, w and other prices must be multiplied by a factor $q<1$,

$$q(wL + \Sigma v_i Z_i) = qp_i X_i = L$$

$$q = \frac{L}{L + \Sigma v_i Z_i}, \qquad w=1 \tag{13.13}$$

If the price of labour is equal to $w=q$, absolute prices will be $p_1^* = qp_1$ and $p_2^* = qp_2$. Consequently, by (13.11) rents will be reduced to $v_1^* = qv_i$ and net output product is equal to labour time. With no rents ($v_i = 0$), $q=1$.

If absolute labour prices are used to evaluate the output at the worst plot (most costly technology), the value of net output of the economy will be higher than labour time currently spent, $p_1 X_1 > L$. But absolute prices are of no particular interest. The allocation of resources is determined by relative prices. If an appropriate multiplier is applied, $q<1$, relative prices are preserved and the required identity of net product and labour time, $p_1 X_1 = L$, will hold as well.

Total rent, $\mathcal{R} = \Sigma v_i Z_i = p_1 X_1 - L$, represents labour time saved because of the cultivation of better qualities of land. Arithmetically – though not institutionally – a symmetric statement is also possible. Suppose prices are determined by the best land, which bears no rent. The cultivation of all other qualities of land is carried out under increasing costs, which may be considered as negative rents. Consequently, $-\Sigma v_i Z_i = L - p_1 X_1$ is labour time lost due to the scarcity of good land.

Analytically, rents must be added to wages in order to exhaust the value of net product. Institutionally they are, of course, an ideal source of taxes.

PART VI

GENERALIZATIONS

14 Many consumer goods

14.1 Constant technology

14.1.1 Quantity equations

Let the economy produce two consumer goods (X_1, X_2) and one producer good (X_3). Labour is expanding (contracting) at a constant rate g. Consequently, with unchanged life-span of machines (n), the replacement rate is also constant, $\delta=\delta(g)$. The quantity equations are as follows:

$$\lambda_1X_1+\lambda_2X_2+\lambda_3X_3=L$$
$$r\kappa_1X_1+r\kappa_2X_2+r\kappa_3X_3=rK=X_3 \qquad r=\delta+g \tag{14.1}$$

With three variables and only two equations, there is one degree of freedom. Set $X_1=1$ so that all variables are expressed as ratios $\left(\frac{X_2}{X_1}, \frac{X_3}{X_1}\right.$ and also $\left.\tilde{L}=\frac{L}{X_1}\right)$:

$$\frac{X_2}{X_1}=\frac{(1-r\kappa_3)\tilde{L}}{\lambda_2+rm_2}-\frac{\lambda_1+rm_1}{\lambda_2+rm_2} \qquad m_1=\kappa_1\lambda_3-\kappa_3\lambda_1$$
$$m_2=\kappa_2\lambda_3-\kappa_3\lambda_2 \tag{14.2}$$
$$\frac{X_3}{X_1}=\frac{r\kappa_2\tilde{L}}{\lambda_2+rm_2}+\frac{rm_3}{\lambda_2+rm_2} \qquad m_3=\kappa_1\lambda_2-\kappa_2\lambda_1$$

The first terms on the right-hand side are the same (except for $\tilde{L}=L/X_1$) to (10.1). With three industries, there are three mechanization possibilities (m_1, m_2, m_3) and they all appear in the second terms. Note that ratios are technologically determined except for the element $\tilde{L}=L/X_1$. If X_1 increases, given labour force, $\tilde{L}$ decreases and so do X_2/X_1 and X_3/X_1; the composition of demand may change even if the stock of machines expands at the constant gross rate r. Since the proportion X_2/X_1 is a decreasing function of X_1, the composition of supply of consumer goods may be adjusted to accommodate any structure of demand. Changes in demand do *not* require any change in technology. We shall assume, however, that consumer preferences are a function of exclusively per capita income. Without technological progress, per capita income does not change and so the structure of demand remains unchanged. This renders $\tilde{L}=L/X_1$ and all other ratios unchanged and the system is fully determined.

In general, with n consumer goods and one machine, there will be $n-1$ degrees of freedom in the system and they may be used to match the changing demand. If the structure of demand remains unchanged, all supply ratios X_i/X_j remain unchanged as well and absolute outputs X_i are fully determined by the technology used and the size of the labour force L.

Now, if the structure of consumption does not change, we can always define a composite consumer good B whose price is p_B and so for n consumer goods:

$$\sum_{i=1}^{n} p_i X_i = p_B B = L$$

B is of course, the output of our standard baskets in the two-industry case. Thus, n consumer goods under uniform growth do not change the initial model in any substantial way.

14.1.2 Price equations

Unlike the asymmetry in the quantity equations, there are as many price equations as there are prices and so prices are always fully determined and do not change whatever happens to the proportions in which quantities are produced (demanded). That, of course, follows from the Constant Technology Theorem:

$$\begin{aligned} rp_3\kappa_1 + \lambda_1 &= p_1 \\ rp_3\kappa_2 + \lambda_2 &= p_2 \qquad w=1 \\ rp_3\kappa_3 + \lambda_3 &= p_3 \end{aligned} \tag{14.3}$$

As there is only one machine industry, the price of machine (p_3) is determined exclusively by the technology of its own industry. The other two prices are now functions of two relative degrees of mechanization:

$$\begin{aligned} p_1 &= \frac{\lambda_1 + rm_1}{1 - r\kappa_3} \qquad m_1 = \kappa_1\lambda_3 - \kappa_3\lambda_1 \\ p_2 &= \frac{\lambda_2 + rm_2}{1 - r\kappa_3} \qquad m_2 = \kappa_2\lambda_3 - \kappa_3\lambda_2 \end{aligned} \tag{14.4}$$

$$p_3 = \frac{\lambda_3}{1 - r\kappa_3}$$
$$\frac{p_1}{p_2} = \frac{\lambda_1 + rm_1}{\lambda_2 + rm_2} \quad \frac{p_1}{p_3} = \frac{\lambda_1 + rm_i}{\lambda_3} \quad i = 1,2 \tag{14.5}$$

Note that $m_3 = \kappa_1\lambda_2 - \kappa_2\lambda_1$ does not enter (14.4) and (14.5): relative mechanization in consumer good industries is irrelevant for the price formation.

Relative prices are equal to ratios of direct labour coefficients if either $r = 0$ or the degrees of mechanization in the respective industries are the same as in the machine industry. This is a general result and applies to any number of consumer good industries.

Rational consumers will spend their income in such a way as to maximize their utility. In the optimum situation the ratios of marginal utilities of any two goods consumed will be equal to the ratios of their prices. Since prices are fully determined by the technology of the system, the goods will be consumed in the proportions that will equalize the rates of commodity substitution with the price ratios for all consumers.

14.2 Heterogeneous labour

It is sometimes assumed that workers represent human capital. Then individual workers ought to be weighted by depreciation of that capital. Since workers are owners of their labour power, they are entitled to profit on their capital. Thus, the number of workers will be modified for the second time. Yet, the firm does not evaluate the costs of education, but productivity of individual workers. This is then the third modification. Assuming that there are only two productivity classes, the number of physical workers in the industry *j* will change to the number of productivity weighted standard workers:

$$zL_j = z_1L_j^1 + z_2L_j^2 = L_j^* \tag{14.6}$$

where z's are productivity factors and L_j^i is the number of workers in industry j belonging to the skill category i. If $z_1 = 1$ represents productivity of unskilled workers, then L_j^* worker-years are measured in 'simple labour time'. And L_j^* represents z times the actual workers employed, L_j.

However, the assessment of productivity, though practised by firms, is to a high degree arbitrary. Measurements of human capital show that wages paid and the return on capital are widely different. Monopoly elements, different access to education and family environment account for part of the difference. Some jobs are dangerous or unpleasant and, therefore, incur specific costs. But it is also true that boring jobs, like work at the conveyor belt, are poorly paid. Next, does elementary education or public health care represent private costs or social services available to everyone? Finally, it depends on social relations whether the income differences will be evaluated as just or excessive. They are great in the United States and relatively low in Sweden. Thus, the best one can do is to assume pure competition, democratic society and labour management whereby those who work evaluate themselves relative wages (Horvat, 1982, ch. 9). Then we can consider actual wages as measures of differential social productivity. The total wage-bill of an industry is obtained by multiplying (14.6) by wage rate w of standard workers:

$$(wz_1)L_j^1 + (wz_2)L_j^2 = w_1 L_j^1 + w_2 L_j^2 = w L_j^* \tag{14.7}$$

The actual wage rates are w_1 and w_2. If L^1 represents the standard labour, then L^2 must be expanded z_2/z_1 times and the number of standard workers is:

$$L_j^1 + \frac{z_2}{z_1} L_j^2 = L_j^* \tag{14.8}$$

Dividing the value of total wage-bill $(w_1 L_j^1 + w_2 L_j^2)$ by L_j^*, we get the standard wage rate w, which is, of course, equal for all standard workers. The labour coefficient is now $\lambda_j^* = L_j^*/X_j$ and if $w = 1$, the value is expressed in standard labour time. All we have to do is to replace the existing variables in quantity and price equations by the standard ones.

14.3 Technological progress

14.3.1 Output growth and demand changes

Technological progress increases per capita income and changes prices. Even with constant consumer preferences, the structure of demand will change due to different income and price elasticities. New and luxury goods will expand faster, old goods and necessities will expand at a lower rate, and the demand for inferior goods will shrink. All these changes can be accommodated by the available degrees of freedom.

A neutral technological progress will leave relative prices unchanged. But per capita income will rise and different income elasticities will change the structure of demand. Thus, there is no point in studying particular patterns of technological progress. We shall assume a completely general case with technological progress changing all prices and quantities differently. Technological progress is unembodied.

If the structure of demand changes, each industry will grow at its own rate of growth h_i. As a result, the sectoral rates of replacement will be different as well. The question arises: what is the appropriate rental rate? In answering the question, we treat the economy as a unified production system and look for an optimum allocation of resources within that system.

Assume that labour force remains unchanged, $L=\text{const.}$, and technological progress affects only labour coefficients: it increases productivity of living labour, differently in each sector, which implies that within a certain period each labour coefficient will decrease by a factor $\Gamma_1=(1+\gamma_1)$. By the end of the period the labour balance in (14.1) assumes the following form

$$\lambda_1\Gamma_1^{-1}X_1+\lambda_2\Gamma_2^{-1}X_2+\lambda_3\Gamma_3^{-1}X_3=\Gamma^{-1}L \qquad (14.9)$$

where Γ represents an average increase of labour productivity in the system. Because of productivity increase, $L-\Gamma^{-1}L=L(1-\Gamma^{-1})$ workers will become redundant. In order to restore full employment, output of each industry must increase by factor $H_i=1+h_i$:

$$\lambda_1\Gamma_1^{-1}X_1H_1+\lambda_2\Gamma_2^{-1}X_2H_2+\lambda_3\Gamma_3^{-1}X_3H_3=(\Gamma^{-1}L)\Gamma=L \qquad (14.10)$$

If capital coefficients do not change, the investment balance in (14.1) becomes:

$$(\delta_1+h_1)\kappa_1X_1+(\delta_2+h_2)\kappa_2X_2+(\delta_3+h_3)\kappa_3X_3=(\delta+h)K=X_3 \quad (14.11)$$

where hK is the number of new machines necessary to equip redundant workers:

$$L(1-\Gamma^{-1})=\frac{\gamma}{1+\gamma}L$$

We have three variables H_i, $i=1,2,3$, and two equations: (14.10) and (14.11). We still need one equation. When technological progress increases per capita net output, the structure of demand becomes a function of income (L^* with higher productivity, $L^*=p_1H_1X_1+p_2H_2X_2$), prices (p_1,p_2) and consumer preferences which may be assumed as given. Prices are fully determined by technology (T). Thus, the proportion in which the two goods are consumed is fully determined by income and technology.

As X_1 and X_2 are initial outputs before technological change, they are known, and so we may write:

$$\frac{H_2}{H_1} = \sigma(L^*, T) \tag{14.12}$$

The proportion σ adds the missing equation; the system is closed and all outputs are fully determined. If there are n consumer goods, there will be $n-1$ proportions $\sigma_i = H_i/H_1$, $i=2, \ldots n$, which will provide an equal number of missing equations. Adding labour and investment balances (14.10) and (14.11), we obtain $n+1$ equations which determined the output of n consumption goods and one machine.

14.3.2 The Pasinetti system

At the beginning of the period, labour and investment (for the period) equations are as follows:

$$\begin{aligned} &\text{Labour equation:} && \lambda_1 X_1 + \lambda_2 X_2 + \lambda_3 X_3 = L \\ &\text{Investment equation:} && r_1 \kappa_1 X_1 + r_2 \kappa_2 X_2 + r_3 \kappa_3 X_3 = rK = X_3, \\ & && r_j = \delta_j + h_j \end{aligned} \tag{14.13}$$

Clearly, if all r_j are different and constant through time, r cannot be constant and vice versa.

Summing up the components of two equations evaluated in corresponding prices, we obtain value balances. Dividing by X_i, we obtain price equations:

$$r_j p_3 \kappa_j + w\lambda_j = p_j, \qquad j=1,2,3 \tag{14.14}$$

The system (14.14) will be called a Pasinetti system.[1] Pasinetti himself calls it 'the natural economic system', but there is nothing particularly natural in it. Pasinetti justifies the approach by pointing out that in this case costs of production represent vertically hyperintegrated labour inputs. That is true, but irrelevant. It only means that each industry finances its own investment costs. But why should it? Besides, why stop at the level of industries? Why not allow that each firm finances its investments and, consequently, earns its own separate rate of profit? The resulting different rates of profit lead to a misallocation of resources. A higher than average rate of profit means a higher price. A higher price than necessary implies that a unit of labour generates greater 'value' in one industry than in another. Assuming diminishing marginal utility, a reallocation of labour from less profitable to more profitable industries (with the concomitant changes in demand prices) increases the welfare of the community. An optimum is achieved when profits are equalized throughout the economy.

A Pareto efficient allocation of resources requires a profit equalization and therefore the Pasinetti system proves unsatisfactory as a final solution. It will be treated as an intermediate stage in our analysis.

14.3.3 The equalization of the rates of profit

Equal profit rates imply equal depreciation charges, which are simply functions of n and h. That may look puzzling, because physical replacement differs from industry to industry. The explanation is simple: an economy must produce *physical* machines to replace an equal number of scrapped machines in the corresponding period; an individual firm faces no physical constraint of this sort. A firm must produce *value* to cover depreciation charges. Whether a firm expands fast or slow, the depreciation rate must be such that depreciation charges accumulated at a common interest rate h will generate value equal to the purchase price of a new machine that will replace the old one at the time it is scrapped. Clearly, if the stock of machines is growing at the rate h, the sum of all replacements and the sum of all depreciations will be equal because they are the same functions of the same parameters n and h.

We have just found that maximization of economic welfare requires an equalization of profit rates. Does that conflict with the formation of labour values? The answer is: No. Consistently derived labour prices also require an equalization of profit rates. Profits are nothing else but investment costs that must be incurred in order to equip labour rendered redundant by technological progress.

If g is a uniform cost incurred by the growth of living labour, h represents the growth of embodied labour when living labour remains constant under technological progress. Both g and h represent systemic costs and, therefore, must be uniform throughout the system. That cost is *one single systemic* cost, regardless of the fact that gross investment may be very different in different industries. Technological progress may be different in different industries in the sense that the same machines and labour will produce different quantities of consumer goods X_1 and X_2. This only means that real wage will increase. It may also mean that a smaller number of workers, equipped with the same number of machines, will produce the same output X_1, X_2 and X_3. Then some workers will be displaced and the production of machines must be increased in order to employ them. This increase in the stock of machines (with unchanged labour) is represented by h. Since machines are the same, the depreciation rate δ is the same for all machines. Since only the systemic technological progress matters, h is the same for all firms. If the depreciation charges $\delta_t K$ are accumulated over n years at the interest rates h, they will provide an investment fund exactly equal to K. This can be proved in the following way.

At the beginning of the period $t=n+1$, the number of machines in the capital stock will be equal to past n investments. Investments increase by unequal factors H_t per period. Starting with a unit investment at $t=1$, the number of machines will increase by the end of $t=n$ to:

$$K_n = 1 + H_1 + H_1 H_2 + \ldots + \prod_{\tau=1}^{n-1} H_\tau \tag{14.15}$$

In $t=n+1$ the first investment will be replaced. $R_{n+1}=1$. Consequently, the replacement rate is equal to:

$$\delta_{n+1} = \frac{R_{n+1}}{K_n} = \frac{1}{1 + H_1 + \ldots + \prod_{\tau=1}^{n-1} H_\tau} \tag{14.16}$$

Depreciation quotas (d=const.) for one machine, set aside annually in the depreciation fund and accumulated at the ruling interest rate, amount to:

$$d\left(\prod_{\tau=1}^{n-1} H_\tau + \prod_{\tau=1}^{n-2} H_\tau + \ldots + H_1 + 1\right) = p_3$$

where h serves as an interest rate and p_3 is the price of the new machine at $t=n+1$. The rate of depreciation to be charged annually in order to recoup the initial unit value after n years is:

$$\delta = \frac{d}{p_3} = \delta_{n+1} \tag{14.17}$$

and it is equal to the rate of replacement at $t=n+1$. It is, however, somewhat artificial to assume a perfect forecast about interest rate changes from year to year. Changes in H_t are likely to be small under full employment. Thus H_t may be approximated by a uniform H. Technological progress in different industries will proceed at different rates which change in time. An overall h is not unrealistic because it only implies that the rate of growth of producer goods remains constant (given labour). Constant H implies constant interest rate and so depreciation and replacement rate simplify to:

$$\delta' = \delta = \frac{h}{H^{n-1}}$$

which is, of course, the same as (4.3).

All that remains is to write down the price equations:

$$
\begin{aligned}
p_3(\delta + h)\kappa_1 + w\lambda_1 &= p_1 \\
p_3(\delta + h)\kappa_2 + w\lambda_2 &= p_2 \\
p_3(\delta + h)\kappa_3 + w\lambda_3 &= p_3
\end{aligned}
\tag{14.18}
$$

Four important consequences follow:

1. The economy may be decentralized because the profit-maximizing firms will move into high-profit industries until profits are equalized throughout the economy.
2. Global gross investment in (14.11) will not change if we take:

   $$\delta_i + h_i = \delta + h = r$$

   But sectoral investment outlays $(\delta_i + h_i)$ and sectoral investment finance $(\delta + h)$ are no longer equal which necessitates the establishment of a financial sector in the economy. Money is introduced in the system in a natural way. It comes as a consequence of the optimizing behaviour.
3. In the process, prices will change: in the heavily investing industries prices will decrease, in the more stagnant ones they will increase as compared with the Pasinetti system.
4. Since prices determine the choice of technology, different techniques will be chosen (substitution activities) in order to minimize costs. As a result, all the parameters of the system will change: labour (and capital) coefficients because of a different technology and replacement and growth rates because of different sectoral growth. Thus, technological progress generates two different types of changes: (1) improvements in technology and (2) substitution of techniques.

If also capital coefficients are changed, h (and, consequently, δ) will change as well. If capital coefficients are reduced, less capital will be necessary and h will be reduced. A reduction of capital coefficients may compensate (as in Neutral II TP) or even overcompensate the investment expanding effects of reduced labour coefficients, rendering h zero or negative.

The growth of labour force simultaneously with technological progress represents no difficulty either. All labour costs increase by investment outlays necessary to equip new workers, i.e. by $g\kappa_i$. Thus, fully generally, the price equations look as follows in an economy with n consumer and one capital good:

$$p_{n+1}(\delta+g+h)\kappa_i+w\lambda_i=p_i, \qquad i=1,\ldots n+1$$

where p_{n+1} is the price of the single capital good. Since capital goods are evaluated in labour prices, $\pi=g+h$ indicates additional labour embodied in new machines.

15 Many capital goods

15.1 Constant technology

15.1.1 Quantity equations

Consider an economy with one consumer good (X_1) and two machines (X_2, X_3). Let the life-span of the two machines be the same ($n_1 = n_2 = n$). The number of quantity equations matches the number of variables:

$$\begin{aligned} &\lambda_1 X_1 + \lambda_2 X_2 + \lambda_3 X_3 = L \\ &r\kappa_1^1 X_1 + r\kappa_2^1 X_2 + r\kappa_3^1 X_3 = rK^1 = X_2, \qquad \kappa_i^1 = \frac{K_i^1}{X_i} \\ &r\kappa_1^2 X_1 + r\kappa_2^2 X_2 + r\kappa_3^2 X_3 = rK^2 = X_3, \qquad \kappa_i^2 = \frac{K_i^2}{X_i} \end{aligned} \tag{15.1}$$

where K^1 and K^2 are stocks of machines of type one and two, and X_2 and X_3 are per period outputs of the same machines.

The last two equations in (15.1) represent a homogeneous system. If X_1 is eliminated from these two equations, X_2 bears a fixed proportion to X_3 as given by:

$$\frac{X_2}{X_3} = \frac{K^1}{K^2} = \frac{rb_2 + \kappa_1^1}{rb_1 + \kappa_1^2}, \qquad \begin{aligned} b_1 &= \kappa_1^1\kappa_2^2 - \kappa_1^2\kappa_2^1 \\ b_2 &= \kappa_1^2\kappa_3^1 - \kappa_1^1\kappa_3^2 \end{aligned} \tag{15.2}$$

In either $r = 0$ or $b_1 = b_2 = 0$, the proportion in which the two types of machines are produced is equal to the ratio of capital coefficients of those machines in the consumer-good industry. Now the role of machine–worker ratio (the degree of mechanization) is replaced by machine–output ratio (capital coefficient); $b_1 = b_2 = 0$ implies:

$$\frac{\kappa_1^1}{\kappa_1^2} = \frac{\kappa_2^1}{\kappa_2^2} = \frac{\kappa_3^1}{\kappa_3^2} = \frac{K^1}{K^2} = \frac{X_2}{X_3}$$

In other words, it is implied that in each industry machines of type 1 and 2 are used in the same proportion in which they are produced.

From $K^1/K^2 = X_2/X_3$ it follows that $X_3/K^2 = X_2/K^1$, i.e., gross investment rates are the same in both industries. Generally, the ratio X_2/X_3 will be a function of the investment rate and all capital coefficients (changing under TP).

The elimination of X_1 from the first two equations gives

$$(rm_3^1 + \lambda_1)X_2 + rm_1^1 X_3 = r\kappa_1^1 L, \quad m_1^1 = \kappa_1^1\lambda_3 - \kappa_3^2\lambda_1, \quad m_3^1 = \kappa_1^1\lambda_2 - \kappa_2^1\lambda_1$$

Use (15.2) to obtain

$$\begin{aligned} X_1 &= \left(\frac{1}{\lambda_1} - \frac{r^2C + rD}{\lambda_1(r^2A + rB + \lambda_1)}\right)L, & A &= \frac{b_2 m_3^1 + b_1 m_1^1}{\kappa_1^1} \\ X_2 &= \frac{r(rb_2 + \kappa_1^1)}{r^2A + rB + \lambda_1}L, & B &= \frac{m_3^1\kappa_1^1 - m_1^1\kappa_1^2 + \lambda_1 b_2}{\kappa_1^1} \\ X_3 &= \frac{r(rb_1 + \kappa_1^2)}{r^2A + rB + \lambda_1}L, & C &= \lambda_2 b_2 + \lambda_3 b_1 \\ & & D &= \lambda_2\kappa_1^1 + \lambda_3\kappa_1^2 \end{aligned} \qquad (15.3)$$

While the proportion between machines (X_2/X_3) is invariant to changes in labour coefficients, the basket-machine proportions (X_1/X_j) depend on λ_1.

The introduction of just one additional machine makes life quite complicated. That explains the popularity of one-machine economies, or of a triangularity of input matrix, or of machines being produced by labour alone.

15.1.2 Price equations

Price equations are also fully determined and also more complicated because each equation has two rental terms corresponding to two capital goods:

$$\begin{aligned} rp_2\kappa_1^1 + rp_3\kappa_1^2 + w\lambda_1 &= p_1 \\ rp_2\kappa_2^1 + rp_3\kappa_2^2 + w\lambda_2 &= p_2 \\ rp_2\kappa_3^1 + rp_3\kappa_3^2 + w\lambda_3 &= p_3 \end{aligned} \qquad (15.4)$$

Machine prices are determined exclusively by the coefficients of their own industries. Once determined, they can be used to find out the consumer good price:

$$p_1 = \frac{r^2(\lambda_1 b_3 + \lambda_2 b_2 + \lambda_3 b_1) + r(m_3^1 + m_1^2) + \lambda_1}{r^2 b_3 - r(\kappa_2^1 + \kappa_3^2) + 1} w, \qquad b_3 = \kappa_3^2\kappa_2^1 - \kappa_3^1\kappa_2^2$$

$$p_2 = \frac{\lambda_2 + rm_2^2}{r^2 b_3 - r(\kappa_2^1 + \kappa_3^2) + 1} w, \qquad \begin{aligned} m_2^1 &= \kappa_2^1\lambda_3 - \kappa_3^1\lambda_2 \\ m_2^2 &= \kappa_2^2\lambda_3 - \kappa_3^2\lambda_2 \end{aligned} \tag{15.5}$$

$$p_3 = \frac{\lambda_3 - rm_2^1}{r^2 b_3 - r(\kappa_2^1 + \kappa_3^2) + 1} w, \qquad \begin{aligned} m_1^2 &= \kappa_1^2\lambda_3 - \kappa_3^2\lambda_1 \\ m_3^1 &= \kappa_1^1\lambda_2 - \kappa_2^1\lambda_1 \end{aligned}$$

For $r=0$, all prices reduce to their labour coefficients, $p_1=\lambda_1, p_2=\lambda_2, p_3=\lambda_3$. If $m_2^1=m_2^2=0$, the ratio of machine prices is equal to the ratio of labour coefficients, $p_2/p_3=\lambda_2/\lambda_3$. Note that m_j^i are not the same mechanization indices as before. For instance, $m_2^1=0$ implies:

$$\frac{\kappa_2^1}{\lambda_2} = \frac{K_2^1}{X_2}\bigg/\frac{L_2}{X_2} = \frac{\kappa_3^1}{\lambda_3} = \frac{K_3^1}{X_3}\bigg/\frac{L_3}{X_3}$$

and

$$\frac{K_2^1}{L_2} \neq \frac{K_2^1}{L_2^1}, \; \frac{K_3^1}{L_3} \neq \frac{K_3^1}{L_3^1}, \; \frac{K_2^1}{L_2^1} \neq \frac{K_3^1}{L_3^1}$$

L_2^1 is the number of workers who operate K_2^1 machines of type one in industry two. L_2 is the total number of workers employed in industry two, $L_2=L_2^1+L_2^2$. Thus, K_2^1/L_2^1 is a proper degree of mechanization, and K_2^1/L_2 may be called *quasi*-intensity of mechanization. But equal quasi-mechanization in machine industries is not a sufficient condition for the two ratios to be equal when consumer good price is considered. For that five additional conditions are required: $m_3^1=m_1^2=0$ and $b_1=b_2=b_3=0$. Note, however, that $b_1=b_2=0$ implies $b_3=0$. In other words, apart from equal quasi-mechanization ratios in all industries, the proportions of machines produced and used in each industry must also be equal.

Price ratios are equal to ratios of labour coefficients, $p_i/p_j=\lambda_i/\lambda_j$, when the organic composition of resources is equal in the three industries, $\omega_1=\omega_2=\omega_3$. The conditions just found imply exactly that:

$$\omega_1=\omega_2 \Rightarrow \frac{p_2\kappa_1^1+p_3\kappa_1^2}{p_2\kappa_2^1+p_3\kappa_2^2}=\frac{\lambda_1}{\lambda_2}$$

$$\omega_1=\omega_3 \Rightarrow \frac{p_2\kappa_1^1+p_3\kappa_1^2}{p_2\kappa_3^1+p_3\kappa_3^2}=\frac{\lambda_1}{\lambda_3}$$

while:

$$m_3^1=0 \Rightarrow \frac{\lambda_1}{\lambda_2}=\frac{\kappa_1^1}{\kappa_2^1}$$

$$m_1^2=0 \Rightarrow \frac{\lambda_1}{\lambda_3}=\frac{\kappa_1^2}{\kappa_3^2}$$

$$b_1=b_2=0 \Rightarrow \frac{\kappa_1^2}{\kappa_1^1}=\frac{\kappa_2^2}{\kappa_2^1}=\frac{\kappa_3^2}{\kappa_3^1}=a$$

Consequently

$$\frac{\lambda_1}{\lambda_2}=\frac{p_2\kappa_1^1+p_3a\kappa_1^1}{p_2\kappa_2^1+p_3a\kappa_2^1}=\frac{\kappa_1^1}{\kappa_2^1}$$

$$\frac{\lambda_1}{\lambda_3}=\frac{p_2\kappa_1^2/a+p_3\kappa_1^2}{p_2\kappa_3^2/a+p_3\kappa_3^2}=\frac{\kappa_1^2}{\kappa_3^2} \qquad \text{Q.E.D.}$$

15.1.3 Wage curve

Per capita consumption of a single consumer good represents the real wage. It follows from the first equation of (15.3) that:

$$\tilde{w}=x_1=\frac{1}{\lambda_1}-\frac{r^2C+rD}{\lambda_1(r^2A+rB+\lambda_1)} \tag{15.6}$$

The curve is now considerably more complicated than before because r^2 appears in the numerator and denominator.

If $w(r)$ is to be made linear, some coefficients must be zero: $C=A=B=0$. That implies uniform quasi mechanization ($m_1^1=m_3^1=0$) and also uniform capital-output intensity ($b_1=b_2=0$). Under these conditions the wage curve reduces to a straight line:

$$\tilde{w}=\frac{1}{\lambda_1}-r\frac{D}{\lambda_1^2} \tag{15.7}$$

Since there is only one consumer good, maximum per capita consumption remains the same as in the standard two-sector model and is determined by the labour coefficient of the first industry, $\tilde{W}(r=0)=\frac{1}{\lambda_1}$. That also follows from the first equation in (15.1) when we put $X_2=X_3=0$. But maximum rental depends apparently on all capital and labour coefficients and is determined by a quadratic equation:

$$R(\tilde{w}=0) \Rightarrow R^2(A-C)+R(B-D)+\lambda_1=0$$

This equation can be somewhat simplified if it is recalled that in the labour system the real wage is the reciprocal of the price of the consumer good. Using (15.5), we obtain:

$$\tilde{w}=\frac{1}{p_1}=\frac{r^2b_3-r(\kappa_2^1+\kappa_3^2)+1}{r^2(\lambda_1b_3+\lambda_2b_2+\lambda_3b_1)+r(m_3^1+m_1^2)+\lambda_1} \tag{15.8}$$

As a ratio of two second degree polynomials, wage curve may have three inflection points (since $d^2w/dr^2=f(r^3)$). For $r=0$ or $b_1=b_2=b_3=m_3^1=m_1^2=0$, the wage curve reduces to a straight line:

$$\tilde{w}=\frac{1}{\lambda_1}-r\frac{\kappa_2^1+\kappa_3^2}{\lambda_1} \tag{15.7a}$$

which is identical with (15.7) because:

$$\frac{D}{\lambda_1^2}=\frac{\kappa_2^1+\kappa_3^2}{\lambda_1}$$

if $m_1^2=m_3^1=0$.

The maximum wage remains, of course, the same, $\tilde{W}(r=0)=\frac{1}{\lambda_1}$, but the maximum $R(w=0)$ results from a simpler quadratic equation:

$$r^2b_3-r(\kappa_2^1+\kappa_3^2)+1=0 \tag{15.9}$$

and depends *exclusively* on capital coefficients in *machine* industries.

An analysis of equation (15.9) and of its solutions:

$$R_{1,2}=\frac{(\kappa_2^1+\kappa_3^2)\pm\sqrt{(\kappa_2^1+\kappa_3^2)^2-4b_3}}{2b_3}$$

reveals the classifying role of b_3, i.e. of the interrelations among four capital coefficients of the two machine industries:

$$b_3<0 \quad : \quad R_1>0,\ R_2<0$$

$$b_3=0 \quad : \quad R=\frac{1}{\kappa_2^1+\kappa_3^2}$$

$$0<b_3<\left(\frac{\kappa_2^1+\kappa_3^2}{2}\right)^2 \quad : \quad R_1,\ R_2>0$$

$$0<b_3=\left(\frac{\kappa_2^1+\kappa_3^2}{2}\right)^2 \quad : \quad R=\frac{2}{\kappa_2^1+\kappa_3^2}$$

$$b_3>\left(\frac{\kappa_2^1+\kappa_3^2}{2}\right)^2 \quad : \quad R_1,\ R_2 \text{ do not exist}$$

R is unique in two cases: for $b_3=0$ and $b_3=\left(\frac{\kappa_2^1+\kappa_3^2}{2}\right)^2$. For negative b_3, only one R is positive and that one is admissible. Both R's are positive for positive b_3 smaller than $\left(\frac{\kappa_2^1+\kappa_3^2}{2}\right)^2$. In this case only the smaller of the two is admissible because $\tilde{W}(r)\geq 0$. Finally, b_3 cannot be larger than $\left(\frac{\kappa_2^1+\kappa_3^2}{2}\right)^2$ because in that case the wage function does not exist. Note that $\frac{\kappa_2^1+\kappa_3^2}{2}$ is an average of the own capital coefficients in two machine industries and $b_3=\kappa_3^2\kappa_2^1-\kappa_3^1\kappa_2^2=0$ implies $\frac{\kappa_3^2}{\kappa_3^1}=\frac{\kappa_2^2}{\kappa_2^1}$, i.e. equal ratios of machine-output intensities in the two machine industries.

15.2 A generalization to two or more capital goods

15.2.1 The possibility of reswitching

Consider a circulating capital two-sector model whose first price equation reads:

$$w\lambda_1^\alpha+(p_1a_{11}^\alpha+p_2a_{21}^\alpha)r=p_1, \qquad r=1+g \tag{15.10a}$$

where α represents the technique in use and $(1+g)$ replaces $(1/v+g)$ in a fixed capital model. The second industry stays with the old technique, while an alternative technique β is introduced in the first industry. It generates an alternative equation with the same price at the switch point $r=r^*$:

$$w\lambda_1^\beta+(p_1a_{11}^\beta+p_2a_{21}^\beta)r=p_1 \tag{15.10b}$$

Take the difference at the switch point:

$$(\lambda_1^\alpha - \lambda_1^\beta) + (a_{11}^\alpha - a_{11}^\beta)\frac{p_1}{w}r^* + (a_{21}^\alpha - a_{21}^\beta)\frac{p_2}{w}r^* = 0 \qquad (15.11)$$

The solution of the equation depends on p_j/w. We know that prices are increasing functions of r because greater r implies more labour time (indirect labour) in the production of every commodity, given technology. Nominal wage w is an arbitrary positive constant.

The same conclusion about p_j/w can also be derived more formally. Let A be a matrix of input coefficients for n industries. Then the system of price equations reads:

$$p = pAr + w\lambda = w\lambda(I - rA)^{-1} \qquad (15.12)$$

and any p_j/w is given by:

$$\frac{p_j}{w} = \lambda(I - rA)^{-1}e_j \qquad (15.13)$$

where e_j is the jth unit column vector. It follows from (15.12) that:

$$pA < \frac{1}{r}p$$

which means that Frobenius eigenvalue (dominant characteristic root) of the semipositive indecomposable matrix A is $\mu^* < \frac{1}{r}$ or $r < \frac{1}{\mu^*}$, which in turn means that $(I - rA)^{-1}$ may be represented by a convergent power series:

$$(I - rA)^{-1} = I + rA + (rA)^2 + \dots$$

Consequently, p_j/w is a strictly increasing function of r. The maximal value of r is equal to the reciprocal of the Frobenius eigenvalue, $R = \frac{1}{\mu^*}$. For $r = R$, the series ceases to converge and p_j/w become infinite.

If one commodity is a pure consumption good, as in our canonical model, $a_{11}^\alpha - a_{11}^\beta = 0$, the equation (15.11) has only one solution because p_2 becomes a linear function in the two-industry case. Generally pure consumer goods do not enter A and its rank depends exclusively on capital goods (pure or mixed capital-consumer goods). That should be obvious because if pure consumer goods never appear as inputs, prices are determined exclusively by capital goods.

As the techniques in (15.11) are efficient, not all brackets can have the same sign. Two cases may be distinguished. If the brackets of capital coefficients are non-negative or non-positive, the equation (15.11) has only one solution because p_j/w are increasing functions (cf. Pertz and Teplitz, 1979). The switch must occur, because otherwise one industry would be dominant. If the a-brackets have opposite signs, reswitching is possible since p_j are ratios of second degree polynomials.

So far we used l-prices. The wage curve implies b-prices. If (15.11) is divided by p_1/w, we get the equation which corresponds to the wage curve:

$$(\lambda_1^\alpha - \lambda_1^\beta)\frac{w}{p_1} = (a_{21}^\beta - a_{21}^\alpha)\frac{p_2}{p_1}r^* + (a_{11}^\beta - a_{11}^\alpha)r^* \qquad (15.11a)$$

Consider the beginning and the end of wage curves. When $r=0, \lambda_1^\alpha = \lambda_1^\beta$, the first industry cannot change the technique (since $wp_1 > 0$) and both wage curves originate in the point $w/p_1 = \frac{1}{\lambda_1}$. For $r=R$, $w/p_1 = w/p_2 = 0$. Now the second industry does not change the technique and the corresponding equation reads:

$$(\lambda_2^\alpha - \lambda_2^\beta)\frac{w}{p_2} = (a_{12}^\beta - a_{12}^\alpha)\frac{p_1}{p_2}r^* + (a_{22}^\alpha - a_{22}^\beta)\,r^* \qquad (15.11b)$$

where the coefficients of the second industry are equal, $a_{12}^\alpha = a_{12}^\beta$, $a_{22}^\alpha = a_{22}^\beta$. The second industry price equation is:

$$w\lambda_2 + (p_1 a_{12} + p_2 a_{22})r = p_2$$

and it does not change with p_1 when $a_{12} = 0$ (pure consumer good). For real wage $w/p_2 = 0$, maximal R is equal to $R = \frac{1}{a_{22}}$.

In a general case, the change of a technique will change the matrix A and its Frobenius eigenvalue $\mu^* = \frac{1}{R}$. Thus, the two alternative wage curves cannot end in the same point R.

In a less formal way it is possible to simplify the reswitching problem. If the wage curves are monotonous and they start or end at the same point, there can and must be only one switch. If there are two or more capital goods, wage curves are ratios of polynomials of second or higher degrees.

Thus, they cease to be monotonous and reswitching becomes possible.

We are now ready to systematize our findings:

1. With any number of pure consumer goods, reswitching cannot occur if
   (a) there is only one capital good or,
   (b) differences of input coefficients have the same signs when two or more capital goods are used.

   Alternatively, for reswitching to occur it is necessary that there are at least two capital goods, regardless of the number of pure consumer goods.
2. If w/p_j is the wage curve, and industry j does not change technique, the two alternative wage curves originate in the same point $\tilde{W}_j = 1/\lambda_j$. The two wage curves can terminate in the same point R only when there is only one capital good or the machine industries do not change techniques. When two wage curves either start or end in the same point, there cannot be reswitching (in a two capital good pure consumer good economy).
3. If the technology remains the same but wage curves are expressed in terms of different commodities ($w/p_j, j = 1,2,\ldots n$), all such wage curves terminate in the same point R, because the matrix A does not change. In fact, different *numéraires* change the dimension of the vertical axis and so wage curves will originate at different points on this axis. But r is a pure number and therefore all wage curves of the same technology terminate at the same point on the horizontal axis.

15.2.2 Six neoclassical postulates

We may now explore whether the six fundamental neoclassical postulates hold true. Neoclassical theory postulates an inverse monotonic relation between prices and quantities of factors of production. It is said that the use of capital, land and labour decreases if interest rate, rent and real wage increase. The same inverse relation holds between prices and quantities of commodities. The four postulates are derived from the scarcity–abundance assumption. Assuming constant returns and diminishing marginal productivity of labour, the first relationship implies an inverse monotonic relation between the rate of profit and labour productivity (output per worker) and also between the rate of profit and consumption per capita. Let us examine these postulates under the condition of resp. wage and distribution curves.

Dual (wage) curves (r=i) It has already been shown that the relation between (1) capital intensity and interest rate depends on relative mechanization. If producer goods industries are more capital intensive, an increase in the interest rate will *increase* general capital intensity – and vice versa.

Next, we found in section 13.3 that (2) the rent postulate may be violated: an increasing rent–wage ratio may induce the application of *more* rather than less *land intensive* (land per worker) technique. (3) Given L, real wage rate may go up or down depending on the production of investment goods. (4) It is known that prices of some commodities may move in the same direction as quantities (so called inferior or Giffen goods, habit forming drugs that generate increasing marginal utility). Now a new class of commodities is added to these perverse cases. Prices are increasing functions of the interest rate and, therefore, of investment rate (more embodied labour). Thus, prices of producer goods *increase* when quantities increase. In general, there is no regularity and non-tautological scarcity assumption appears false.

The first and fifth postulate (5) hold true only if the basket industry is more mechanized. If there are several technologies, at the switch points these postulates will always hold true. (6) Since both, wage curves and technology frontier, are downward sloping, $d\tilde{w}/dr = dc/di < 0$, the sixth postulate will never be violated. Consequently, in the canonical model at switch points all three postulates hold true; along individual wage curves – i.e. between switch points – the first and fifth may be violated, but not the sixth one.

Distribution curves$(r > i)$ It was shown in section 10.3.3 that along individual distribution curves all postulates may be violated. Some postulates are preserved at the switch points if the distribution curves never cross more than once as in the canonical model. If a technique reappears at the technology frontier, at the first switch point capital, output and consumption per worker will decrease, but as *r increases* the old technique will switch back and so the three quantities – even per capita consumption – will *increase*. Reswitching *need not* actually occur; it is sufficient that individual distribution curves cross below technology frontier, as noticed already by I. Steedman (1972a).

In Fig. 15.1 investment is kept at i_0 while r varies causing the techniques to switch. At the first switch point r_1^1, everything is in order, the inverse relationships hold. But at r_2^* all three quantities behave perversely: as r *increases*, capital per worker *increases* (as indicated by the slopes of the chords $\overline{ab}$ and $\overline{ad}$), output per worker *increases* (as indicated by the intercepts of the chords on the i axis) and consumption per worker *increases* from c_β to c_γ (while the wage rate always decreases). The consumption perversity is considered to be particularly damaging to neoclassical theorizing. All three perversities are due to the fact that distribution curves cross twice, once at the technology frontier and then also below it.

The conditions for the perverse behaviour of consumption may also be

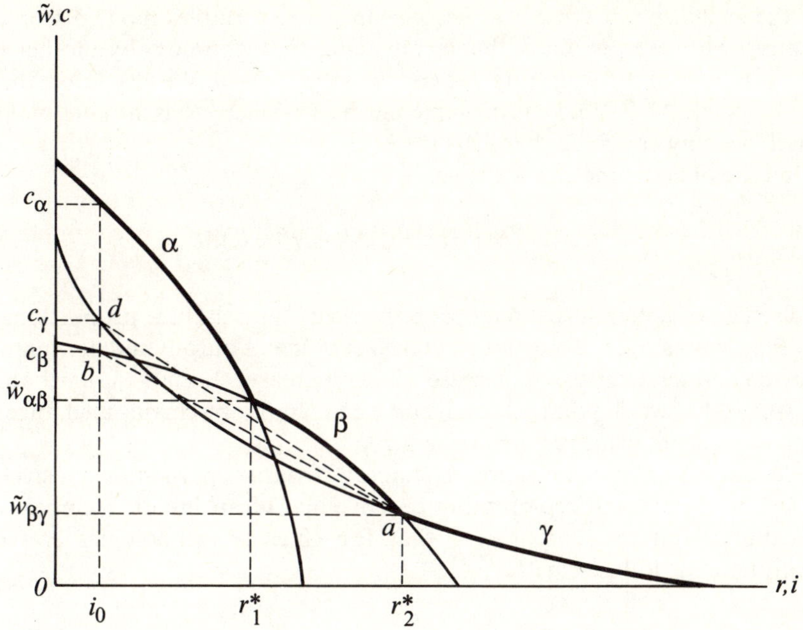

Figure 15.1 The violation of neoclassical postulates without reswitching

stated algebraically. Consider possible changes at the switch point r^* of a downward sloping technology frontier $\tilde{w}(r)$. For each of the two distribution curves, income distributed must be equal to the value of output produced, while the investment rate i_0 is fixed:

$$\tilde{y} = \tilde{w} + r\tilde{k} = c + i_0\tilde{k}$$

from which it follows that:

$$c = \tilde{w} + \tilde{k}(r - i_0)$$

In the case of dual curves ($r = i$), consumption and wages are equal, $c = \tilde{w}$, and no perversity can occur. In the case of distribution curves ($r - i_0 > 0$), c and $\tilde{w}$ may move in different directions when changes in r induce changes in techniques. Consider first changes in output for an infinitesimal increase of r at the switch point:

$$\Delta\tilde{y} = \Delta\tilde{w} + \tilde{k}\Delta r + r^*\Delta\tilde{k} \qquad \text{(a)}$$

At the switch point there is a discontinuity, i.e. variables move discontinuously. However, we know that by replacing one technology by another at the switch point the wage rate does not change, $\Delta\tilde{w}=0$. We also know that $\tilde{k}\Delta r>0$ while $\Delta\tilde{k}\gtreqless 0$ and has the same sign as $\Delta\tilde{y}$. Since $\tilde{k}\Delta r$ is infinitesimally small, we may conclude that $\Delta\tilde{y}=r^*\Delta\tilde{k}$.

In case of consumption we have:

$$c=\Delta\tilde{w}+\tilde{k}\Delta r+(r^*-i_0)\Delta\tilde{k}=(r^*-i_0)\Delta\tilde{k}$$

and so consumption also moves proportionally to $\Delta\tilde{k}$ but the proportionality factor is smaller. Thus both the basket value of output and consumption may either decrease or increase when r increases. For $r^*=i_0$, $c=\tilde{w}$ and $\Delta c=0$: at the switch point of a dual curve consumption remains unchanged because the real wage remains unchanged.

Consider, finally, a continuous technology frontier consisting exclusively of switch points and representing an envelope of an infinite number of distribution curves and assume that for efficient technologies $c(r)$ is continuous. It follows that:

$$\frac{dc}{dr}=\left(\frac{d\tilde{w}}{dr}+\tilde{k}\right)+(r-i_0)\frac{d\tilde{k}}{dr}$$

If the envelope is globally concave, then $-\dfrac{d\tilde{w}}{dr}>\tilde{k}$ because the slope of the tangent is steeper than that of any chord passing through the same point on the frontier and a point *below* frontier. The first bracket is negative, but the second is positive because $d\tilde{k}/dr>0$ and the perversity becomes possible (cf. also Steedman, 1990, pp. 147–8). If the envelope is globally convex, $d\tilde{k}/dr<0$, it is the other way round.

Consumption perversity destroys the sacrifice and time preference theories of interest: if an increase in the interest rate increases consumption (greater consumption leads to greater profits), sacrifice is impossible and time preference meaningless.

15.3 Technological progress

15.3.1 Capital coefficients unchanged

Let us again consider labour augmenting unembodied technological progress. As two different machines are produced, we now have two investment equations:

Labour equation: $$\sum_{i=1}^{3} (\lambda_i \Gamma_i^{-1}) X_i H_i = (\Gamma^{-1} L)\Gamma = L$$

Investment equations: $$\sum_{i=1}^{3} \kappa_i^1 X_i (h_i^1 + \delta_i^1) = (h^1 + \delta^1) K^1 = X_2 \tag{15.14}$$

$$\sum_{i=1}^{3} \kappa_i^2 X_i (h_i^2 + \delta_i^2) = (h^2 + \delta^2) K^2 = X_3$$

The system of equations (15.14) is basically the same as (15.1) with γ replacing g. Since there is only one consumer good, the structure of demand – the composition of the basket – cannot change. As capital coefficients do not change either, the structure of investment demand does not change. Thus the system moves at one single rate $h = \gamma$ determined by the rate of labour productivity growth. The usual vertical summation gives price equations

$$(p_2 \kappa_i^1 + p_3 \kappa_i^2) r + w \lambda_i \Gamma_i^{-1} = p_i \Gamma_i^{-1} \tag{15.15}$$

Due to technological progress all prices decrease. In case all factors Γ_i are the same, prices decrease and quantities increase by equal factors Γ(15.5 and 15.1), organic composition of resources remains the same:

$$\omega_i(t) = \frac{(p_2 K_i^1 + p_3 K_i^2)\Gamma^{-1}}{L_i} = \frac{(p_2 K_i^1 + p_2 K_i^2)\Gamma^{-1}}{\lambda_i \Gamma^{-1}} = \omega_i(0)$$

and technological progress is neutral I.

With uniform r, prices are labour prices constructed in such a way that individual stationary costs are augmented by the (average) investment costs (corrected for replacement reduction) incurred by the economy in order to employ workers rendered redundant by technological progress.

If working hours are also changing, the (positive or negative) rate of change must be included in the rental rate:

$$r = \delta + \pi, \qquad \pi = GH - 1 \tag{15.16}$$

If the durability of machines differs, $n_i \neq n_2$, there will be two different δ's. They will be related as follows:

$$\frac{\delta^1}{\delta^2} = \frac{\pi}{\Pi^{n_1} - 1} \bigg/ \frac{\pi}{\Pi^{n_2} - 1} = \frac{\Pi^{n_2} - 1}{\Pi^{n_1} - 1}, \qquad \Pi = 1 + \pi \tag{15.17}$$

If $n_2 > n_1$, then $\delta^1 > \delta^2$. For $\pi = \text{const.}$, (15.17) holds strictly; if π changes in time, (15.17) is an approximation.

Now all rental rates are different:

$$r^j = \delta^j + \pi, \quad j = 1,2 \tag{15.16a}$$

where the superscript j indicates the type of the machine. The profit rate is uniform:

$$\pi = GH - 1 = g + h$$

and it may be positive, zero or even negative for a sufficiently large contraction of labour ($g < 0$).

15.3.2 Capital coefficients change

If both labour productivity and capital efficiency improve, the situation becomes somewhat messy. Let L_j^s represent the number of workers in industry j operating machines of type s. Productivity of that group of workers increases by Γ_j^s and output by H_j^s. The output of corresponding machines must also increase by H_j^s. Their efficiency increases by $^*\Gamma_j^s$. The labour and machine balances amount to:

$$\begin{aligned}
(\Gamma_1^1)^{-1}L_1^1H_1^1 + (\Gamma_2^1)^{-1}L_2^1H_2^1 + (\Gamma_3^1)^{-1}L_3^1H_3^1 &= (\Gamma^1)^{-1}L^1H^1 \neq L^1 \\
(\Gamma_1^2)^{-1}L_1^2H_1^2 + (\Gamma_2^2)^{-1}L_2^2H_2^2 + (\Gamma_3^2)^{-1}L_3^2H_3^2 &= (\Gamma^2)^{-1}L^2H^2 \neq L^2 \\
(\Gamma^1)^{-1}L^1H^1 + (\Gamma^2)^{-1}L^2H^2 &= L = L^1 + L^2 = L_1 + L_2 + L_3 \\
(^*\Gamma_1^1)^{-1}K_1^1H_1^1 + (^*\Gamma_2^1)^{-1}K_2^1H_2^1 + (^*\Gamma_3^1)^{-1}K_3^1H_3^1 &= (^*\Gamma^1)^{-1}K^1H^1 \neq K^1 \\
(^*\Gamma_1^2)^{-1}K_1^2H_1^2 + (^*\Gamma_2^2)^{-1}K_2^2H_2^2 + (^*\Gamma_3^2)^{-1}K_3^2H_3^2 &= (^*\Gamma^2)^{-1}K^2H^2 \neq K^2
\end{aligned} \tag{15.18}$$

L^1 and L^2 are the initial numbers of workers operating machines of type 1 and 2. Due to differential technological progress, labour is reallocated between these two types of machines so that the new numbers of workers are $(\Gamma^1)^{-1}L^1H^1$ and $(\Gamma^2)^{-1}L^2H^2$, but the available work force remains the same. For that reason workers will be reallocated among industries but their total number will remain the same ($L_j^r \neq L_j$ but $\Sigma L_j^r \neq \Sigma L_j = L$, L_j^r is reallocated labour in industry j). If the number of workers operating machines of type s increases by factor H^s, so must the number of machines. But their efficiency increases by factor $^*\Gamma^s$ and so the actual number of machines increases by factor $(^*\Gamma^s)^{-1}H^s$. The total number of machines of both types will generally *not* be equal to the initial number.

It will be assumed that the output of the two types of machines installed in the same industry increase by the same factor:

$$H_1^1 = H_1^2 = H_1$$
$$H_2^1 = H_2^2 = H_2 \qquad (15.19)$$
$$H_3^1 = H_3^2 = H_3$$

and that these gross factors are constant. Constant gross factors of output of machines mean also that stocks of machines expand at the same rates (for $n = \text{const.}$):

$$({}^*\Gamma^1)^{-1} H^1 = H_2$$
$$({}^*\Gamma^2)^{-1} H^2 = H_3$$

These expressions ought to be substituted in the last two equations of (15.18). The first two equations of (15.18) may be substituted into the third thus reducing the number of equations to three. All individual technological progress factors Γ_j^s and ${}^*\Gamma_j^s$ are exogenously given. Thus, there are nine variables ($H_1^1, H_2^1, H_3^1, H_1^2, H_2^2, H_3^2, H_1, H_2$ and H_3) and nine equations (15.18 and 15.19). Outputs of machines X_2 and X_3 are at the same time gross investment. Since it is assumed that the pattern of technological progress is such that they expand at constant rates, replacements are known functions of those rates, $\delta = \delta(h_i)$.

Different H_i indicate a Pasinetti system with different interest rates for each industry. For efficient pricing we need one single h_1 common to the entire system. That problem will be considered in the next chapter.

There is one final remark. K^s represents the number of machines of type s. Machines remain physically unchanged and can be counted. This is a logical construction and not a realistic assumption. Technological progress not only increases efficiency, but also changes machines physically. In order to preserve the possibility of aggregation, one would have to express the machines in terms of baskets at the current productivity of labour. In this way heterogeneous products would be reduced to one homogeneous commodity that could be counted.

16 The general case: many consumer and producer goods

16.1 Constant technology

16.1.1 Price and quantity equations

The economy operates with homogeneous labour and m machines and produces n consumer goods. We first consider a restricted case where there is no technological progress and the structure of demand remains unchanged. Physical work time spent in production changes at a constant rate $g \gtreqless 0$. Consequently, all industries expand (contract) at the same rate. We shall also assume that all machines have the same durability ($n_i = n$ for all i). With these assumptions the rental rate will be uniform throughout the economy ($r = \delta + g$).

The system of price equations consists of two blocks: consumer good prices ($p_1, \dots p_n$) and machine prices ($p_{n+1}, \dots p_{n+m}$).

$$
\begin{array}{ll}
C\text{-prices} & \begin{array}{l} rp_{n+1}\kappa_1^1 + \dots + rp_{n+m}\kappa_1^m + w\lambda_1 = p_1 \\ \cdots\cdots\cdots\cdots\cdots\cdots \\ rp_{n+1}\kappa_n^1 + \dots + rp_{n+m}\kappa_n^m + w\lambda_n = p_n \end{array} \\
M\text{-prices} & \begin{array}{l} rp_{n+1}\kappa_{n+1}^1 + \dots + rp_{n+m}\kappa_{n+1}^m + w\lambda_{n+1} = p_{n+1} \\ \cdots\cdots\cdots\cdots\cdots\cdots \\ rp_{n+1}\kappa_{n+m}^1 + \dots + rp_{n+m}\kappa_{n+m}^m + w\lambda_{n+m} = p_{n+m} \end{array}
\end{array}
\qquad (16.1)
$$

A capital coefficient $\kappa_1^s = \dfrac{K_1^s}{X_i}$ represents the number of machines of type s ($s = 1, \dots, m$) per unit of output in industry i ($i = 1, \dots, n+m$).

There are $n+m+2$ variables ($n+m$ prices, w and r) and $n+m$ equations so that real wage $\tilde{w} = w/p_i$ can be expressed as a function of r.

The solution of the system is simplified if we first solve block M of machine prices and then substitute these prices into block C. In more compact notation:

$$
K^C = \begin{bmatrix} \kappa_1^1 \dots \kappa_n^1 \\ \cdots\cdots \\ \kappa_1^m \dots \kappa_n^m \end{bmatrix}, \qquad \begin{array}{l} \lambda^0 = [\lambda_1 \dots \lambda_n] \\ p^C = [p_1 \dots p_n] \end{array}
$$

$$
K^M = \begin{bmatrix} \kappa_{n+1}^1 \dots \kappa_{n+m}^1 \\ \cdots\cdots \\ \kappa_{n+1}^m \dots \kappa_{n+m}^m \end{bmatrix}, \qquad \begin{array}{l} \lambda^M = [\lambda_{n+1} \dots \lambda_{n+m}] \\ p^M = [p_{n+1} \dots p_{n+m}] \end{array}
$$

Consequently:

$$p^M = rp^M K^M + w\lambda^M = w\lambda^M (I - rK^M)^{-1} \tag{16.2}$$

$$p^C = rp^M K^C + w\lambda^C = w[\lambda^C + \lambda^M (I - rK^M)^{-1} rK^C] \tag{16.3}$$

It is of some interest to note the algebraic implications of our industry classification. If all commodities are used directly or indirectly in the production of each commodity, the matrix of input coefficients K is indecomposable and its rank is equal to the number of commodities $(n+m)$. If some commodities are not used in the production of other commodities but only appear as inputs in their own production (Sraffian 'non-basics'), the input coefficient matrix can be decomposed into a block-triangular matrix with two or more indecomposable square submatrices located on the diagonal:

$$K = \begin{bmatrix} A^1 & & 0 \\ \dots & \ddots \; A^r & \\ K^C & & K^M \end{bmatrix}$$

In a decomposable matrix, circularity is replaced by a unidirectional relation between inputs and outputs. That property has two economic consequences. First, the isolated submatrix of 'basics' (K^M) is sufficient for the determination of prices of 'basics', and the determination of the profit rate of the entire system. On the other hand, the output of 'non-basics' requires the input of not only their own commodities but also the input of 'basics' (K^C). Thus, secondly, for the rate of profit to be uniform for the entire system, nonbasics in isolation ($K^C = 0$) must generate higher rate of profit than 'basics' as otherwise they would be unable to absorb the input of 'basics' at positive prices of their own outputs (Zaghini, 1967).

If 'non-basics' are pure consumption goods, as in our classification of industries, the input matrix is decomposed in a special way:

$$K = \left[\begin{array}{c:c} 0 & 0 \\ \hdashline K^C & K^M \end{array}\right]$$

and its rank is reduced by n. That simplifies the analysis. Consumption goods are pure in the sense that they cannot be used as durable producer goods but they may enter production as intermediate goods. In the process they disappear being absorbed into full capital and labour coefficients.

Machine prices have an interesting feature. Use (16.2) with $w=1$ to obtain exact labour prices:

$$p^M=\lambda^M(I-rK^M)^{-1}, \quad w=1$$

These prices are 'full' labour coefficients, $p^M=\bar{\bar{\lambda}}^M$ as can easily be demonstrated:

$$\bar{\bar{\lambda}}^M=\lambda^M+(rK^M)\bar{\bar{\lambda}}_M=\lambda^M(I-rK^M)^{-1} \tag{16.4}$$

But coefficients λ^M themselves represent full labour coefficients with respect to vertical integration of intermediate goods (ch. 2.2):

$$\lambda=\hat{\lambda}(I-A)^{-1}$$

where $\hat{\lambda}$ represent original, direct labour coefficients and A the original matrix of input–output coefficients. Thus machine prices represent doubly integrated labour coefficients (therefore lambda double-bar): first with respect to intermediate goods and second with respect to capital goods.

Machine prices may also be derived by repeated rounds of vertical integration. To produce one machine of type one, it is necessary to use κ_1^1, κ_1^2, κ_1^3, etc. machines of type one, two, three etc. These machines must also be produced, and for their production it is necessary to use $\lambda_{n+1}\kappa_1^1$, $\lambda_{n+2}\kappa_1^2$, $\lambda_{n+3}\kappa_1^3$, etc. quantities of labour. We may repeat the same calculation for yet another round of production and still another etc. Let $\lambda_{-1}^M=\lambda^M K^M$ be the row vector of labour requirements in the first round back and the corresponding prices be $p_{-1}^M=p^M K^M$. Multiplying the price equation (16.2) by K^M, we may write:

$$p^M K^M=p_{-1}^M=\lambda^M K^M+rp^M K^M K^M=\lambda_{-1}^M+rp_{-1}^M K^M$$

and similarly:

$$p_{-1}^M K^M=p_{-2}^M=\lambda_{-1}^M K^M+rp_{-1}^M K^M K^M=\lambda_{-2}^M+rp_{-2}^M K^M$$

We may continue repeating the rounds of integration as far as we like. The substitution into (16.2) gives:

$$p^M=\lambda^M+r\lambda_{-1}^M+r^2\lambda_{-2}^M+r^3\lambda_{-3}^M+\ldots$$

The series is clearly convergent for all $0\leq r<R$. Machine prices turn out to consist of the sums of successively vertically integrated labour requirements

weighted by the increasing powers of the rental rate (for similar reasoning see Pasinetti, 1980, pp. 18–30).

Price equations (16.1) may be written even more compactly:

$$\left[\begin{array}{c:c} p^M & w \end{array}\right]\left[\begin{array}{c:c} rK^C & r\bar{K}^M \\ \hdashline \lambda^C & \lambda^M \end{array}\right]=\left[\begin{array}{c:c} p^C & 0 \end{array}\right]$$

or as

$$\bar{p}^M T=\bar{p}^C \tag{16.5}$$

where the symbols used are:

$$\bar{p}^M=[p^M \vdots\, w],\quad T=\left[\begin{array}{c:c} rK^C & r\bar{K}^M \\ \hdashline \lambda^C & \lambda^M \end{array}\right],\quad \bar{K}^M=\begin{bmatrix} \kappa^1_{n+1}-1 \ldots \kappa^1_{n+m} \\ \ldots\ldots\ldots\ldots\ldots\ldots \\ \kappa^m_{n+1} \quad \ldots \kappa^m_{n+m}-1 \end{bmatrix}$$

$$\bar{p}^C=[p^C \vdots\, 0],$$

Similarly quantity equations are:

$$\left[\begin{array}{c:c} rK^C & r\bar{K}^M \\ \hdashline \lambda^C & \lambda^M \end{array}\right]\begin{bmatrix} X^C \\ \ldots \\ X^M \end{bmatrix}=\begin{bmatrix} 0 \\ \ldots \\ L \end{bmatrix},\quad \begin{bmatrix} X^C \\ \ldots \\ X^M \end{bmatrix}=X,\quad \begin{bmatrix} 0 \\ \ldots \\ L \end{bmatrix}=\bar{L}$$

$$TX=\bar{L} \tag{16.6}$$

There are $m+1$ equations and $m+n$ variables so that $n-1$ degrees of freedom are available to accommodate changes in consumer demand.

The labour value of consumer goods – net product – is equal to currently available labour time:

$$\sum_{i=1}^{n} p_i X_i=\bar{p}^C X=(\bar{p}^M T)X=\bar{p}^M(TX)=\bar{p}^M\bar{L}=L$$

The result also follows directly from the equality of supply and demand, $\Sigma p_i X_i=wL$, $w=1$.

From $p^C X^C=L$ and (16.3), we can find how current labour time is divided between consumer goods industries:

$$\lambda^C X^C=\sum_{i=1}^{n}\lambda_i X_i=\sum_{i=1}^{n} L_i$$

and producer goods industries:

$$[\lambda^M(I-rK^M)^{-1}rK^C]\,X^C = L - \sum_{i=1}^{n} L_i = \sum_{i=n+1}^{n+m} L_i$$

As the technology and the structure do not change, the division of labour between two groups of industries remains constant through time and so λ^C indicates living labour and $\lambda^M(I-rK^M)^{-1}rK^C$ embodied labour in the formation of consumer goods prices. The embodied labour is an increasing function of r.

16.1.2 Relative prices

Two blocks of prices generate three types of relative prices:

$$\frac{p_i}{p_j} = \frac{rp^M K_i^C + w\lambda_i}{rp^M K_j^C + w\lambda_j}, \qquad i,j = 1, \ldots n \tag{16.7a}$$

$$\frac{p_r}{p_s} = \frac{rp^M K_r^M + w\lambda_r}{rp^M K_s^M + w\lambda_s}, \qquad r,s = n+1, \ldots n+m \tag{16.7b}$$

$$\frac{p_r}{p_j} = \frac{rp^M K_r^M + w\lambda_r}{rp^M K_j^C + w\lambda_j}, \qquad \begin{array}{l} j = 1, \ldots n \\ r = n+1, \ldots n+m \end{array} \tag{16.7c}$$

There are four characteristic cases of relative prices. I shall call them – somewhat arbitrarily – the Marxian, Sraffian, uniform ω and general case.

1. *Marxian case*: $r=0$, and wages are maximal, $\tilde{w} = \tilde{W}$. Price ratios are fully determined by labour coefficients:

$$\frac{p_i}{p_j} = \frac{\lambda_i}{\lambda_j}, \qquad i,j = 1, \ldots n+m \tag{16.8}$$

   For $w=1$, absolute prices are equal to labour coefficients.

2. *Sraffian case*: $w=0$, and profits are maximal, $r=R$. Rentals cancel out, and relative prices are again fully determined by technology

$$\frac{p_i}{p_j} = \frac{p^M K_i^C}{p^m K_j^C}, \qquad i,j = 1, \ldots n \tag{16.9}$$

   where K_i^C is the ith column of the matrix of capital-coefficients K^C. Similar relations hold for the other two types of relative prices. Relative prices remain invariant from r even if wages are positive, but are included in the technology matrix as reproduction costs. However, then K^M, K^C and p^M are different from the ones used here.

3. *Uniform organic composition of resources*: $\omega = p^M K_i^u / w\lambda_i$, $u = C, M$. *Absolute* prices *vary* with r, but *relative* prices remain invariant.

$$\frac{p_i}{p_j} = \frac{rp^M K_i^C + w\lambda_i}{rp^M K_j^C + w\lambda_j} = \frac{w\lambda_i(r\omega + 1)}{w\lambda_j(r\omega + 1)} = \frac{p^M K_i^C\left(r + \frac{1}{\omega}\right)}{p^M K_j^C\left(r + \frac{1}{\omega}\right)}$$

$$\frac{p_i}{p_j} = \frac{\lambda_i}{\lambda_j} = \frac{p^M K_i^C}{p^M K_j^C}, \qquad i,j = 1, \ldots n \tag{16.10}$$

and similarly for p_r/p_M and p_r/p_j. It turns out that the cases termed Marxian and Sraffian are special cases of the uniform organic composition of resources when either $r = 0$ or $w = 0$.

Besides, R and ω are related in a simple fashion. From (16.2):

$$p^M = Rp^M K^M, \qquad w = 0 \tag{16.11}$$

Thus, $1/R = \lambda^*$ is the Frobenius eigenvalue of the indecomposable semipositive matrix K^M. Consequently there is only one vector of postive prices p^M determined up to a multiplicative constant. Since:

$$p^M K^M = \omega w \lambda^M$$

we may also use (16.2) to derive:

$$p^M = W\lambda^M = \frac{1}{\omega} p^M K^M, \qquad r = 0 \tag{16.12}$$

It follows from (16.11) and (16.12) that:

$$R = \frac{1}{\omega} \tag{16.13}$$

maximal rental rate is equal to the reciprocal value of the uniform organic composition of resources.

4. *The general case of relative price invariance*: $p_i/p_j = \text{const}$. Consider any two price ratios invariant to r:

$$\frac{p_i}{p_K} = \frac{rp^M K_i^u + w\lambda_i}{rp^M K_k^u + w\lambda_k} = \mathrm{a}$$

$$\frac{p_j}{p_K} = \frac{rp^M K_j^u + w\lambda_j}{rp^M K_k^u + w\lambda_k} = \mathrm{b}$$

where a and b are constants. Multiply both fractions by their denominators and rearrange:

$$rp^M(K_i^u - aK_k^u) = w(a\lambda_k - \lambda_i)$$
$$rp^M(K_j^u - bK_k^u) = w(b\lambda_k - \lambda_j)$$

Divide the two relations through each other:

$$\frac{p^M(K_i^u - aK_k^u)}{p^M(K_j^u - bK_k^u)} = \frac{a\lambda_k - \lambda_i}{b\lambda_k - \lambda_j} = c$$

where c does not change with r and w.

Rewrite to obtain:

$$p^M[K_i^u - cK_j^u - (a + bc)K_k^u] = 0 \qquad (16.14)$$

Since $p^M > 0$, the relation in square brackets must be zero if it is to hold for every p^M and not only by fluke. This implies linear dependence of the columns of capital coefficients matrix K^u. That is exactly what equalization of organic composition of resources does: the columns of K^u become proportional to each other. From (16.10)

$$\lambda_i P^M K_j^u - \lambda_j p^M K_i^u = p^M(\lambda_i K_j^u - \lambda_j K_i^u) = 0$$

$$K_j^u = \frac{\lambda_j}{\lambda_i} K_i^u \qquad (16.15)$$

16.1.3 The wage curve

Nominal wage w in (16.2) and (16.3) may be deflated either by the price of a consumer good or by the price of a basket of the same standard assortment of consumer goods. Under our assumptions, the structure of consumer demand does not change and so total consumption behaves like a single composite good.

I choose the simpler procedure and express wages in terms of consumer good number one, $\tilde{w} = w/p_1$. The wage curve is then determined by the relation:

$$\tilde{w}[\lambda^C+\lambda^M(I-rK^M)^{-1}rK^C]e_1=1 \tag{16.16}$$

where e_1 is a unit column vector with the first element unity and other zero. The inverse $(I-rK^M)^{-1}$ implies a polynomial of the mth degree (which is the order of the matrix K^M) in r. Since there is another r associated with K^C, the wage curve is a polynomial of the $m+1$st degree.

For $r=0$, maximum wage is equal to $\tilde{W}=1/\lambda_1$. For $\tilde{w}=0$, consumer goods are not produced and maximum R is determined from (16.2) as a reciprocal of the Frobenius eigenvalue of the matrix K^M. If a technique is changed in a consumer good industry, machine prices remain unchanged, $p^M=$const., and so does R. If a change occurs in a producer good industry, all prices and R change, but maximum $\tilde{W}$ remains unchanged (assuming, of course, that the real wage is expressed in consumer goods). Since at a switch point only one technique can change (otherwise prices would generally not be equal), the existence of one switch implies that two wage curves either originate or terminate in the same point depending on whether the technique is changed in a producer or a consumer good industry. If there is more than one switch, and the techniques changed belong to the same $(K_j^u\lambda^u)$ block, all wage curves will have either the same beginning or the same end. If changes occur in both blocks, wage curves will originate and terminate in different points.

Between the two points there may be many switches and reswitches of techniques. In Fig. 16.1 point 2 represents reswitching when technology α recurs. At each switch point only one (consumer good) technique is changed.

Reswitching may imply, but need not, capital reversal. Consider the organic composition of resources:

$$\omega=\frac{\sum_s p_{n+s}K^s}{L}$$

The same technology recurs at higher r, but the value of capital remains undetermined. Prices must rise, because rentals increase, while technical coefficients remain the same.[1] But at the same time the output of consumer goods will decrease and the replacement of C-capital by M-capital may generate composition effect, which may outweigh the price effect. If instead of dual curve, we consider the distribution curve (K and L remain the same, $\tilde{w}$ and r change), reswitching will necessarily imply capital reversal.

Even that conclusion does not hold if capital is measured in terms of a consumer good and not in labour prices. Let it be the first consumer good:

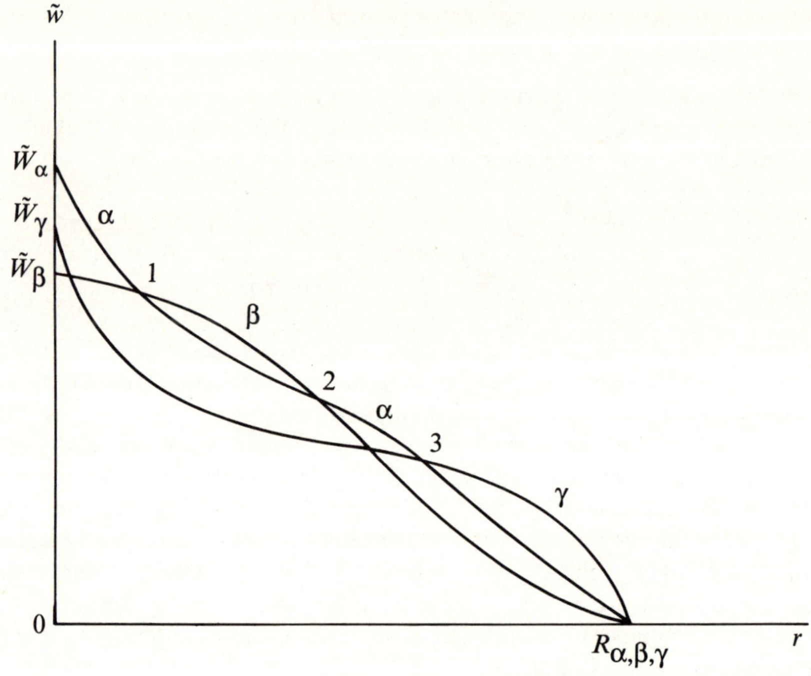

Figure 16.1 Technological frontier with reswitching of techniques in consumer good industries

$$\tilde{k} = \frac{\frac{1}{p_1} \sum_s p_{n+s} K^s}{L}$$

If p_1 happens to rise faster than any of p_{n+s}, then also prices of capital goods, p_{n+s}/p_1, may decrease.

In general, higher rental may increase or decrease the use of capital measured either in labour time or in terms of consumption goods. Reswitching may or may not imply capital reversal except for the distribution curve where ω necessarily increases.

16.1.4 Linear wage curves

A linear wage curve implies that relative prices are invariant to changes in r. We have already systematically examined the conditions for invariance of relative prices. We shall now restate the problem in a slightly different way.

There is only one ω, one R and one vector of prices that satisfy the invariance requirement, as shown in section 16.1.2. Consumer prices are determined by a system of linear equations (16.3):

$$rp^M K_i^C + \lambda_i = p_i, \qquad i = 1, \ldots n$$

which has a unique solution for any $0 < r < R$ because p^M is unique and technical coefficients are fixed. In order that relative consumer goods prices be also invariant, their production must be constrained by a uniform ω (not necessary the same as the former).

If relative prices are unique and invariant, there is a unique linear relation between wages and rentals, represented by a decreasing linear function of r:

$$\frac{w}{p_1} = \tilde{w} = a - br \tag{16.17}$$

The constants a and b may be determined as follows.

Since relative prices are constant and unique for all admissible values of r, the following must hold:

$$\tilde{W}^M = R\frac{p^M}{p_1}K^M = r\frac{p^M}{p_1}K^M + \tilde{w}\lambda^M$$

Eliminating λ^M or $(p^M/p_1)K^M$ from the two equations, the third yields the required linear relation:

$$\tilde{w} = \tilde{W}\left(1 - \frac{r}{R}\right) \tag{16.17a}$$

where $\tilde{W} = a$, $\dfrac{\tilde{W}}{R} = b$.

Linear wage curves, i.e. wage straight lines, intersect, of course, only once and technological frontier has nice neoclassical properties.

Contrary to the first impression, linear wage curves are not unrealistic. If real wage is expressed in consumer goods actually produced, which is a natural procedure to apply, i.e.:

$$p^C X^C = 1, \qquad \tilde{w} = \frac{w}{p^C X^C}$$

(16.16) is transformed into:

$$\tilde{w}[\lambda^C + \lambda^M (I - rK^M)^{-1} rK^C] X^C = 1 \tag{16.16a}$$

When applied in empirical work,[2] this formula generated linear wage curve. Why?

The block of X^C industries is likely to have the ratio of aggregate value of output to aggregate value of input (a sort of Sraffian R) rather close to that of X^M industries although the output–input ratios of individual industries may greatly deviate. It is *not* necessary that every industry has the same R throughout the economy. If we measure output in terms of a composite good, it is sufficient that the R of that good is the same as that of the rest of economy.

Express (16.2) and (16.3) as value balances, i.e. multiply the equations by X^M and X^C:

$$\begin{aligned} rp^M K^M X^M + w\lambda^M X^M &= p^M X^M \\ rp^M K^C X^C + w\lambda^C X^C &= p^C X^C \end{aligned} \tag{16.18}$$

Impose the same R on both sectors:

$$R = \frac{p^M X^M}{p^M K^M X^M} = \frac{p^C X^C}{p^M K^C X^C}$$

so as to obtain:

$$\begin{aligned} w\lambda^M X^M &= p^M X^M \left(1 - \frac{r}{R}\right) \\ w\lambda^C X^C &= p^C X^C \left(1 - \frac{r}{R}\right) \end{aligned} \tag{16.19}$$

The ratio of values of the two outputs is equal to:

$$\frac{p^M X^M}{p^C X^C} = \frac{\lambda^M X^M}{\lambda^C X^C} = \frac{L^M}{L^C} \tag{16.20}$$

and is independent of r for the distribution curve (i = const.).

Equal standard ratio $R(w=0)$ implies, of course, equal organic composition $\omega(r=0)$. Substitute uniform:

$$\omega = \frac{p^M K^M X^M}{w\lambda^M X^M} = \frac{p^M K^C X^C}{w\lambda^C X^C}$$

into value balances (16.18) to obtain:

$$(r\omega+1)w\lambda^M X^M = p^M X^M$$
$$(r\omega+1)w\lambda^C X^C = p^C X^C$$

The ratio of value of outputs is the same and independent from r as in (16.20). However, a caveat is necessary:

$$\frac{p^M X^M}{p^C X^C} = \frac{L^M}{L^C} = \text{const.}$$

holds for the *distribution curve only* (i=const.), not for the dual curve, because any change in $r=i$ will change the distribution of labour (L^M/L^C) between the two sectors. Also, unlike in a two sector economy, $p_i/p_j \neq \lambda_i/\lambda_j$ = const. because individual industries have widely different organic compositions and only two average ω's are assumed equal.

Divide the second value balance of (16.18) by $p^C X^C$, and the linear relation emerges:

$$r = R(1 - \tilde{w}L^C)$$

For $r=0$, $L^C=L$ and maximum wage from (16.18) is $\tilde{W}=1/L$. The substitution gives the Sraffian relation:

$$r = R\left(1 - \frac{\tilde{w}}{\tilde{W}}\right)$$

valid for the distribution curve.

The price of machine s is given by $rp^M \kappa^M_{n+s} + w\lambda_{n+s} = p_{n+s}$, $\kappa^M_{n+s} = \{\kappa^1_{n+s}, \ldots, \kappa^m_{n+s}\}$. If all prices are expressed in terms of machine s, the equation changes into:

$$r\frac{p^M \kappa^M_{n+s}}{p_{n+s}} + \tilde{w}\lambda_{n+s} = 1, \qquad \tilde{w} = \frac{w}{p_{n+s}}$$

The wage curve is given by:

$$\tilde{w} = \frac{1}{\lambda_{n+s}}\left(1 - r\frac{p^M \kappa^M_{n+s}}{p_{n+s}}\right) \tag{16.21}$$

It will be linear if $(p^M/p_{n+s})\kappa^M_{n+s} = c$ = const. The condition is satisfied in the following three cases:

1. There is a constant relation between capital cost and price $p^M \kappa^M_{n+s} = cp_{n+s}$.
2. There is a constant relation between the value of aggregate inputs and the value of aggregate outputs, $p^M \kappa^M X^M = cp^M X^M$, which implies uniform organic composition of machine industries with $c = \omega/(1+\omega)$.
3. There is only one capital good and so $p^M = p_{n+1}$, $\kappa_{n+s} = \kappa_{n+1}$.

   The conclusion is simple. If real wage is expressed in terms of machines, and there is only one type of machines, wage curves are always straight lines. If there exist more than one type of machines in the economy, the organic composition of resources in the machine industries must be uniform. Prices in consumer goods industries may vary in whatever fashion.

We may conclude. In order to linearize the distribution curve, it is not necessary to use the artificial Sraffian standard commodity as a *numéraire* and be subject to a critique that no one consumes such a commodity. There exists a real commodity that will do the trick: the basket of consumer goods or any single commodity produced under conditions of average ω. The actual basket of consumer goods as a *numéraire* will produce approximate linearization. For strict linearity we have to impose uniform ω or R on both sectors. Empirically, the correction proves negligible, except for the beginning and the end of the distribution curve (Petrović, 1986).

16.1.5 Linear wage curve and changing relative prices in consumer goods industries

The economy consists of pure wage goods industries and mixed producer goods industries. In such a case r is uniquely determined in the producer goods sector, whatever the price in the consumer goods sector. Express the real wage in terms of one producer good price or the value of producer goods. If the relation is linear, then also $\tilde{w}$ can be determined in the producer goods sector. Since r and $\tilde{w}$ are the same for both sectors, we can determine them without considering the consumer goods sector at all.

16.2 Industrial interdependence effects

If a theoretical paradigm is based on the behaviour of individual economic agents – as is the case with classical and neoclassical theories – there is a natural tendency to succumb to the 'fallacy of composition': to simply extend microeconomics into macroeconomics while failing to study the system's effects. This tendency is the stronger the more counter-intuitive such effects are. Throughout the present study the interdependence effects have been encountered quite frequently. Now four more are added.

1. *Changes in nominal wage rates*. If there is unemployment, a reduction of wages (e.g. by reducing social insurance contributions paid by firms) is often suggested as a cure. The suggestion is justified by two different reasons: (a) due to falling marginal productivity of labour, lower wages will induce greater employment and (b) cheaper labour makes labour intensive technology more profitable and that also increases employment. Now, if (a) lower wages simply result in greater unspent profits, and not in greater investment, the ensuing fall in the aggregate demand will even *increase* unemployment – as Keynes already knew. If (b) wages are reduced as well but less than proportionally since wages represent only a fraction of the cost of production. But in an interdependent economy output of one industry is input to another and so there will be a second round of price reduction. When the process of adjustments comes to an end in the new long-run equilibrium, nominal prices will be reduced in exactly the same proportion as wages, relative prices will remain the same and there will be no incentive to substitute a more labour intensive technology and increase employment.[3] As equations (16.2) and (16.3) demonstrate, that applies equally to consumer and producer goods industries.

   The foregoing deductive reasoning must not be confused with an empirical theory. Economic processes occur in time, time dependent technological progress, expectations, etc. change the decision parameters and the long-run equilibrium is, in fact, never reached. Also the processes occur within a set of social institutions: a planned economy will react differently from a *laissez-faire* one. Thus, an empirical theory is much richer in variables and relations. Yet, however rich, its pure deductive set of propositions must be logically valid.

2. *Changes in nominal prices*. By postulating diminishing marginal utility and diminishing marginal productivity, a universal inverse relationship between prices and quantities demanded is deduced. And, indeed, if the price of an input is reduced, the profit maximizing firm will try to substitute it for another, more expensive one and, thus, increase the demand for the cheaper commodity. A consumer will react similarly. Macroeconomically, that is different. If there is no technological progress, the price of commodity can be lowered only if wages in industry producing that commodity are lowered (given profits). In a competitive (or heavily unionized and planned) economy with equal wage and profit rates, that will imply lowering prices and wages throughout the economy with the final result as in (1). Consequently, lower prices of an input will not increase the demand for that producer good. Neither will it increase demand for a pure consumer good regardless of the fact that consumer goods do not enter inputs and so

the circularity within the system is interrupted. As is evident from (16.2) and (16.3), prices are determined exclusively by wages and technology. Since technology does not change and wages are equally reduced in all industries, relative prices of consumer goods and real wages do not change. Consequently, neither can the aggregate demand for any consumer good change (given the preferences).

The other possibility for changing nominal prices is to change r. As is shown in Table 10.1, an increase in basket prices (due to an increase in r) leads to a reduction of quantities produced and the inverse relationship is preserved. But an *increase* in machine prices *increases* the number of machines produced (because of an increase in investment) and that perversity destroys the inverse relationship.

3. *Changes in real wages*. The foregoing effects are clearly due to the fact that, under the postulated conditions, changes in nominal prices and wage rates leave relative prices and real wages unchanged. Consider now real magnitudes and take the first consumer good as a *numéraire* ($p_1 = 1$). It is, of course, a separate question how in a real world economy real wages can be reduced or increased. Either somehow investment is changed or real profits are changed or both. Suppose the change occurred and real wages are reduced.

Lower $\tilde{w}$ implies a different $(\tilde{w}, r)$ point on the technology frontier which, in turn, generally implies a different profit maximizing technology. This new technology may well be less rather than more labour intensive and may decrease rather than increase employment. The effect is most clearly seen if we employ our canonical model again.

Consider Fig. 11.1. In cases (a) and (b) the machine industry changes technique, in (c) and (d) the basket industry does that. In all cases, and in the two not shown, the lowering of wages induces a switch from a less labour intensive to a more labour intensive technique ($\lambda_j^{\alpha} < \lambda_j^{\beta}$). Thus, *total* (living and embodied) labour intensity changes regularly. But labour productivity based on living labour only may change differently. Take Fig. 11.2 (11.1c) for further consideration.

The relation between direct and full coefficients as given by (2.8) is:

$$\hat{\lambda} = \lambda(I - A)$$
$$\hat{\kappa} = \kappa(I - A)$$

In our case the technique changes in the first industry so that $\lambda_1^{\alpha} < \lambda_1^{\beta}$. Since the techniques are efficient, capital coefficients must be inversely related, $\kappa_1^{\alpha} > \kappa_1^{\beta}$. The second industry technique (λ_2, κ_2) remains unchanged. Consider the simplest possible case when machines enter production as producer durables and baskets enter production as intermediate goods and there are no other intermediate goods. Thus, input matrix A has only one row of coefficients:

$$A=\begin{bmatrix} a_{11} & a_{12} \\ 0 & 0 \end{bmatrix}$$

We can now derive unknown direct coefficients from the known full coefficients:

$$\hat{\lambda}_1=\lambda_1(1-a_{11}) \qquad \hat{\lambda}_2=\lambda_2-a_{12}\lambda_1$$
$$\hat{\kappa}_1=\kappa_1(1-a_{11}) \qquad \hat{\kappa}_2=\kappa_2-a_{12}\kappa_1$$

The implications are as follows:

(a) If A remains unchanged, direct labour coefficients in the first industry move in the same direction as full coefficients, $\hat{\lambda}_1^{\alpha}<\hat{\lambda}_1^{\beta}$. An increase of the rental rate beyond the switch point r^* increases both direct and full labour intensity of output. That may be called the *regular* change.

(b) Although (λ_2, κ_2) does not change, $(\hat{\lambda}_2, \hat{\kappa}_2)$ does: a change of *full* coefficient technique in one industry implies changes of *direct* coefficient techniques in both industries.

(c) Moreover, $\hat{\lambda}_2^{\alpha}>\hat{\lambda}_2^{\beta}$, which implies a *perverse* change since labour intensity of output diminishes as r increases.[4]

(d) Capital coefficients also change differently, κ_1 regularly and κ_2 perversely.

(e) Since (λ_2, κ_2) remains unchanged, so does the price of machines. Consequently, value capital coefficients change as technical coefficients in (d).

(f) Mechanization (capital–worker) ratios:

$$k_1^{\alpha}>k_1^{\beta}, \quad k_2^{\alpha}<k_2^{\beta}, \quad k_i=\frac{\kappa_i}{\lambda_i}$$

change regularly in the first and perversely in the second industry and so do their values. But the aggregate value of capital per worker (the slope of the tangent to wage curves α and β at r^*) changes regularly, as already found in section 11.3.

(g) If A also changes at the switch point r^*, direct coefficients in either industry may move in any possible way in relation to full coefficients.

4. *Changes in relative prices.* As Table 10.1 demonstrates, all depends on the relative mechanization m. For $m=0$, relative prices will not change, while nominal prices may increase or decrease with the effects described under point (2). Whenever p_1 and p_2 increase, the output of baskets will decrease and the output of machines increase regardless of what happens to the relative price $p_2/p_1=\tilde{p}_2$. At the same time $\tilde{p}_2$ is an increasing function of r for $m<0$, and a decreasing function for $m>0$.

   In general, there is no universally valid relationship between prices and quantities in the general equilibrium setting. They may move together or in opposite directions depending on whether a commodity is a consumer or a producer good, depending on the organic composition of resources and on whether direct or total labour input is considered.

16.3 Technological progress

Unembodied technological progress affects all labour and capital coefficients and at different rates. Each machine has a different life-span n_m. Rising income and consumer preferences generate changes in the demand structure. Consequently, each industry expands (contracts) at a different rate h_j and replacement rates are not only different for different machines but also for the same machines installed in different industries. Let δ_j^s be the replacement rate of the sth machine installed in the jth industry, and h_j^s rate of expansion of the stock of the machines s in industry j. Since all replacement and growth rates are different, so are gross investment rates $r_j^s=\delta_j^s+h_j^s$.

16.3.1 Quantity equations

At the beginning of the period, the labour balance is given by:

$$\sum_{j=1}^{n+m} L_j=L$$

Let $g=0$ and let technological progress affect labour coefficients. The new labour balance at the end of the period is:

$$\sum_{j=1}^{n+m} \Gamma_j^{-1}L_jH_j=(\Gamma^{-1}L)\Gamma=L \tag{16.22}$$

where Γ_j^{-1} is an average for L_j workers operating m machines in industry j, $\Gamma=(1+\gamma)$ is the grand average productivity growth of living labour for the economy and $H_j=1+h_j$ are growth factors by which various industries must change their outputs in order to keep full employment and satisfy changed demand.

At the beginning of the period the number of machines of type s installed in various industries j is given by:

$$\sum_{j=1}^{n+m} K_j^s = K^s, \qquad s=1,\dots m$$

At the end of the period the capacity balance for various machines – which determines the necessary new investment during the year – will be:

$$\sum_{j=1}^{n+m} K_j^s H_j = K^s H^s, \qquad s=1,\dots m \tag{16.23}$$

Since TP is uneven and the structure of demand changes, all growth factors are generally different, $H_i \neq H_j$, $H^r \neq H^s$. If capital coefficients do not change, machine–worker ratios in various industries will increase by Γ_j, $j=1,\dots n+m$, as the number of machines increases proportionally to the output, i.e. by H_j.

If capital coefficients also improve, individual machine–worker ratios will increase by less than Γ_j, albeit unequally, depending on individual improvements of κ_j^s. For given H_j the new capacity balance will amount to:

$$\sum_{j=1}^{n+m} (\Gamma_j^s)^{-1} K_j^s H_j = (\Gamma^s)^{-1} K^s H^s, \qquad s=1,\dots m \tag{16.24}$$

Γ^s is the average efficiency factor for the stock of machines of type s in the case of unchanged distribution of machines among industries. H^s is the factor of increase of the same stock in case capital coefficients do not change (but labour productivity increases). $(\Gamma^s)^{-1} H^s = h_{n+s} = 1 + \mu^s$ is the actual factor of change of the number of s-machines. If labour is also increasing, this factor will have to be multiplied by $G = 1 + g$.

Improved efficiency of machines means generally a smaller number of machines and, consequently, smaller new investment. This will make possible a reallocation of labour in favour of consumer good industries.

Technological progress will render some of the commodities obsolescent and their production will be discontinued. At the same time new products will be introduced. Thus, the number of industries will change, $n+m$ will usually increase.

Assuming that technological coefficients (κ_j^s, λ_j) change and all adjustments have been carried out, initial labour distribution at the beginning of the period will provide employment in the next period for workers displaced because of technological progress assumed to come to fruition by the end of the current period:

$$\text{Labour equations: } \lambda_1 X_1 + \ldots + \lambda_{n+m} X_{n+m} = L$$

$$\text{Investment equations: } \frac{\kappa_1^1 X_1 r_1^1 + \ldots + \kappa_{n+m}^1 X_{n+m} r_{n+m}^1 = K^1 r^1 = X_{n+1}}{\kappa_1^m X_1 r_1^m + \ldots + \kappa_{n+m}^m X_{n+m} r_{n+m}^m = K^m r^m = X_{n+m}} \quad (16.25)$$

$$r_j^s = \delta_j^s + \mu_j^s, \qquad r^s = \delta^s + \mu^s, \qquad \mu_j^s = (\Gamma_j^s)^{-1} H_j - 1$$

where $X_{n+1}, \ldots X_{n+m}$ represent outputs of m different machines in the current period.

Since every machine improves differently, every μ_j^s will be different. As replacements are functions of the growth rates of the stock of machines, even with the same durability every δ_j^s will be different.

If it is assumed that the efficiency of every machine increases equally in all its uses, the number of machines s and t installed in industries i and j will change as

$$\frac{(\Gamma^s)^{-1} H_i}{(\Gamma^t)^{-1} H_i} = \frac{(\Gamma^s)^{-1} H_j}{(\Gamma^t)^{-1} H_j} = \frac{\Gamma^t}{\Gamma^s}, \quad \frac{(\Gamma^s)^{-1} H_i}{(\Gamma^s)^{-1} H_j} = \frac{H_i}{H_j}$$

In other words, the number of different machines installed in the same industry varies as technological progress while the number of the same machines installed in different industries varies in proportion to outputs of those industries. Since $r_j^s = f(\Gamma^s, H_j)$, there will still exist $m \times (m+n)$ different r_j^s even with a uniform n.

Note that growth rates are no longer uniform. Since $\delta_j^s = f(\mu_j^s)$, r_j^s will remain constant if μ_j^s does. That implies that either technological progress (Γ_j^s) and output growth rate (H_j) remain constant, or their changes compensate each other. Even if all r_j^s remain constant, r^s will not and will tend to increase in time because industries with higher r_j^s will increase their weights. Nor is this the end of the story, because the factors r^s will have to be averaged. But, of course, neither technological progress nor demand changes proceed uniformly. Thus, strict calculations are possible only on the year-to-year basis. And approximations are possible on the assumption that the numerous changes that proceed in the real world tend to offset each other and leave the relevant growth rates approximately constant.

In (16.25) technological coefficients (and technological progress) are given and so are outputs planned in the preceding period under perfect foresight. Labour equation, which accommodates improvements in labour productivity, sets one restriction for $(n+m)$ growth rates h_j. If $n-1$ outputs of consumer goods are determined, so is the nth output as well. Thus we have additional $(n-1)$ equations generated by consumer demand which is a function of income and preferences. Investment equations, which incorporate changes in efficiency of machines, add the remaining m restrictions on investments in $n+m$ industries. Economic planners will take initial outputs, demand elasticities and exogenously given changes in technical coefficients as data and will use quantity balances (16.25) to compute the necessary new output for each industry $(X_j H_j)$.

16.3.2 Price equations

Summing up vertically the components of the system (16.25) evaluated at the corresponding prices and using growth rates μ^s for each type of machines, we obtain a modified Pasinetti system, which will serve as an intermediary. It is modified because the profit rate (π^s) is now uniform and different for each type of machine instead of being uniform and different for each industry. Technological progress changes differently different machines and so their number does not expand at the same rate as industrial output. Industrial π_j would remain uniform only if (a) TP affected the efficiency of all machines equally or (b) if differential industrial growth were exactly matched by differential TP. Each μ^s is a profit rate – there are $(n+m)$ of them – which renders the price system non-optimal. We would like to have a price system with one single profit rate π. In other words: we would like to design prices in the following way: use individual living labour cost (λ_i) and add stationary embodied labour costs augmented for the systemic cost of full employment. That implies an equality of the value produced and distributed for the economy as a whole, not for each industry or firm. The systemic costs consist of an increase in new investments to keep labour employed minus a decrease of unit replacement due to capital growth.

The system must generate funds to finance depreciation and new investment. The actual increase in the number of machines by type of machine is equal to:

$$K^s(1+\mu^s)G - K^s = K^s[(1+\mu^s)G - 1], \quad (1+\mu^s)G - 1 = \pi^s, \quad s = 1, \ldots m \tag{16.26}$$

The factor of increase of s-machines may also be written as:

$$(1+\mu^s)(1+g) = 1 + \mu^s + g + g\mu^s$$

the small multiplicative term $g\mu^s$ may be neglected, and so we get an approximation $\pi^s \doteq g + \mu^s$.

The uniform profit rate is obtained by equating the value of investment in different machines with the total investment fund:

$$\sum_{s=1}^{m} p_{n+s} K^s \pi^s = \pi \sum_{s=1}^{m} p_{n+s} K^s, \tag{16.27}$$

The average replacement rates by types of machine are given by:

$$\sum_{j=1}^{n+m} \delta_j^s K_j^s = \delta^s K^s, \qquad s = 1, \dots m$$

These rates assure that physical production of various machines will be sufficient for replacement of scrapped machines. There are as many rates as there are types of machines. A replacement rate δ^s is a function of the increase of a stock of machines (given durability) and their rates of increase which are different for different machines. A depreciation rate d^s depends on the growth of the value of capital at a single rate π. Thus, $\delta^s = d^s$. Again the value distributed and produced must be equal:

$$\sum_{s=1}^{m} p_{n+s} \delta^s K^s = \sum_{s=1}^{m} p_{n+s} d^s K^s \tag{16.28}$$

If all machines have the same durability, there will be one single d determined by (16.28). If the durabilities differ, we need an additional set of equations that determine $m-1$ ratios:

$$\frac{d^r}{d^s} = \frac{\Pi_s^n - 1}{\Pi_r^n - 1}, \qquad \begin{matrix} r = 1 \\ s = 2, \dots m \end{matrix} \qquad \Pi = 1 + \Pi \tag{16.29}$$

If capital $\sum_{s=1}^{m} p_{n+s} K^s$ expands at a constant rate π, (16.29) will be an approximation.

Although the profit rate is uniform, each rental rate is different because each depreciation rate is different due to unequal durability of machines:

$$r^s = d^s + \pi$$

And now, at long last, we are able to write down the price equations:

$$\sum_{s=1}^{m} d^s p_{n+s}\kappa_j^s + \pi \sum_{s=1}^{m} p_{n+s}\kappa_j^s + w\lambda_j = p_j, \qquad j=1,\ldots n+m \qquad (16.30)$$

$$\pi \doteq g+\mu, \qquad w=1 \text{ implies labour time prices}$$

The price has three components: (1) individual depreciations which depend on the life-spans of machines installed and on the growth of capital $d^s = d^s(n_s, \pi)$; (2) systemic costs due to investment necessary to equip new and redundant workers and expressed in a uniform profit rate $\pi = (1+g)(1+\mu) - 1 \doteq g+\mu$, and (3) cost of living labour λ_j. Thus the labour value of a commodity depends (a) on the specific technological conditions of production (λ, κ, n) and (b) on the systemic conditions of production (g, μ). Labour costs are costs of production under full employment and so (a) consists of living and embodied labour of individual production while (b) adds labour necessary to preserve full employment when labour force changes, technological progress displaces hitherto employed workers and the structure of demand changes.

In a general case technological progress will change both labour and capital coefficients and a full employment uniform rate of profit will amount to:

$$\pi = (1+g)(1+\mu) - 1, \qquad \mu = \frac{\sum_{s=1}^{m} p_{n+s} K^s \mu^s}{\sum_{s=1}^{m} p_{n+s} K^s} \qquad (16.31)$$

where μ is the rate of growth of value of all machines and μ^s is the rate of increase in number of machines of type s. In the case of a decline of population or of a reduction of the work hours, g will be negative and the profit rate may disappear or even become negative.

Since the gross investment rate cannot be negative:

$$\delta^s + \mu^s + g \geq 0, \qquad s = 1,\ldots m$$

the largest admissible negative g is $(\delta^s + \mu^s)$ and so negative profit rate cannot fall below:

$$\pi = \mu - \min(\delta^s + \mu^s), \qquad s = 1,\ldots m$$

if the output capacity is to be fully used.

16.4 Stable price level

If all wages are spent on consumer goods and all profits on investment goods, cost of living is equal to per capita consumption which, in turn, is equal to the wage rate:

$$\frac{\sum_{i=1}^{n} p_i X_i}{L} = \sum p_i x_i = w, \qquad x_i = \frac{X_i}{L}$$

The composite consumer good that may be bought by one wage will be called a wage basket. Let the standard wage basket be the one bought by one wage in the initial period:

$$\sum_{i=1}^{n} p_i^0 x_i^0 = w^0 = 1 \tag{16.32}$$

Now, normalized w^0 is both a nominal and a real wage because it buys exactly one standard wage basket, $\sum_i p_i^0 x_i^0 = 1$.

Technological progress increases labour productivity. As a consequence, economy produces more wage goods. The real wage, measured in constant initial prices (Laspeyres index of quantities), increases exactly as much as labour productivity in consumption goods industries:

$$\sum_{i=1}^{n} p_i^0 x_i^0 H_i = \tilde{w}^t = \Gamma w^0, \qquad w^0 = 1 \tag{16.33}$$

where Γ is generally different from Γ in (16.22). With the same amount of labour, economy now produces Γ times more baskets equivalent to standard baskets. They are called equivalent because multipliers H_j change the composition of wage baskets.

The nominal wage, expressed in labour time, remains the same:

$$w^t = 1 = \sum_{i=1}^{n} p_i^t x_i^0 H_i \tag{16.34}$$

Thus, the initial basket of wage goods (w^0) and the current basket (w^t) contain the same amount of labour time[5] but the latter contains more goods. As a consequence, the Paasche index of prices decreased as much as the Laspeyres index of quantities (labour productivity) increased, i.e. by factor $\Gamma = \tilde{w}^t/w^0$. If all labour prices are increased by that productivity factor, the Paasche cost of living index will remain constant:

$$\sum_{i=1}^{n} (\Gamma p_i^t) x_i^0 H_i = \sum_{i=1}^{n} p_i^0 x_i^0 H_i \tag{16.35}$$

In other words, the cost of living index will be stabilized if the currently produced wage goods ($x_i^0 H_i$) are evaluated in prices which leave the labour time contained equal to the one at the base year productivity of labour.

Since all prices are multiplied by the same factor Γ, relative prices remain the same. And absolute prices increase as much as they would increase if w^0 is replaced by $w^t = \Gamma w^0$ in the formation of current prices. Thus, the cost of living index will be stabilized if wages increase at the rate of productivity increase in consumer goods industries. Note that the wage baskets undergo a twofold change: not only composition but also prices change. The change may also include the introduction of new products (with imputed p_i) and the disappearance of some of the old products. Note also that Γp_i^t:

$$\Gamma p_i^t = \frac{\tilde{w}^t}{w^0} p_i^t = \frac{\tilde{p}_i^t}{w^0} = \bar{\tilde{p}}_i^t \tag{16.36}$$

is nothing else but standard prices of section 9.2.

The foregoing exercise helps to give precise meaning to various types of prices used. Nominal wages and prices (w, p_i) are measured by conventional units of account, say by money. Taking wage rate as a *numéraire* ($w = 1$), prices measure current labour time contained in commodities. If a particular consumer good is used as a *numéraire*, we obtain particular real wages and prices measuring values in equivalent amounts of that commodity ($\tilde{w} = w/p_j$, $\tilde{p}_i = p_i/p_j$). If the current wage basket is taken as a *numéraire*, by (16.35):

$$w^t = \sum_i p_i^t x_i^t = \Gamma^{-1} \sum_i p_i^0 x_i^t \tag{16.37}$$

and the real wage ($w/\Sigma p_i x_i$) buys one basket currently and Γ^{-1} equivalent baskets in the base year. Prices in terms of baskets are *b*-prices ($p_j/\Sigma p_i x_i$). If *b*-values are expressed in base period real wages, we obtain standard prices:

$$\frac{p_j^t/\Sigma p_i^t x_i^1}{w^0} = \frac{p_j^t/(\Gamma^{-1}\tilde{w}^0)}{\tilde{w}^0} = \Gamma p_j^t = \bar{\tilde{p}}_j^t \tag{16.36a}$$

For the same reasons as above, the general price index will be stabilized if wages increase at the average rate of labour productivity where the average is calculated for *all* industries. The initial value of total outputs is $\sum_{i=1}^{n+m} p_i^0 X_i^0$.

This output can be produced with L workers in the base period and with $\Gamma^{-1} L$ workers in the period t. L workers produce Γ times greater output, and this is the factor of productivity increase:

$$\sum_{i=1}^{n+m} p_i^0 X_i H_i = \Gamma \sum_{i=1}^{n+m} p_i^0 X_i \tag{16.33a}$$

where Γ is now the same as in (16.22).

If it happens that the division of labour between consumer good and producer good industries remains unchanged, $\sum_{j=1}^{n} L_j^0 = \sum_{j=1}^{n} L_j^t$, $\sum_{j=n+1}^{n+m} L_j^0 = \sum_{j=n+1}^{n+m} L_j^t$, the *aggregate* labour value of consumer and producer goods (with $L=$const.) will remain the same in both periods

$$\sum_{i=1}^{n+m} p_i^0 X_i^0 = \sum_{i=1}^{n+m} p_i^t X_i^0 H_i$$

This means that new prices must be inflated by factor Γ in order to preserve the same price level. Consequently, wages must be increased by the same productivity factor, $w^t = \Gamma w^0$. Since, by assumption, the relation between living and embodied labour does not change, which seems to be a good approximation of reality since the share of wages and salaries in social product changes slowly over longer periods – the same wages will also stabilize the cost of living index. Alternatively: nominal wages expanding at the rate of growth of per capita production of consumer goods, when the shares of labour employed in consumer and producer good sectors do not change, stabilize both the cost of living and general price indices.

In general, the *constant productivity* labour keeps the average level of *nominal* prices constant.

To keep increases of wages within the confines of productivity increase is, of course, one of the well-known rules of economic policy designed to stabilize prices.

16.5 The interest rate

As investment is not self-financed, the economy needs a financial sector that will redistribute investment finance. Real economy must be supplemented by financial economy also because consumption is not self-financed either. Consumer loans generate interest rates.

If a commodity is borrowed now in order to be returned at time t, its own interest rate is zero. For other commodities, however, the interest rates may be positive (if their prices relatively decline) or negative (if their prices relatively increase). Changes in prices reflect, of course, changes in labour productivity in different industries.

One commodity is again of special analytical interest. That is the wage basket. Suppose the *numéraire* of the price system is the wage rate ($w^0 = w^t = 1$) and all loans, in terms of the wage rate, are stipulated at zero interest rate ($i = 0$). The wage baskets will have the same value now and at t when the loan expires. Since prices decline through time, a wage basket lent now will be repaid by Γ equivalent wage baskets at t. Thus, the interest rate, in terms of equivalent wage baskets – which keeps the price level constant – is equal to the productivity growth, $i_r = \Gamma - 1 = \gamma$. Since prices are constant, this is at the same time real interest rate (Pasinetti calls it the natural rate of interest, 1981, p. 174).

If Γw^0 keeps prices constant, any further growth of wages will generate inflation. If w^t is the money wage rate at t, then:

$$w^t = \phi\Gamma \doteq 1 + \gamma + \phi, \qquad w^0 = 1$$

where ϕ is the rate of inflation. The nominal value of the wage basket at t will increase by factor ϕ, and the interest rate by $\phi\Gamma - 1 - \gamma \doteq \phi$. Thus, in general case, the real interest rate is given by:

$$i_r \doteq i_m - \phi = \gamma$$

where i_m is the money rate of interest and i_r is Fisherian real interest rate. If inflation is present, say 20% or more per year, I found it more advisable to calculate the money interest rate in an alternative way: evaluate capital in inflating prices and apply the same real interest rate:

$$i_m K = i_r(\phi K) \qquad \therefore \qquad i_m = \phi i_r$$

In other words, instead of adding the rate of inflation to the real interest rate, it is being multiplied by the factor of inflation which makes money interest rate increase much less. If $i_r = 5\%$, $\psi = 20\%$, the Fisherian interest rate is $i_m = 5\% + 20\% = 25\%$ and the alternative $i_m = 5\% \times 1.2 = 6\%$ or four times less. But the principal has to be revalued and annual repayments of a loan are greater though still several times less than inflation. Thus, inflationary pressure on prices is much less.

It is generally thought that interest is incompatible with the socialist distribution of income regulated by the principle of distribution according to labour performed. In a system of labour time prices, current distribution of income is by definition based on labour inputs. The measurement of individual labour contributions is in practice somewhat complicated, but the problem has been solved (Horvat, 1982, ch. 9).

The intertemporal distribution of income looks puzzling. If loans are stipulated in terms of labour, certain quantity of labour now will be exchanged for the same quantity of labour in the future when the loan expires. Consequently, the rate of interest is zero, and the socialist principle of distribution is fully respected. However, since the productivity of labour increases, the corresponding real interest rate is γ.

If labour force remains unchanged, $g=0$, and the relation between living and embodied labour does not change either, inflating labour prices by productivity factor Γ keeps the general level of prices constant. This is equivalent to saying that, in terms of constant current prices, the output has increased by Γ.

$$\Gamma = H = 1 + \pi$$

$$\gamma = h = \pi$$

The consumer rate of interest and the producer rate of profit are the same. In a general case there will be a difference, $\gamma \neq \pi$ because $g \neq 0$ and the value composition of social product may change.[6] Under these assumptions the neoclassical assumption of a unique interest rate, $i_r = \gamma = \pi$, is impossible under full employment conditions because it renders the equation system overdetermined.

In the production system, π plays the role of the discount rate for financial loans. Assuming banking costs to be zero, depreciation allowances accumulated at the 'interest' rate π will, by the time a machine is scrapped, amount to the price of a new machine. Similarly, the profits earned on financial loans given to deficit industries will be exactly equal to the profits of the borrowing industries. In any period the available financial means are exactly equal to the full employment gross investment. In this sense financial assets match real assets and make possible unimpeded reproduction under optimum allocation of resources. If banking costs are positive, they may be absorbed into full coefficients as intermediate goods.

What about the equilibrium on the consumer loans market? The supply of loans is determined by income and the saving habits and may be taken as exogenously given. The demand for loans depends on consumer interest rate γ, the period of repayment t and the required collateral c. Since γ – the growth of labour productivity – is exogenously determined, it is t and c that may be varied in order to equilibrate demand and supply if it is desired that labour is always exchanged for the same amount of labour either in simultaneous or in intertemporal transactions.

16.6 Conclusion

It has proved possible to work out a rigorous theory of value and prices starting from the insights of classical economists. Apart from being logically consistent, the new theory is different from the classical labour theory of value in another important respect: it is not only descriptive but also normative. As a normative theory, it provides criteria for an optimal allocation of resources. As a descriptive theory, it is differently descriptive from the invisible hand of classical economists: it approaches the economic problem as do macroeconomic planners or, if you prefer, economic policy-makers.

The new theory differs much more from the neoclassical theory. Marginal adjustments and marginal substitutions with given resources are neglected as relatively unimportant. The long-run equilibrium, not the short-run, is at the centre of the stage. *Ex post* – after the installation of equipment – substitution possibilities are negligible. *Ex ante*, marginal products may not exist because of discontinuities or because inputs are qualitatively different for different techniques. From the point of view of macroeconomic planner the important issues are: structure, growth, technological progress and full employment. The neoclassical theory is ill-equipped to tackle these problems. Besides, it is unable to explain the origin of profit and interest rates, its main theoretical building blocks. The much used time preference turns out to be an ideological parable, not a part of a scientific theory. Neoclassical theory also generates paradoxes in capital theory and is often misleading in policy applications (i.e. that unemployment – always, at least partly, technologically determined – can be cured by reducing wages or that low wages make labour intensive industries more profitable). As the survey of aporiae showed, the logical foundations of the mainstream theory are shaky or unsustainable.

The demonstration that six fundamental theoretical postulates are invalid – because they represent special and not general cases – delivers a serious blow to neoclassical theory. Also the welfare theory will have to be reworked from scratch. In an unemployment economy – where by additional employment at least some individuals can be made better off without anybody being left worse off – the Pareto optimum loses theoretical rationale. And if you must fall back to the second best theory, the theory provides no guidance for economic policy. In the systemic theory, the criteria are clear: whatever increases the real wage is a desirable or optimum approaching activity. Growth is in focus and not allocation of resources which, as calculations show, may generate losses, due to distorted prices, not more than a fraction of 1%.

The long-run equilibrium has a different meaning from that inherited from Marshall. It has nothing to do with fixed capital but means an equality of supply and demand of commodities given the supply of labour. It means fully synchronized development in which at every period of time the quantity and structure of supply just matches demand of the fully employed labour. Since every (reproducible) good can be produced, given time and resources, the equilibrium prices must be cost prices. This is at the same time a fundamental insight of classical economists and observed practice of firms (full cost or mark up prices). Perhaps they may be called gravitational prices.

If investment is determined by the need to provide replacement and new jobs, it cannot be determined by something else. The same applies to consumption, which must absorb the remaining part of GNP. Since in equilibrium demand and supply are synchronized, the case of many consumer and producer goods represents in fact general equilibrium without an auctioneer, contingent goods, infinite horizon, scarcity determined prices and the rest. In the decentralized market economy one has to consider supply and demand only as a means to achieve general equilibrium. To achieve this goal, market failures – whatever they are – must be corrected by deliberate economic policy measures.

Finally, the systemic theory appears to be related to real world and its assumptions reproduce the actual activities of economic agents. It takes care of dynamic synergetic effects and produces the necessary criteria for decision-making. It reverses the usual procedure and provides macroeconomic foundations of microeconomics. It allows theory of consumer choice to be grafted on the production theory developed but that theory is shown to be economically non-essential – like in the thinking of classics. It can easily be extended to international trade (open economy), public finance (taxes and public goods) and to other areas of economics. The extension to economic policy provides hardly any difficulty. For instance, divide the economy into business and household sectors. In the business sector make sure that investment is exactly equal to that necessary to replace worn out and obsolete equipment and the creation of new jobs. Once firms engage in investment, the necessary savings will be forthcoming automatically. In the household sector there may be surplus or deficit saving (i.e. aggregate personal income earmarked for current consumption amounts to less or more than required consumption). Planning authority has to use policy instruments to equalize saving and dis-saving in the household sector – a sort of interpersonal borrowing and lending of purchasing power – and thus make sure that consumption and investment make up to the potential national income. The necessary reserve stocks and reserve output capacities provide for uncertainties and unexpected shocks.

In short, the new theory is also a new paradigm, an economic planners' paradigm. It does not see the world through the eyes of individual business people and individual consumers. It treats economy as a system, which must be designed properly in order to function efficiently. The invisible hand does a good deal of work in the market, but not all the work. The rest must be done by macroeconomic planning. This implies neither administrative planning nor the absence of political democracy. Individual initiative is precious and ought to be preserved and maximally enhanced. It implies better working and more competitive markets – because of reduction of uncertainties and market failures – and more profound democratic life and, therefore, liberation of initiative – because to political and social democracy, economic democracy is added and the place of work democratized. But this is already subject of a different book (see Horvat, 1982).

The two theories are not mutually exclusive. The systemic theory sets standards and, once developed, provides a basis for macroeconomic policy. The (corrected) neoclassical theory is basically microeconomic and studies the behaviour of individual economic agents. It provides criteria for *ex ante* (not *ex post*!) maximization of profit by equalizing marginal cost and marginal revenue. The two theories reconciled will hopefully elevate the scientific status of economics.

Notes

Chapter 1

1. This is the definition of T. Kotarbiński, the author of the first comprehensive study of the subject (1955). O. Lange raises objections and defines praxiology as the science of *rational* activity:

   > using the word rational in the methodological sense; the effectiveness of an activity is connected with its factual rationality which, however, is not an attribute of activity as a mode of behaviour and is therefore not a question of praxiology but of technology (1959, p. 189).

   The first to discuss the relation of economics to praxiology was the unavoidable Eugene Slutsky (1926). His term for pure economics is *formal* economics which 'establishes and develops the relations among basic categories that constitute the phenomenal being of economic conditions' (p. 238). Slutsky reaches the conclusion that 'formal economics is no independent science but is only a discipline within the framework of formal Praxiology' (p. 249). A. Lowe singles out economics, as the provision of material means, from praxiology, as the universal logic of choice (1965, p. 10). However, this distinction can hardly be sustained because hobby activities may provide material means and do not belong to economics.
2. The term describes Marshall's scissors whose classical blade represents cost and the 'neo'-blade represents utility; both are necessary to cut out prices.
3. For that reason John Hicks (1979) suggested that the appellation 'neoclassical' be replaced by an old term, *catallactics*, meaning the theory of exchange. Using Lakatosian terminology, Robert Fisher enumerates the following six hard core elements of the neoclassical research programme (1986, p. 172): the individual as a key unit of analysis; the law of utility maximization; the marginal utility/total utility distinction; the law of diminishing marginal utility; the prevalence of competition; the potency of the equilibrating mechanism. If this research programme is to get a name, it should clearly be called catallactics.
4. Not at all in the view of neoclassical economists. Ronald Jones explains:

   > ... the relatively rich production structure of the Heckscher–Ohlin model has made it a source of fruitful hypotheses for empirical testing (whose usefulness is *not* diminished by the fact that in the simplest form – two goods, two factors and identical technologies worldwide – the model's predictions are *overwhelmingly rejected* by the data) as well as a useful vehicle for the study of a wide range of theoretical issues (p. 20, italics mine).

   Charles Kindleberger stands almost alone in deriving a natural conclusion that what Leontief proves 'is not that the USA is capital-scarce and labour-abundant but that the Heckscher–Ohlin theorem is wrong' (cited by de Marchi, 1976, p. 124).

5. Stephen Marglin notes that it is necessary to assume full employment of labour and capital in order to be able to argue that marginal productivity of labour determines the real wage and the marginal productivity of capital determines the profit rate. 'By contrast – he adds – in the neo-Marxian and the neo-Keynesian models, causality runs in the opposite direction, factor prices determining marginal productivities' (1984, p. 330). Alfred Eichner writes:

   > Under modern techniques of production, with workers employed in teams to operate a fixed stock of equipment, it is not possible to determine the 'marginal product of labour' in any meaningful sense of that term ... it is ... even more difficult to determine marginal contribution of the other employees, including any white-collar professionals and middle-level managers. Indeed, no evidence that it is possible to vary the amount of labour inputs in the short period, relative to the other inputs, while still maintaining the same level of output has ever been adduced (1987, p. 881).

6. Referring to empirical studies, Eichner concludes:

   > It has proven impossible to derive these curves [isoquants] from the available empirical data on production by individual firms.... The implication of isoquants – namely, that firms are able to produce a given quantity of output, even in the absence of technical progress, by employing varying combinations of labour and other inputs – is strongly contradicted by the available evidence. Empirical investigation in a number of manufacturing industries has shown that production requires the use of labour, material, and other inputs in relatively fixed proportions ... (1983, p. 212).

   Laurence White provides a survey of empirical studies and concludes: 'The economist's smoothly curved production isoquant is rarely present' (1978, p. 47).

Chapter 2

1. Equation (2.7) is a commonplace in modern input–output analysis. It is of historical interest to note that the first to compose this equation was V.K. Dmitriev (1898, p. 44). He was also the first to formalize the wage–profit relation (wage curve) (p. 59).
2. Some of the similarities are quite direct: the praxiological rationality corresponds to the principle of least action (extremum principle), equality of the value of annual inputs and outputs corresponds to conservation of energy, replacement and employment effects correspond to relativity effects, the concept of the market corresponds to that of the field. Lowe noted the extremum and conservation economic counterparts. Regarding the conservation principle, he writes that:

   > its validity has always been taken for granted. From the early beginnings when the ultimate economic matter was defined as 'the sum total of the annual produce of the land' (Quesnay) or the 'fund' constituted by 'the

annual labour of every nation' (Smith), the market process was understood as the circulation and transformation of an indestructible aggregate of energy' (1965, p. 106).

Earlier economists (Jevons, Walras, Fisher and others) made an explicit use of the mechanical paradigm, which still dominates economics (the concept of equilibrium, reversibility, no distinction between analytical and historical time, etc.). Kennet Boulding (1966, p. 6) describes the paradigm as follows: in Newtonian mechanics all quantities may be reduced to some combination of three basic dimensions, length, mass and time. For instance, distance has length, velocity is length per unit of time and acceleration is the change of velocity per unit of time. Similarly in economics there are three basic dimensions, commodity (in fact many commodity dimensions, otherwise utility), money and time. For instance, stock of a commodity, production as the flow of a commodity per unit of time, price as money per unit of a commodity and the rate of growth as a change of a quantity per unit of time. The basic difference between physics and economics lies, of course, in the fact that unlike physics in economics agents exist endowed with conscience and acting teleologically.

For an early attempt to depart from mechanics and of treating economics as thermodynamics, see the book-length treatise by Kosta Stojanović (1910). He identifies work in physics and economy and likens warmth with capital, energy with wealth, pressure with supply and temperature with demand. These conceptual analogies are then used to derive parallels to the first (conservation of energy) and second (entropy) laws of economodynamics. The most recent book-length treatise is that by Nicholas Georgescu-Roegen (1971). He points out that: '... only an analysis of the intimate relationship between the Entropy Law and economic process can bring to the surface those decisively qualitative aspects of this process for which the mechanical analogue of modern economics has no room' (p. 3). Like Stojanović, Georgescu-Roegen maintains 'thermodynamics is largely physics of economic value' (p. 276) and that 'the basic nature of economic process is entropic' (p. 283), but unlike Stojanović abstains from any attempt to construct an operational thermodynamic value calculus (p. 18).

Chapter 4

1. The effect has a long history that starts with Senior and Marx, but they did not know what to do with it. First published paper with the formulae I am using is that by E. Domar (1953). Domar thought that the effect – a surplus of depreciation over replacement in his analysis – was a matter of depreciation methods and would disappear in the case of linear decay when linear depreciation is applied. That this conclusion had been erroneous was demonstrated in Horvat (1958a). In my papers (1973a), also linear and proportional changes were studied, as well as a related phenomenon which I dubbed 'depreciation multiplier'. For a comparison with relativity effect in physics see Horvat (1973b). For a brief history of the discovery of the phenomenon see Horvat (1964, pp. 168–72). Nothing is substantially changed if the service life of assets varies stochastically. Since the process is ergodic, the system will tend towards a constant replacement rate regardless of initial distribution of assets. The limiting age distribution of assets is independent of the initial distribution and depends only on the scrapping distribution (Feller, 1950, pp. 272–7); Lange, 1975, Ch. 3.3); Jorgenson, 1974).

2. Ricardo uses a similar example to derive a different conclusion:

> Suppose I employ twenty men at an expense of £1000 for a year in the production of a commodity, and at the end of the year I employ twenty men again for another year, at a further expense of £1000 in finishing or perfecting the same commodity, and that I bring it to market at the end of two years, if profits be 10 per cent, my commodity must sell for £2310; for I have employed £1000 capital for one year, and £2100 capital for one year more. Another man employs precisely the same quantity of labour, but he employs it all in the first year; he employs forty men at an expense of £2000, and at the end of the first year he sells it with 10 per cent profit, or for £2200. Here then are two commodities having precisely the same quantity of labour bestowed on them, one which sells for £2310 – the other for £2200 (1821, p. 37).

The reasoning is quite illustrative for the mistake usually committed by the labour theorists and their critics. First of all, the summation of labour inputs must not be diachronic (as visualized by a single firm) but synchronic (pertaining to the system as a whole). As demonstrated in the text, the systemically necessary labour is not 2 (i.e. 2×20 workers) but 2.31, which is exactly the figure reported by Ricardo for the value of output.

Next, the alternative (one-year) technique sells output at £2200 because the labour input is lower (2×20 workers plus 10% for the increase of the labour force). Under competition, both techniques cannot coexist and the systemically less productive two-year technique will be abandoned.

Finally, Ricardo does not ask himself why the rate of profit should be 10%. Evidently, he takes it as an exogenously determined quantity simply given at the market. However, if (1) the technology applied does not change, (2) all profits are invested in the creation of new jobs and (3) all workers are employed, the equilibrium rate of profit is equal to the rate of increase of active population. Consequently, labour theory is a general equilibrium normative theory. Obviously, if there is unemployment and there exists a class of capitalists who consume a part of profits, prices will be different. But such a price structure makes optimal allocation of resources impossible.

The problems are not unlike those in physics where the formula of the free fall ($gt^2/2$) applies in a vacuum. In other media, depending also on its shape and mass, the object falls differently. Free fall in a vacuum is a limiting and, therefore, a normative case. The formula expresses a natural law from which deviations can be measured when the conditions are not fulfilled. Similarly, when the rate of profit differs from the rate of employment growth, the actual prices will deviate from the labour prices. Given the preferences, the output will be smaller than the optimal output and the magnitude of deviations is a measure of misallocation of resources in space and time.

3. The first to use the term 'synchronized labour cost' were Ch. Weizsächer and P. Samuelson (1971) in a paper designed to show the falsity of Marx's labour theory of value and the correctness of 'bourgeois prices calculated at dated labour requirements, marked-up by compound interest, at a profit or interest rate equal to the system's rate of exponential growth ...' (p. 1192). Samuelson believed that he 'proved the following theorem: If labour grows at exponential rate $1+g$ and goods are priced at their "synchronized labour costs", then the

bourgeois pricing formula $A_0(g)=a_0(1+g)[I-a(1+g)]^{-1}$ must be charged by rational planners' (1971, p. 429; a_0 stands for direct labour coefficients, a for production coefficients). The formula is not correct. In terms of our concepts, Samuelson's theorem implies using the combined matrix:

$$G\begin{bmatrix} A \\ \hat{\lambda} \end{bmatrix}$$

instead of equivalent matrix GA. The summation down the columns at the consistent set of prices produces the above formula:

$$p=G(pA+\hat{\lambda})=G\hat{\lambda}\,[1-GA]^{-1}$$

The error consists in using 'the bourgeois' $G\hat{\lambda}$ instead of $\hat{\lambda}$. This is done rather frequently (cf. Steedman, 1976; Morishima and Catephores, 1978; Fujimori, 1982) and is called *ex ante* remuneration of labour. If wages are advanced, the resulting wage fund functions as capital and, it is argued, requires that interest be charged. The procedure is illegitimate even if labour fund does not consist of money but of stored commodities. Whatever happens to work force and its wage fund, technology remains the same:

$$T=\begin{bmatrix} A \\ \hat{\lambda} \end{bmatrix}$$

If labour expands, new workers must be employed at $t+1$ and therefore additional producer goods (gA) must be produced at t. That looks *as if capital coefficients are augmented* to GA. Labour coefficients remain unaffected, because they remain outside A in any case. Unlike X_2 goods, X_1 goods do not enter A and represent the net residual (to be maximized as the end goal of production). Its changes do not affect A or $\hat{\lambda}$ in any way.

The same conclusion will be reached by using the price–quantity duality of a given technology:

$$\begin{array}{lll} p_1 & \begin{bmatrix} a_{11} & a_{12} \\ a_{21} & a_{22} \end{bmatrix} & g(a_{11}\hat{X}_1+a_{12}\hat{X}_2)+x_1 \quad \hat{X}_1 \\ p_2 & & g(a_{21}\hat{X}_1+a_{22}\hat{X}_2)+x_2 \quad \hat{X}_2 \\ g & [pA_1 \quad pA_2] & \\ w & [\ \hat{\lambda}_1 \quad\ \ \hat{\lambda}_2\ ] & \\ & \ \ p_1 \qquad\ p_2 & \end{array} \qquad A_j=\begin{bmatrix} a_{1j} \\ a_{2j} \end{bmatrix}, A_1+A_2=A$$

Summation across the rows and down the columns gives:

$$A\hat{X}+gA\hat{X}+x=\hat{X} \Rightarrow \hat{X}=(I-GA)^{-1}x$$
$$pA+gpA+w\hat{\lambda}=p \Rightarrow p=w\hat{\lambda}(I-GA)^{-1}$$

In both instances prices are the same and the value added is the same. In addition profits are equated to investment:

$$g[(p_1a_{11}+p_2a_{21})\hat{X}_1+(p_1a_{12}+p_2a_{22})\hat{X}_2]=g[(a_{11}\hat{X}_1+a_{12}\hat{X}_2)p_1 + (a_{21}\hat{X}_1+a_{22}\hat{X}_2)p_2]$$

and wages are equal to consumption:

$$w(\hat{\lambda}_1\hat{X}_1+\hat{\lambda}_2\hat{X}_2)=p_1x_1+p_2x_2$$

Producer goods production has to increase (gA) in order to equip *new* labour, but it is produced by the *same* labour ($\hat{\lambda}$). Next year the available labour will have increased to $GL=G\hat{A}\hat{X}$, but this is not the result of the production process. Moreover, labour may remain unchanged and the number of machines can increase because of technological progress. Neoclassicals still have to learn that labour is *not* symmetrical to other factors of production.

Chapter 5

1. We have discovered ... that the rate of interest must be dethroned from its unquestioned place as one of the central concepts of the theory. In its place must be substituted an intertemporal price system (*Bliss*, 1973, p. 346).

Chapter 6

1. In the literature usually called 'disembodied'. But only ghosts are disembodied.
2. Marx himself expected a biased capital-using technological progress, i.e. an increasing ω.

Chapter 7

1. That neoclassical defect was already noticed by Reed (1968) and Rymes (1971).

Chapter 8

1. In general empirical evidence suggests that the vintage assumption is not analytically important. Gregory and James survey the empirical research elsewhere and also analyse the data of Australian industry to conclude 'that vintage effects are quantitatively insignificant as an explanation of cross-section productivity dispersion in most industries' (1973, p. 1154). It appears that the unembodied technological progress may be a good approximation of reality. If the rate of growth remains constant, the assumption of unembodied technological progress can make no harm. But beware. If in a year a change in investment is contemplated, the effects of embodied TP may be approximated by a simple formula. For instance, let a steadily growing GNP be estimated by the Cobb–Douglas function:

$$Y=e^{\gamma(g)+\Delta\gamma(\Delta g)}L^{\alpha}K^{1-\alpha}, \qquad \Delta\gamma\geq 0 \text{ if } \Delta g\geq 0, \qquad 0<\alpha<1$$

If the rate of growth (g) is constant, $\Delta\gamma=0$, the function reduces to the ordinary Cobb–Douglas function. The elasticity α is usually $\alpha=0.7$ and so $1-\alpha=0.3$. This implies that by increasing capital by 1%, leaving labour unchanged (although reallocated), one would increase GNP by 0.3%. As every national planner knows, that is patently wrong, because for moderate increase of investment over a steady rate of growth, capital coefficient remains approximately the same, $\kappa \doteq$ const. We know that additional new more productive technology, increasing returns to scale and replacement effect are responsible for the absence of diminishing returns. The three effects increase technological progress as a function of increased K and are usually known as Verdoorn Effect.

If capital coefficient remains constant, $\kappa=K/Y=400/100=4$ and the share of investment is $s=0.20$, the system grows at $g=s/\kappa=5\%$. Thus, the current increase of investment is $20.0.05=1$. It represents $\Delta I/K=1/400=0.0025\%$ of existing capital. This increases the share of investment in GNP from $s=I/Y=20/100$ to $s=21/(100+1{:}4)=21/100.25=20.9\%$. If labour force remains constant, an increase in TP, $\Delta\gamma$, may be calculated as follows:

$$1=\frac{1/\kappa^*}{1/\kappa}=\frac{Y^*/K^*}{Y/K}=\frac{e^{\gamma+\Delta\gamma}L^{\alpha}(K+\Delta I)^{1-\alpha}K}{e^{\gamma}L^{\alpha}K^{1-\alpha}(K+\Delta I)}=\frac{e^{\Delta\gamma}(K+\Delta I)^{-\alpha}}{K^{-\alpha}}$$

$$=e^{\Delta\gamma}(1+\Delta I/K)^{-\alpha}$$

Take logarithms on both sides

$$0=\Delta\gamma-\alpha\ln(1+\Delta I/K)$$

to obtain:

$$\Delta\gamma=\alpha\ln(1+\Delta I/K)\doteq\alpha\frac{\Delta I}{K}=0.7\frac{1}{400}=0.00175$$

The increase of technical progress of $\Delta\gamma=0.175\%$ due to the increase of capital of $I/K=0.25\%$ may very roughly be attributed to TP. The elasticity is now one, $\frac{\Delta Y K}{\Delta K Y}=\frac{1\,400}{4\,100}=1$, which is more than three times higher than the previous figure and so is the marginal product of capital, '$\Delta Y/\Delta K$'.

2. The effects (1), (2) and (4) have already been observed by Hans Brems, but his approach was very different. Brems considers the case where capital stock is built by labour only, various rates of interest and technological progress are given and the criterion for the truncation is the maximization of the present net worth of the endless stream of all future acquisitions of durable goods by the firm. He finds that the optimum life of producer durables will be longer the slower the technological progress, the costlier they are and the higher the rate of interest (Brems, 1968, pp. 152–65).

Chapter 9

1. As mentioned earlier (section 5.5), γ represents the own rate of interest in the general equilibrium theory. If relative prices do not change, (9.9) holds also for machine prices:

$$p_2(t) = p_2(0)(1+\delta)^{-t}$$

This is an expression suggested by S.G. Strumilin (1946). He argues that the rising productivity of labour reduces the value of capital assets and this loss must be recuperated by augmenting the cost of production to be covered by price. In his words: 'Losses in the value of past labour embodied in our funds ought to be replaced fully during the period of exploitation of these funds' (p. 169). Strumilin was unable to substantiate his idea and so it was dismissed by both Marxist and non-Marxist writers.

Chapter 10

1. This curve is often called *w–r* and *c–i* possibility frontier, which is misleading. It does not satisfy the condition of the use of the most productive techniques except at one point. Even more misleading is to call it 'factor-price frontier', because that ignores the *c–i* relation.
2. The translation into Sraffa's system of circulating capital is straightforward, for $\tilde{w}=0$, $X_1=0$. Net output reduces to $X_2=RK$ and the standard ratio is given by:

$$R = \frac{\text{net output}}{\text{capital used}} = \frac{1}{\kappa_2}$$

since in my system κ_i is capital coefficient based on net output.
3. It may be argued that even if capitalists consumed nothing, $\pi = i$, they would still exploit workers as long as they use ownership right to hire labour and dispose of surplus. That is logically correct, but empirically vacuous: employers will never forget their family and themselves when distributing income. Next, Marxian surplus value includes the entire difference $\tilde{y}-\tilde{w}$, not only $c-\tilde{w}$. Thus, eliminating exploitation means eliminating private control over the entire difference $\tilde{y}-\tilde{w}$. Again, empirically that must follow as soon as $\pi - i = 0$. Finally, theoretically it is possible to design public finance in such a way that $\pi = i$ and $\tilde{w} = c$ and then workers are taxed so that gross wages are reduced for $c-\tilde{w}$. The same amount – or part of it – is transferred to capitalists in order to provide them with consumable income. Such a scheme is also empirically impossible and for obvious reasons. Government expenditures financed by taxation introduce complications. And so does saving out of wages. It is important to note that π serves to choose the correct technology and i must be such to secure full employment.
4. The value of final output ($\tilde{y}$) in Fig. 10.5 does not change with r only when $i=0$. In that case $\tilde{y}$ is equal to the intercept of distribution curve on the $\tilde{w}$ axis. In a general case it is different (cf. Harcourt, 1972, pp. 148–9).
5. The *Non-substitution* Theorem is a misnomer because with one primary factor there is nothing to be substituted for. The minimum cost techniques do not

change whatever the composition of demand. With technological progress, technology changes in time and so do the prices. But at any moment of time the book of blueprints is given and so are minimum cost techniques for particular industries that *do not change* if the composition of demand changes (cf. Pasinetti, 1977).

Chapter 11

1. Properties **1–7** are essentially the same as described by Pasinetti (1979, pp. 158–63).
2. That property was first established by M. Bruno, E. Burmeister and E. Sheshinski (1966, pp. 536–7).

Chapter 13

1. In Marx's view land ownership is the cause of absolute rent because land is not freely accessible for capital investments.

   > If capital meets an alien force ... which limits its investment in certain spheres, admitting it only under conditions which wholly or partly exclude that general equalization of surplus value to an average profit, then it is evident that the excess of the value of commodities in such spheres of production over their price of production would give rise to a surplus-profit, which could be converted into rent.... Such an alien force and barrier are presented by landed property' (Marx, 1894, pp. 761–2).

   As our analysis shows, it is true that a more mechanized technique will not be applied as soon as it becomes profitable, but only when it also generates the already established rent. Since free entry of new capital is prevented, the organic composition of capital is lower than it *could be under rational institutions.* However, whether it is also lower than in manufacturing depends on technical conditions. In fact, modern agriculture tends to be more mechanized than manufacturing on the average. Marx had a correct intuition, but confused two separate issues.
2. In this and the next few paragraphs the reader will notice the trail marked by P. Sraffa (1960).
3. The same model, but based on circulating capital with two capital goods, was first used by J.S. Metcalfe and I. Steedman (1972). Later also G. Abraham-Frois and E. Berrebi use the same model but apparently are not aware of the intricacies involved (1976, pp. 216–23).

Chapter 14

1. Compared with actual model worked out by Pasinetti, there are two technical differences. Instead of replacement rates $\delta^i = 1/v_i$, Pasinetti uses linear depreciation rates $1/n$, ($1/T_i$ in his notation). And machines are produced only by labour and not by other machines. The former is erroneous and the latter is an unnecessary simplification (Pasinetti, 1981, chs VII and VIII).

Chapter 16

1. Elements of the matrix $(I-rK^M)^{-1}>0$ in (16.2) and (16.3) increase with $r(0<r<R)$ because $K^M \geq 0$ and indecomposable and $1/R$ is the Frobenius eigenvalue of K^M.
2. W. Krelle (1977) and C. Özol (1984) produced wage curves for West Germany, Great Britain, France, Italy, Japan and the United States; P. Petrović (1986) and my graduate student Barbara Bojnec for Yugoslavia. The last author gives also the summary of the empirical research conducted so far (1989). Petrović and Özol use the largest number of industries (47 and 85). Petrović shows that the empirical wage curves are convex or concave depending on which commodity is used as a *numéraire*. The finer the industrial division (the greater the number of industries in input–output tables), the more pronounced is the curvature of the wage curves. The most pronounced convex curve in Petrović's sample was obtained when electricity generation was used as a *numéraire*; the most pronounced concave curve was due to productive services as a *numéraire*. If the consumption basket is taken as a *numéraire*, wage curves become approximately linear. Technological progress shifts the wage curves upwards. Note that empirical curves are really quasi-wage curves: they do *not* show different technologies used by the *same* industries to produce the *same* commodities at different rental rates; they depict the observed *points* that correspond to the use of *different* technologies by *different* industries. Note also that reswitching – i.e. the recurrence of the same technique at a different rental rate – belongs to analytical and not to real time. In real time – in the observed empirical world – technological progress changes the books of blueprints and, assuming the indecomposability of the matrix of technical coefficients, the same technique cannot recur. The upward shifts of empirical wage curves imply that they belong to different technology frontiers. Even if some such wage curves cross once for high interest rates – as those drawn by Krelle do – the cross points are not switch points, i.e. they do not belong to the same commodities produced by the same industries at the same prices.
3. The same conclusion was reached by Pasinetti (1981, pp. 191–2).
4. Ian Steedman (1985, p. 377) was first to demonstrate the possibility of that perversity. He used the simpler, circulating capital model and did not consider other implications.
5. This reminds one of the famous Ricardo's quest for a commodity with 'absolute value' which would provide an 'invariable standard of value'. Such a commodity (a) must always contain the same quantity of labour and (b) must be invariant to changes in income distribution. (*Works*, Vol. IV, p. 382; Vol. I, p. 17). Requirement (b) is satisfied by Sraffa's 'standard commodity' (which implies a uniform organic composition of capital) and requirement (a) by changing wage basket, which Pasinetti calls 'dynamic standard commodity' (1981, p. 105). Both requirements would formally be satisfied by wage baskets with uniform organic composition of capital. Now, the former is artificial and the latter has a restrictive economic meaning; the same physical quantity of labour, but of different productivity, is a different quantity of labour as a factor of production. Such heterogeneous labour cannot be added or compared.
6. The necessity to distinguish consumer and producer rates of interest under socialism was noticed a long time ago (cf. Horvat, 1964, ch. 4).

References

This list of references is not a bibliography. Any reasonable bibliography of writings on value and capital would run into many pages. References in the list refer to books and articles quoted in the text. The following criteria were applied in selecting the items for quotations: (1) Texts which directly influenced my thinking and to which I owe particular solutions of the problems. (2) Texts of which I was unaware at the time of writing, but which preceded my own thinking. (3) Texts which represent elaborations of points I am making. That in particular applies to the citations of my own writings made in order to avoid the need of repeating the argument already published. (4) Texts that serve as historical illustrations. A conscious praxiological effort was made to keep the number of references down to a necessary minimum in order to maximize the information efficiency of the list. (The quotations 'reprinted in *S.E.*' refer to I. Steedman, ed., *Sraffian Economics*.)

Abraham-Frois, G. and Berrebi, E. (1976), *Théorie de la valeur, des prix et de l'accumulation*, Paris: Economica.

——(1988), 'Optimisation et prix de production', *Revue d'économie politique*, 66–77.

Bhaduri, A. and Robinson, Joan (1980), 'Accumulation and exploitation: an analysis in the tradition of Marx, Sraffa and Kalecki', *Cambridge Journal of Economics*, 103–15.

Bhagwati, J. (1964), 'The pure theory of international trade', *Economic Journal*, 1–84.

Blaug, M. (1980), *The Methodology of Economics*, Cambridge University Press.

——(1984), 'Paradigms vs. research programmes in the history of economics', in D.M. Hausman (ed.), *The Philosophy of Economics*, Cambridge University Press, 360–88.

Bliss, C.J. (1973), *Capital Theory and the Distribution of Income*, Amsterdam: North-Holland.

Böhm-Bawerk, E. von (1889), *The Positive Theory of Capital*, London: Macmillan, 1891.

Bojnec, Barbara (1984), 'Distributive curves for the Yugoslav economy', *Economic Analysis and Workers' Management*, 253–72.

Boulding, K. (1966), *Macroeconomics*, New York: Harper & Row.

Bowen, H.P., Reamer, E.E. and Sveikauskos, L. (1987), 'Multicountry, multifactor tests of the factor abundance theory', *American Economic Review*, 791–809.

Brems, H. (1968), *Quantitative Economic Theory*, New York: John Wiley.

Bruno, M., Burmeister, E. and Sheshinski, E. (1966), 'The nature and implications of the reswitching of techniques', *Quarterly Journal of Economics*, 526–53.

Buchanan, D.H. (1929), 'The historical approach to rent and price theory', *Economica*, 123–55; reprinted in *Readings in the Theory of Income Distribution*, Philadelphia: Blakiston, 1951, pp. 599–637.

Clark, J.B. (1899), *Distribution of Wealth*, New York: Macmillan.

Conant, J.B. (1947), *On Understanding Science*, New Haven, Conn.: Yale University Press.

Craven, J. (1977), 'On the marginal product of capital', *Oxford Economic Papers*, 472–7.

De Marchi, N. (1976), 'Anomaly and the development of economics: the case of the Leontief paradox', in S. Latris (ed.), *Method and Appraisal in Economics*, Cambridge University Press.

Dewey, D. (1965), *Modern Capital Theory*, New York: Columbia Press.

Dickinson, H.D. (1932), *Institutional Revenue*, London: Williams & Norgate.

Dixit, A. (1977), 'The accumulation of capital theory', *Oxford Economic Papers*, 1–29.

Dmitriev, V.K. (1898), *Economic Essays on Value, Competition and Utility*, trans. by D.M. Nuti, Cambridge University Press, 1974.

Domar, E.D. (1953), 'Depreciation, replacement and growth', *Economic Journal*, 1–32; reprinted in *Essays in the Theory of Economic Growth*, New York: Oxford University Press, 1957.

Dorfman, R., Samuelson, P.A. and Solow, R.M. (1958), *Linear Programming and Economic Analysis*, New York: McGraw-Hill.

Duhem, P. (1906), *The Aim and Structure of Physical Theory*, Princeton University Press.

Eichner, A.S. (ed.) (1983), *Why Economics Is Not Yet a Science*, New York: Sharpe.

——(1987), *The Macroeconomics of Advanced Market Economies*, New York: Sharpe.

Feller, W. (1950), *Probability Theory and Its Applications*, vol. I, New York: John Wiley.

Fisher, I. (1907), *The Rate of Interest*, New York: Macmillan.

——(1930), *The Theory of Interest*, reprinted New York: Kelley & Millman, 1954.

Fisher, M.R. (1986), *The Logic of Discovery*, Brighton: Wheatsheaf.

Friedman, M. (1953), *Essays in Positive Economics*, Chicago University Press.

Fujimori, Y. (1982), *Modern Analysis of Value Theory*, Berlin: Springer.

Georgescu-Roegen, N. (1971), *The Entropy Law and the Economic Process*, Cambridge, Mass.: Harvard University Press.

Goodwin, R.M. (1982), *Essays in Economic Dynamics*, London: Macmillan.

Gregory, R.G., and James, D.W. (1973), 'Do New Factories Embody Best Practice Technology', *Economic Journal*, 1133–55.

Harcourt, G.C. (1972), *Some Cambridge Controversies in the Theory of Capital*, Cambridge University Press.

——(1976), 'The Cambridge controversies: old ways and new horizons – or dead end?', *Oxford Economic Papers*, 25–65.

Harris, J.D. (1973), 'Capital, distribution and the aggregate production function', *American Economic Review*, 101–13.

——(1978), *Capital Accumulation and Income Distribution*, London: Routledge & Kegan Paul.

Harrod, R.F. (1939), 'An essay in dynamic theory', *Economic Journal*, 14–33.

Hausman, J. (ed.) (1984), *The Philosophy of Economics*, Cambridge University Press.

Heilbroner, R. (1983), 'The problem of value in the constitution of economic thought', mimeographed paper.

Hicks, J.R. (1979), '"Revolutions" in Economics', in S. Latsis (ed.), *Method and Appraisal in Economics*, Cambridge University Press, pp. 207–18.

——(1983), 'The factor price equalization theorem', in *Classics and Moderns*, Cambridge, Mass.: Harvard University Press.

Horvat, B. (1958a), 'The depreciation multiplier and a generalised theory of fixed capital costs', *Manchester School*, 136–59.

——(1958b), 'The optimum rate of investment', *Economic Journal*, 747–67.

——(1962), *Interindustry Analysis*, Zagreb: Narodne novine.

——(1964), *Towards a Theory of Planned Economy*, New York: Sharpe.

——(1965), 'The optimum rate of investment reconsidered', *Economic Journal*, 572–76.

——(1968), 'The rule of accumulation in a planned economy', *Kyklos*, 239–68.

——(1972), 'A model of maximal economic growth', *Kyklos*, 215–28.

——(1973a), 'Real fixed capital costs under steady growth', 'Fixed capital cost, depreciation multiplier and the rate of interest', *European Economic Review*, 83–103, 163–79.

——(1973b), 'Certain similarities between inertial systems in physics and steadily growing systems in economics', *Economic Analysis*, 47–57.

——(1982), *The political economy of socialism*, New York: Sharpe; Oxford: Martin Robertson.

——(1985), 'Political economy', in A. and J. Kuper (eds), *The Social Science Encyclopedia*, London: Routledge & Kegan.

——(1986a), 'The theory of worker-managed firm revisited', *Journal of Comparative Economics*, 9–25.

——(1986b), 'The theory of rent', *Economic Analysis*, 109–18.

——(1987), *Radna teorija cijena (The Labour Theory of Prices)*, Beograd: Rad.

——(1991), 'Stabilization and monetary restriction', Zagreb University, seminar paper, mimeo.

Jevons, W.S. (1871), *The Theory of Political Economy*, New York: A.M. Kelley, 1965.

Jones. R. and Neary P. (1984), 'The positive theory of international trade', in R. Jones and P. Kenen (eds), *Handbook of International Economics*, vol. I, Amsterdam: North-Holland, 1–62.

Jorgenson, D. (1966), 'The embodiment hypothesis', *Journal of Political Economy*, 1–17.

——(1974), 'The economic theory of replacement and depreciation', in W. Sellekaerts (ed.), *Econometrics and Economic Theory*, New York: IASP, pp. 189–222.

Knight, F.H. (1944), 'Diminishing returns from investment', *Journal of Political Economy*, 29–41.

Kotarbiński, T. (1955), *Traktat o dobrej robocie (Treatise on Good Work)*, Warszawa: PWN.

Krelle, W. (1977), 'Basic facts in capital theory: some lessons from the controversy in capital theory', *Revue d'économie politique*, 282–329.

Kuhn, T.S. (1962), *The Structure of Scientific Revolutions*, Chicago University Press.

Kurz, H. (1978), 'Rent theory in a multisector model', *Oxford Economic Papers*, 16–37, reprinted in *S.E.*

Lakatos, I. (1970), 'Falsification and the methodology of scientific research programmes', in I. Lakatos and A. Musgrave (eds), *Criticism and the Growth of Knowledge*, Cambridge University Press, pp. 91–196.

Lane, R.E. (1991), *The Market Experience*, Cambridge University Press.

Lange, O. (1936), 'The place of interest in the theory of production', *Review of Economic Studies*, 159–92.

——(1959), *Political Economy*, vol. I, Oxford: Pergamon Press, 1963.

——(1975), *Ekonomia Polityczna*, Dziela 3, Warsaw: PWE.

Leibenstein, H. (1966), 'Allocative efficiency vs. *X*-efficiency', *American Economic Review*, 393–415.

Leontief, W.W. (1953), 'Domestic production and foreign trade: the American capital position re-examined', *Proceedings of the American Philosophical Society*, pp. 336–9.

Lerner, A. (1972), 'A note on "understanding the Marxian notion of exploitation"', *Journal of Economic Literature*, 50–2.

Lipsey, R. and Lancaster, K. (1956), 'The general theory of the second best', *Review of Economic Studies*, 11–32.

Lowe, A. (1965), *On Economic Knowledge*, New York: Harper & Row.

Machlup, F. (1978), *Methodology of Economics and Other Sciences*, New York: Academic Press.

MacVane, S.M. (1887), 'Analysis of cost of production', *Quarterly Journal of Economics*, 481–7.

Mainwaring, L. (1984), *Value and Distribution in Capitalist Economies*, Cambridge University Press.

Marglin, S. (1984), *Growth, Distribution and Prices*, Cambridge, Mass.: Harvard University Press.

Marshall, A. (1920), *Principles of Economics*, 8th edn, London: Macmillan, 1961.

Marx, K. (1954–9), *Capital: A Critique of Political Economy*, Moscow: Progress Publishers.

——(1867), vol. I, *The Process of Capitalist Production*.

——(1885), vol. II, *The Process of Circulation of Capital*.

——(1894), vol. III, *The Process of Capitalist Production as a Whole*.

Metcalfe, J.S. and Steedman, I. (1972), 'Reswitching and primary input use', *Economic Journal*, 140–57; reprinted in I. Steedman (ed.), *Fundamental Issues in Trade Theory*, London: Macmillan, 15–37.

Mill, J.S. (1848), *Principles of Political Economy*, Fairfield, N.J.: A.M. Kelley, 1987.

Morishima, M. (1966), 'Refutation of the nonswitching theorem', *Quarterly Journal of Economics*, 519–25.

——(1973), *Marx' Economics: a Dual Theory of Value and Growth*, Cambridge University Press.

Morishima, M. and Catephores, G. (1978), *Value, Exploitation and Growth*, New York: McGraw-Hill.

Nell E. (ed.) (1980), *Growth, Profits and Property*, Cambridge University Press.

Notkin, A.I. (1948), *Ocherki teorii socialisticheskogo vosproiz vodstva*, Moskva: OGIZ-GOSPOLITIZDAT.

Nuti, D.M. (1977), 'Price and composition effects and the pseudo-production function', *Revue d'économic politique*, 232–43.

Özol, C. (1984), 'Parable and realism in production theory: the surrogate wage function', *Canadian Journal of Economics*, 352–68.

Pasinetti, L.L. (1977), 'On "non-substitution" in production models', *Cambridge Journal of Economics*, 389–94; reprinted in *S.E.*

——(1979), *Lectures on the Theory of Production*, London: Macmillan.

——(1981), *Structural Change and Economic Growth*, Cambridge University Press.

Pasinetti, L.L. (ed.) (1980), *Essays on the Theory of Joint Production*, London: Macmillan.

Pertz, K. and Teplitz, W. (1979), 'Changes of technique in neo-Ricardian and neoclassical production theory', *Zeitschrift für gesamte Staatswissenschaft*, 247–55.

Petrović, P. (1986), 'Shape of a wage–profit curve: some empirical evidence', *Working Paper No. 376*, Ithaca: Cornell University.

Phelps, F.S. (1966), *Golden Rules of Economic Growth*, New York: Norton.

Poincaré, H. (1908), *Science et Méthode*, Paris: Flammarion.

Popper, K. (1968), *The Logic of Scientific Discovery*, 3rd edn, London: Hutchinson; transl. Beograd, Nolit, 1973.

Reed, L.M. (1968), 'The measure of total factor productivity', *Canadian Journal of Economics*, 349–58.

Ricardo, D. (1821), *The Principles of Political Economy and Taxation*, 3rd edn, reprinted in P. Sraffa and M.H. Dobs (eds), *The Works and Correspondence of David Ricardo*, vol. I, New York, 1951.

Robbins, L. (1932), *An Essay on the Nature and Significance of Economic Science*, London: Macmillan.

Robinson, Joan (1956), *The Accumulation of Capital*, London: Macmillan.

——(1961), *Exercises in Economic Analysis*, London: Macmillan.

——(1964), *Economic Philosophy*, Harmondsworth: Penguin.

Rymes, K.T. (1971), *The Concepts of Capital and Technological Change*, Cambridge University Press.

Samuelson, P.A. (1948), 'International trade and the equalization of factor prices', *Economic Journal*, 163–84.

——(1971), 'Understanding the Marxian notion of exploitation: a summary of the so-called transformation problem between Marxian values and competitive prices', *Journal of Economic Literature*, 399–431.

——(1976), 'Interest rate determination and oversimplifying parables: a summing up', in M. Brown, K. Sato and P. Zarembka (eds), *Essays in Modern Capital Theory*, Amsterdam: North-Holland, pp. 3–23.

Schefold, B. (1978), 'On Counting Equations', in N. Salvadori and I. Steedman (eds) (1990), *Joint Production of Commodities*, Aldershot: Edward Elgar, pp. 126–38.

Schumpeter, J. (1912), *Theorie der wirtschaftlichen Entwicklung*, Leipzig: Duncker and Humboldt.

——(1954), *History of Economic Analysis*, New York: Oxford University Press.

Senior, N.W. (1836), *An Outline of the Science of Political Economy*, New York: Kelley Reprint, 1965.

Slutsky, E. (1926), 'Ein Beitrag zur Formalprakseologischen Grundlegung der Oekonomik', in *Zapiski social'no-ekonomichnogo viddilu*, vol. 4, Kiev: Ukrainskaja Akademija Nauk.

Solow, R.M. (1963), *Capital Theory and the Rate of Return*, Amsterdam: North-Holland.

Spaventa, L. (1970), 'Rate of profit, rate of growth and capital intensity in a simple production model', *Oxford Economic Papers*, 130–48; reprinted in *S.E.*

Sraffa, P. (1960), *Production of Commodities by Means of Commodities*, Cambridge University Press.

Steedman, I. (1972a), 'An expository note on the switching of techniques', *Bulletin of the Conference of Socialist Economists*, Autumn, 5–21.

——(1972b), *Marx after Sraffa*, London: NLB.

——(1976), 'Positive profits with negative surplus value', *Economic Journal*, 873–6.

——(1985), 'On input "demand" curves', *Cambridge Journal of Economics*, 165–72; reprinted in *S.E.*

——(1990), 'Perversity without complementarity', *Review of Political Economy*, 138–48.

Steedman, I. (ed.) (1979), *Fundamental Issues in Trade Theory*, London: Macmillan.

——(1988), *Sraffian Economics*, vols I and II, Aldershot, Hants.: Edward Elgar.

Stojanović, K. (1910), *Osnovi teorije ekonomskih vrednosti* (Principles of the Theory of Economic Values), Beograd: Srpska kraljevska akademija.

Strnad, J. (1989), 'O fizici čestica i kosmologiji' (Particle Physics and Cosmology), *Scientia Yugoslavica*, 101–9.

Strumilin, S.G. (1946), 'Factor vremeni v proyektirovkah kapitalnykh vlozenii', *Izvestija Akademii nauk SSSR, Otdeleniye ekonomiki i prava*, no. 3; translated into English in *International Economic Papers*, vol. 1, London: Macmillan, 1951, pp. 160–85.

Sylos-Labini, P. (1990), 'Sraffa's critique of Marshall', in Krishna Bharadwaj and Bertrand Schefold (eds), *Essays on Piero Sraffa: Critical Perspectives on the Revival of Classical Theory*, London: Unwin Hyman.

Thurow, C.L. (1983), *Dangerous Currents, the State of Economics*, Oxford University Press.

Uhr, C.G. (1951), 'Knut Wicksell: a centennial evaluation', *American Economic Review*, 829–60.

Verdoorn, P.J. (1980), 'Verdoorn's law in retrospect', *Economic Journal*, 382–5.

Walras, L. (1874), *Elements of Pure Economics*, transl. by W. Jaffé, Fairfield, N.J.: A.M. Kelley, 1977.

Walsh, V. and Gram, H. (1980), *Classical and Neoclassical Theories of General Equilibrium*, Oxford University Press.

Ward, B. (1972), *What's Wrong with Economics?*, London: Macmillan.

Weber, M. (1922), *Gesammelte Aufsätze zur Wissenschaftslehre*, Tübingen: Mohr (Siebeck).

Weizsäcker, Ch. and Samuelson, P.A. (1971), 'A new labour theory of value for rational planning through use of the bourgeois profit rates', *Proceedings of the National Academy of Sciences*, June, 1192–4.

Whalley, J. (1976), 'Thorton's estimate of efficiency losses in Soviet industry: some fixed-point method recalculations', *Journal of Political Economy*, 153–9.

White, J.L. (1978), 'The evidence on appropriate factor proportions for manufacturing in less developed countries: a survey', *Economic Development and Cultural Change*, 27–60.

Woods, J.E. (1987), 'A note on rent', *Oxford Economic Papers*, 388–411.

——(1990), *The Production of Commodities*, London: Macmillan.

Works and Correspondence of David Ricardo, ed. by P. Sraffa (1951), vol. I and IV, Cambridge University Press.

Zaghini, E. (1967), 'On non-basic commodities', *Schweizerische Zeitschrift für Volkswirtschaft und Statistik*, 257–66; reprinted in *S.E.*

Ziercke, M. (1988), 'Rente, Bodenpreise', *Handwörterbuch der Wirtschaftswissenschaft*, Stuttgart: Fisher, Mohr, Vandenhoeck, vol. 2, 548–67.

Name index

Subject index